CAVA DEI TIRRENI
(SALERNO)
✉ ROTOLO
☎ 39

Darling Biti,

the first days after I
came back home I cannot write; I must
settle. Otherwise I could only send a _cri de
coeur_ saying "Oh, how I wish I had not
left you!" But, when settled. I love to
join you with words, as letters consent.
I am very busy with my work as - if I
am to give it - I must give it for the 15
september. I am hypnotized by it - but
just now, in the middle of it, I have one
of these dreadful _écoeurement_ and the
temptation of letting it go. But I will
not, and decide. on the contrary. to finish.
and then let other people judge it.
One thing I realized is this: that one
begins with a certain plot, a certain scheme
and then. the _personnages_ once they move
they have as a life of their own, and

A MATTER OF PASSION

The publisher gratefully
acknowledges the generous
contribution provided by
the Director's Circle of the Associates
of the University of California Press,
whose members are

Edmund Corvelli, Jr.
Leslie and Herbert Fingarette
Diane and Charles L. Frankel
Florence and Leo Helzel
Sandra and Charles Hobson
Valerie and Joel Katz
Robert Marshall
Ruth and David Mellinkoff
Joan Palevsky

A Matter of Passion

LETTERS OF

BERNARD BERENSON

AND

CLOTILDE MARGHIERI

EDITED BY DARIO BIOCCA

UNIVERSITY
OF CALIFORNIA PRESS
BERKELEY · LOS ANGELES
OXFORD

University of California Press
Berkeley and Los Angeles, California

University of California Press, Ltd.
Oxford, England

© 1989 by The Regents
of the University of California

LIBRARY OF CONGRESS
CATALOGING-IN-PUBLICATION DATA

Berenson, Bernard, 1865–1959.
A matter of passion:
letters of Bernard Berenson
and Clotilde Marghieri / edited by Dario Biocca.

p. cm.
Includes index.

ISBN 0-520-06527-1 (alk. paper)

1. Berenson, Bernard, 1865–1959—Correspondence.
2. Art historians—United States—Correspondence.
3. Marghieri, Clotilde.   I. Marghieri, Clotilde.
II. Biocca, Dario.   III. Title.

N7483.B47A4 1989
709'.2'2—dc19
[B]
88-36522
CIP

Printed in the United States of America

1   2   3   4   5   6   7   8   9

The paper used in this publication
meets the minimum requirements of
American National Standard for Information Sciences—
Permanence of Paper for Printed Library Materials,
ANSI Z39.48–1984. ∞™

Friendship, affection, stimulus of heart
even more than of mind, but both
together are what remain at my age,
and the Gods have given me this and much
else in loving friends like you.
What a beautiful world today.
I wish I was with you
in your Realm of Gold.

BERNARD BERENSON,
MARCH 19, 1955

✤ CONTENTS ✤

✤ PREFACE ✤

THE ARCHIVES OF Villa I Tatti, which Harvard University acquired after Bernard Berenson's death in 1959, hold no records of the correspondence between the American art historian and Clotilde Marghieri. Many of Berenson's friends knew of his methodical habit of spending at least one hour each day on letter writing, but only a few intimates were aware of his close relationship with the Neapolitan novelist.

Shortly before his death, Berenson returned to Clotilde Marghieri all the letters he had received from her. He had earlier told her that the correspondence could be published, but trusted she would "keep them for the day they can be printed without disturbing survivors" (letter of February 27, 1945). Only in 1981 did Marghieri make the letters public, publishing a selection translated into Italian and entitled *Lo specchio doppio* (The Double Mirror).

Although a more generous selection than *Lo specchio doppio,* the present volume still contains only part of the correspondence. Of the sixteen hundred letters Berenson and Marghieri wrote one another—this, a cautious estimate—eleven hundred letters have survived. Some letters were lost during the war; many others Marghieri disposed of to protect both her privacy and Berenson's.

Bernard Berenson and Clotilde Marghieri first met in the hall of a Neapolitan hotel in the summer of 1925. They were introduced by Pellegrina Rosselli del Turco, a longtime friend of Marghieri's who had become Berenson's secretary and who described him as an "old sage, curious, witty, and eager to make new acquaintances." Berenson was then in his sixties, a world-famous art critic, and married to Mary Logan Pearsall Smith. Born into a cultivated family from Naples, Marghieri was in her early thirties, a would-be journalist and novelist. She was married to a successful lawyer, Gino Marghieri, and they had a son, Massimo; the following year their daughter, Lucia, was born. Berenson was captivated by the young woman's charm and intelligence; he wrote her several times and invited her to visit I Tatti, the Berensons' villa in Settignano, outside Florence. Three years later, when the two met in Florence, their acquaintance developed into a passionate relationship.

Marghieri felt at home in Florence. Her parents had sent her there "to learn Italian with a Tuscan accent," and most of her friends, including Pellegrina Rosselli, had spent many years with her at the Medicean Villa La Quiete, a private boarding school run by Montalvo nuns. Marghieri's novel *Le educande di Poggio Gherardo* (1963) is a vivid recollection of those memorable years when none of the young women was ever allowed to leave the school even for a day. Thereafter, Marghieri spent several weeks each year in Florence with the closest of all her Tuscan friends, Vittoria De' Pazzi.

Naples, however, was Marghieri's home, and in the 1930s it was still regarded as the most cosmopolitan city on the shores of southern Europe. Fourteen newspapers were published daily; bookstores and private libraries provided scholars with formidable collections of manuscripts and rare books; and foreign travelers included Capri, Pompei, Paestum, and Ercolano in their grand tour of southern Italy. Since the Italian unification, however, Naples had been plunged into economic and social crisis. "Neapolitan philosophers," one critic noted, "seem nowadays to think and argue only among themselves, and as if they were in Berlin."[1] Alienation from public life and politics, coupled

1. Antonio Ghirelli, *Napoli italiana* (Turin 1981), p. 44.

with a keen interest in foreign culture, was a common trait of many Neapolitan intellectuals.

From the turn of the century until World War II, Benedetto Croce was at the core of Neapolitan, indeed, all Italian cultural life. His home was open to scholars of all nations, faiths, and opinions, and occasionally provided shelter to those prosecuted by Fascism. Croce's circle was not, however, open to women. Berenson regarded this aspect of Neapolitan life as "paleolithic." Nevertheless, Marghieri ultimately did gain access to all the most exclusive intellectual circles, including Croce's. "Doors are closed," she explained to Berenson, "but never really shut."

While still in her twenties, Clotilde Marghieri met with people such as Giuseppe Antonio Borgese, Gino Doria, Roberto Pane, Lorenzo Giusso, and Ugo Ojetti: artists, writers, and journalists who helped her enter the literary world. Under the pen name Clovis, she began to write book reviews for Neapolitan newspapers. Her mentors encouraged her to read foreign literature and philosophy, but she hardly needed such advice: "I used to read everything," she recalled in the early 1960s, "books of all qualities and concerning any subjects, good books and bad books alike, provided they would fill my days with printed words." Among these books was Berenson's *Italian Painters of the Renaissance,* which had won him the admiration of scholars of Italian art throughout the world.

Clotilde Marghieri's marriage to Gino Marghieri lasted sixty years; she loved her husband, and he respected her independence. But the clan of Marghieri in-laws criticized her nonconformism and discouraged her from pursuing her own interests and her literary career. Gino Marghieri's father, Alberto, was a distinguished lawyer, senator, and chairman of the University of Naples. His family's traditional values allowed for little individual freedom, particularly for women. The family felt deeply scandalized when, in the

1930s, Clotilde moved out of her husband's home and into La Quiete, a country house on the slopes of Mount Vesuvius that she named after her Florentine school.

Gino Marghieri never attempted to disrupt his wife's correspondence with Bernard Berenson. The two men met on several occasions and exchanged letters in which they expressed mutual respect. Berenson, however, did not enjoy the company of children, never had any of his own, and met Marghieri's children only when they were young adults. In his letters he conveyed a sense of repulsion for any nonelective relationship, including that between parent and child. He insisted that Clotilde enjoy a society free from family obligations, in which men and women were considered equal. Such a society, in his view, could only be found at I Tatti.

When Marghieri first visited Berenson's home, I Tatti was a large, square hilltop villa that had been renovated over the years and furnished with a vast library and art collection. The villa was surrounded by a magnificent garden, where Bernard and Mary Berenson had been married on December 18, 1900. Mary Berenson made I Tatti home to scores of Americans, English, French, German, and Italian friends. Guests were free to read in the library until eleven o'clock in the morning, and then would join the Berensons for a walk in the gardens until noon. B.B. would later return to his study and attend to his correspondence. The company would meet again at one o'clock for lunch. The afternoon, except for a short break at tea time, was also devoted to reading and writing. Though scores of friends would join in for dinner, evenings never lasted past eleven.

Beyond this civilized and contemplative cloister lay an Italy under the grip of Fascism. The authorities did not harass the Berensons, nor did they bother their foreign friends and visitors. Nevertheless, during the 1930s more and more of Berenson's Italian acquaintances migrated to France, England, and the United States. The late 1930s, as Berenson's letters to Marghieri show, brought an increasing isolation to the "society of kindred souls" centered in Settignano. Eventually, racial persecution and the prospect of a war between Berenson's two countries, Italy and the United States, led him to consider returning to Boston.

But on the eve of World War II, Bernard Berenson decided that he and his wife should remain in Italy. She accepted although, in B.B.'s words, she did so "reluctantly." The art collection of Villa I Tatti was hidden in various places in and out of Florence; the library was closed and books were stored in walled-up rooms. Berenson wrote to his friend Sylvia Sprigge that after Italy had declared war on the United States, a high-ranking member of the Fascist government asked the U.S. ambassador whether there was anything he could do after the embassy had closed. "Yes," the diplomat replied. "Look after the Berensons."[2] Nonetheless, as soon as German troops invaded Italy, Berenson was forced to go into hiding. Mary Berenson, by then an invalid, stayed at I Tatti and guarded the house against looting and vandalism. Soon after the Allied liberation, and before it was possible to restore the villa to its original splendor, she died with B.B. at her bedside.

Upon his return to I Tatti, Berenson suffered another loss: the death of Pellegrina Rosselli. For many months Berenson clung to the hope that she might have survived the war, but Pellegrina, a member of the Resistance, had been executed by German soldiers in the city of Forlì.

A new "Archangel," as Berenson called his young Polish-born librarian, soon revived I Tatti. Nicky Mariano had first been employed by Berenson in 1919 to attend to the library and correspond with foreign publishers and art dealers. Later she was entrusted with a variety of administrative duties, including the arrangement of travel and invitations. After Mary Berenson's death, Mariano devoted herself entirely to B.B. and remained always at his side. Her ministra-

2. Sylvia Sprigge, *Berenson: A Biography* (Boston 1960), p. 164.

———

tions were particularly invaluable after Berenson, out on his daily walk near I Tatti, was hit by the door of a passing car and fell some twenty-five feet down the edge of a steep hill. At the time of the accident, in December 1954, Berenson was eighty-nine years old. He recovered sufficiently enough to travel to North Africa in the spring of 1955, and on his return he visited Marghieri for the last time at Villa La Quiete.

A few months before Berenson's death, Marghieri began work on her first novel. Berenson had constantly encouraged her to write. So also had Mary Berenson, who read all the articles, plays, and book reviews—published and unpublished—that Marghieri periodically sent to I Tatti. Marghieri's literary work grew in the following years, as if to make up for lost time: *Vita in villa* recalls the years she spent at La Quiete, at the foot of Mount Vesuvius; *Il segno sul braccio* is a gallery of portraits of friends and acquaintances, including Edith Wharton, Sibilla Aleramo, and Umberto Zanotti Bianco; *Amati enigmi* is a calm reflection on aging and death. Upon the publication of *Lo specchio doppio* in 1981, Natalino Sapegno, one of Italy's most astute literary critics, wrote: "Berenson was the first to realize that Marghieri would become an accomplished writer and eventually reveal her true self. . . . Thus, the correspondence with B.B. chronicled not only a long friendship, but most importantly the making of a writer and a free human spirit."[3]

Bernard Berenson and Clotilde Marghieri conducted their correspondence in English, though neither was a native speaker of the language. Throughout the years both of them used British and American spelling interchangeably, and these are here reproduced unaltered. However, I have occasionally corrected some spelling errors and supplied, in brackets, a few necessary words obviously omitted in haste.

3. Natalino Sapegno, unpublished manuscript.

I have made no other changes nor abridged any of the letters—with the exception of some of the details concerning the death of Pellegrina Rosselli. For foreign phrases that may not be immediately understood or recognized as cognates, I have supplied, again in brackets, English translations.

As Clotilde Marghieri's grandson, I had the opportunity to discuss with her some passages that would otherwise have remained unclear. She also taught me how to decipher Berenson's minute handwriting.

I am grateful to all the relatives, friends, and scholars who have made this publication possible. I would like to thank Lucia Marghieri Biocca and Massimo Marghieri, who gave me permission to publish the letters; professor James Burge, who initially transcribed portions of the correspondence; professor Gene Brucker, who urged me to submit the manuscript for publication; and professor Randolph Starn, who gave me valuable advice. Ingrid Mirner and Susan Etlinger helped me throughout the transcription. I am particularly grateful to Krystyna von Henneberg; she prepared the footnotes with me and revised the manuscript with great patience. Finally, I would like to thank James Clark and Laird Easton, at the University of California Press, for their patience and encouragement. Amy Einsohn has edited the final draft of the manuscript with the greatest care and attention.

The reproduction of photographs and manuscripts was made possible by a Humanities Research Grant offered by the University of California, Berkeley.

Berkeley, California
March 1989

D.B.

PART ONE
1927–1932

I Tatti
Settignano
June 3, 1927

Dearest Clotilde,

A rumour reaches me that you may be coming for the wedding of a friend. So I hasten to beg you to come before we go. We shall be leaving the 20th and the sooner will be the better.

Since you were here last, I have never been able to get you out of my thoughts. I long for the chance of seeing you a great deal more for I have a sense that we are destined, or at least could be if the chance presented itself, to be great, very great friends.

We expect to be gone for six or seven months first in Germany and then in Scandinavia, Holland and Belgique; and then London and Paris. Is there any possibility for you to join us anywhere?

With affectionate expectation,
Yours,
B.B.

Sainte-Claire Le Château[1]
Hyères (Var)
January 6, 1930
Dearest Clotilde,

I love people who, as you say of yourself, give themselves to others "only in talking." Conversation, the give and the take of talk, has been from my earliest years and remains more than ever today the crowning joy of my life. And there is no greater happiness than a *chant-fable* which lifts the faculties of two people attracted to each other into a subtler, swifter, more delicate mode of exercise. So come, dearest Friend, and let us be happy together. Come just as soon as you can. And give me all of yourself that you can. And despair not. You are young, I am not yet decrepit. I may even live to join you often at Capri. Meanwhile, you must come to me at I Tatti. I am returning there in a few days.

Affectionately,
B.B.

Sainte-Claire Le Château
Hyères (Var)
January 15, 1931
Dearest Clotilde,

Yes, I expect to get back no later than January 20 and I hope you know how glad, how very glad I shall be to see you. And you will let me see a lot of you, won't you?

Aldous Huxley lunched here today and I read to him what you said about *Point Counter Point*.[2] He was pleased. I liked the book very much for its talk, some of the most bril-

---

1. The residence of Edith Wharton, located on the French Riviera between Nice and Marseilles. The expatriate American novelist was a close friend of the Berensons'.
2. Huxley spent a good deal of his life in Italy and France before finally settling in California. His house in France was located near Edith Wharton's, and he and the Berensons exchanged frequent visits.

liant I have ever seen in print. It is surpassed, however, in the first story of Huxley's *Brief Candles*.

If you care to see ideas carried further and more violently than usual, I recommend *Mort de la Pensée Bourgeoise* (Grasset) and *Mort de la Morale Bourgeoise* (Berl).[3]

How I wish I could spend a month in continuous conversation with you as I am now doing with Mrs. Wharton. That is the way to get the real sap out of people, and how I should like to get yours! Write again, and don't fail me at Florence.

Your cordial and affectionate,

B.B.

I Tatti
Settignano
March 6, 1931

Your little note of last Monday rejoiced my heart when it reached me Tuesday. I had written Sunday a very long letter which you must have received if you were in Rome. Monday afternoon I have by every post been expecting a letter from you.

I deliberately do not speak of an answer. It is between us not a matter of question and answer, but of a dialogue in which each should say what he has to say to express himself while stimulating the other to do likewise. There is a great deal to be said on that score but not now. I wonder rather why, if you care for me, you let so many days go by without writing to me after receiving such a screed as I dashed off to you a week ago. Your vanishings and silences fill me with anguish and it is not too strong a word because I have never encountered them before, and therefore do not know how to

3. Two major works by French essayist Emmanuel Berl, published in 1929 and 1930. Berenson has inadvertently named Grasset, the publisher of the first volume, in the first parenthesis. In both works Berl denounces the suffocating traditionalism of the bourgeois classes of early twentieth-century Europe.

interpret them. And unluckily I am so made that I cannot abide by facts or events, but must construct some reasons for them.

No doubt my reasoning, like all reasoning, is not mathematical, leads only to myths, and is in vital relations perhaps misleading and dangerous. I can see from the kind of myth that you have constructed about me, how little mine about you is likely to strike you as corresponding to anything that you should recognize as being yourself. And yet, if I had the training and the leisure, what a novel I could write with you as a heroine!

I should come in only as the spectator, eager out of sympathy to understand, and baffled at every attempt. If only I could get rid of this puerile passion. It is only the continuation of that metaphysical age children go through. I did at the age of six or seven. Some years later I read Schiller's *Disciple of Sais*. He insisted Isis unveil herself and he drew away the curtain hiding the dread Goddess, and is neither struck dead for his sacrilege, nor illuminated by the revelation of divinity. Nothing happens. There is nothing behind the veil.

At least so Schiller told me nearly fifty years ago. Perhaps if I re-read the poem now, I should discover that what the poet meant to say was this: You cannot get to the heart of a mystery by violence. If you try, you find nothing. You must ripen into understanding of yourself, and then there are no more secrets. But I am far from ripeness. After sixty years I am still the small boy who broke into pieces the first watch that was given to him to see what made it go. Am I still that small boy? Then, I have lived in vain, lived like the rest of us; not as well even as Ibsen's Peer Gynt.

And you, my obsession, projection of alternate thought that passes through my mind, object of my yearning and longing and desire, what happens to you when you disappear into an interlunar cave?

A lady dined yesterday here, the famous musician Landowska.[4] She said: If you want to go on loving people, don't look into them too much. But I am not made like that, hélas! I must feel and conceive and imagine all together, or I perish.

I am a good bit of a wreck myself and Mary's progress is very slow.[5]

Your so loving,
B.B.

I Tatti
Settignano
March 15, 1931

It made me happy, my beloved, to get your little note, the one of the 12th. Of course I will write to you often, very often, and you must take what you receive as nothing else, no more, no less, than expressions of my longings for your Real Presence. In love I remain an Orthodox Thomistic Catholic, and will have no compromise with sublimations which leave nothing for my senses and yearnings to embrace, enfold and possess.

Baffled and frustrated, I want the real psycho-physical entity within my present grasp, just as I want it when I take the Communion, to be sure that I am taking the body of the Lord and not mere symbols. But suspense has for *Lebenskünstler* [lovers of life] like you and me something to offer. It is not a substitute for palpability, but has certain compensations.

I was walking along the Rue Royale, some twelve or

4. Wanda Landowska (1877–1959), Polish harpsichordist, pianist, and composer. Her masterly harpsichord concerts in Europe and the United States established her as an authority on old music, and she founded a school for the study of early modern music outside Paris, before emigrating to the United States in 1941.

5. In 1931, following a trip to North Africa, and as a consequence of a poorly performed operation, Mary Berenson's already poor health took a turn for the worse. She spent the rest of her life as a semi-invalid, fending off periodic and increasingly long bouts of pain and depression.

thirteen years ago, and a charming gentleman *très ancien ré-
gime* stopped me and asked me about a lady whom we both
frequented. I told him she had gone to Brittany for a fortnight. "Elle y est allée," he replied, "pour mieux rêver de
vous." [She went there, the better to dream of you.] There is
not only compensation but something delicious in weaving
about a loved one a pattern of living and being not too bru-
tally determined by time as it goes, and space as it stays.

You say nothing about your health. You must not fail to
send me a bulletin each time you write, for it is a matter that
preoccupies me.

Yesterday Maria Teresa Rasponi[6] appeared unexpectedly
at tea and she talked at great length about you and so lovingly that had we been alone I should have embraced her. I
confess that I was surprised, under such a placid exterior, so
much understanding not only of you as an individual, but of
what you and I mean for each other.

About a week ago I met your host De Vecchi,[7] and the
few minutes we talked were all about you.

We are in a fever of finishing things up and there is so
much to do that but for Nicky,[8] the Archangel and Minister
of Genius, I should give up in despair. We leave the 19th via
Civitavecchia and Cagliari. Our next address will be Hotel
Transatlantique, Tunis.

And please, love me.

B.B.

6. Countess Maria Teresa Rasponi Dalle Teste, née Chiari.
7. Vittoria De Vecchi, née De' Pazzi, wife of Bindo De Vecchi,
   chairman of the University of Florence. Vittoria De' Pazzi was
   one of Clotilde Marghieri's closest friends, and Marghieri dedicated her novel *Le educande di Poggio Gherardo* (1963) to her.
8. Nicky Mariano had been hired in 1919 as the librarian at I Tatti.
   She remained a lifelong companion of the Berensons', aiding
   them in everything from health matters and social engagements to
   travel and research. Mariano recounts her experiences in *Forty
   Years with Berenson* (London 1966).

Hotel Transatlantique
Tunis
March 23, 1931
Dearest Clotilde,

Do send me the photo of your little girl's portrait done by your friend Pane.[9] It will interest me to see what his talent is like and what resemblance to her parents he discovers in her face.

I dare say Pellegrina[10] has written to you that she came on to Civitavecchia and spent the forenoon with us. I was very glad to see her, as I remain so tenderly fond of her. She started confessing at once, and like all who confess she instinctively minimized how much she felt for the person she talked about, and made out that he was as clay in her hands, that he had no backbone of his own, but that she had the strength to send him away, to toss him upon the ocean of life to sink or swim. No doubt. No doubt but she was vibrating with excitement as she spoke. I expect the young man will fulfill the prophecy of the Bible which says: "Throw your bread upon the waters and after many days it will come back to you." We were interrupted and couldn't talk to the end. When I see her again, I shall not attempt to advise her. I never advise in the sense of offering a program of conduct. I shall however try to make her descry her own intentions. The one certainty that I carried away was that she did feel free to leave for Cithera. Not that she herself was at all clear on this point.

We stopped over at Cagliari and at the museum I saw the famous Sardinian bronzes. They amused me a great deal and

9. Roberto Pane (1878–1987), architect, architectural historian of Renaissance and Baroque Naples, painter, and author of *L'Architettura dell'età Barocca a Napoli* (1935), and *L'Acquaforte di Piranesi* (1938). Pane was one of Marghieri's closest friends.

10. Countess Pellegrina Paulucci de Calboli, née Rosselli del Turco, Berenson's secretary and a long-time friend of Clotilde Marghieri; it was she who first introduced them. Berenson called her "Pel-

seemed to hold about the same relation to the Ionian art that the late Siamese, or better still the Javanese theater figures do to the Gupta art of India.

We got here to *La Terre Africaine*. It is an enchanting disappointment, for instead of being flat and sandy as I vaguely expected, it is almost as lovely and hilly as your own native landscape. Almost at once we plunged into society. Sunday was the day of the Erlangers. They have a Moorish villa beyond Carthage and the site was of fairy-like splendor and the house good for its kind. But the hostess was a mummified beauty who thought only of making people for bridge, and the company consisting of what I can call the lower classes of the intellect. For I severely divide bipeds, regardless of their worldly stations, into upper, middle and lower classes of the mind. Of *Unsereiner* [people like us], nothing.

Of our further adventures I will tell you next time. I look forward to our meeting in Naples and you must come to La Consuma[11] in August. We can and must be great friends.

Yours,
B.B.

Hotel Transatlantique
Tunis
April 27, 1931
Dearest Clotilde,

I found your note of the 20th here on arrival yesterday evening. You speak of yourself as being an "unstable creature, physiologically condemned to variableness." Every

---

legrinchen" because of her love of German poetry; she is also sometimes referred to as "Pelly."
11. A small town in the hills northeast of Florence, La Consuma was the site of Poggio allo Spino, the Berensons' summer residence until 1937.

syllable that you say of yourself is as true of me, except that I doubt whether I even attempt to discipline myself to present to others a presentable aspect. I change from hour to hour, from quarter of an hour to quarter of an hour, as if I were swimming in an ocean constantly varying in temperatures and currents.

Perhaps the most sensitive people are like that: *Himmelhoch Jauchzend / Zum Tode Betrübt.*[12] They are, however, the only people I care for and get on with. Invariably eupeptic people, even tempered, full of sense, reason and judgement, I am ready to entrust with all practical and administrative affairs. They can even be artists, perhaps very big ones, but they are not company for me. Nor do they yearn for my society either.

Is Raniero[13] a sensitive or a crank? I fear he is only a crank. It will be very awkward if he comes with Pellegrina, for who will entertain him? However, his disgust for my Freemasonic principles and my black magic, let alone the other reasons he gives himself for disapproving of me, will drive him quickly back to his cave.

There is no discrepancy between mysticism and physiology, for the latter is purely instrumental and serves for perception as a telescope or a microscope does. As a matter of fact, I am a good bit of mystic, but the object of my craving is no mythical one, whether Xtian or other, but *IT,* and there is *ITNESS* in all things not mechanized.

Do write again and again. I love to hear from you. Address as I told you to Hotel Aletti, Alger.

With so much love,

B.B.

12. The lines are from Goethe's *Egmont:* "Rejoicing as high as the heavens / Grieving as low as death."
13. Count Raniero Paulucci de Calboli, Pellegrina's husband.

Piazza dei Martiri 30[14]
Naples
June 5, 1931

My dearest Bibi,

We met in the same wish: to remember each other as soon as we departed. You must have found my word in Rome at your arrival, as I received yours when you were still in journey. When I read your letter, dear, I burst into tears. I am not too haughty to tell you this. I felt like a girl of fifteen, her heart broken by a separation. I was just like that school-girl I was telling you about, and I could feel so young and lively in my pain as I had been, and yet so miserable. Through my pain I could feel myself again sticking to life.

You represent to me all that is charm and loveliness and courtesy, apart from what I admire in your spirit, so that when I am near you I forget all that is difficult and hard and harsh. In the atmosphere that is around you I build my home of fantasy and fancy. I think that we never know thoroughly what we mean for each other. But why investigate?

I went to hear some music last night. As one of the authors was a Bolshevik, people in the theater thought it necessary to make a demonstration. Idiots. I felt ashamed of human kind.

Dearest, we must meet soon.

For ever and ever,
Clotilde

Hotel de la Ville
Rome
June 8, 1931

Darling,

Your little note made me happy. You tell me how much I mean to you, how much I do to you just because of my

14. The address of Palazzo Calabritto, the Marghieris' residence in Naples.

way of being, because of some qualities you find in me. I rejoice that it is so, and I rejoice the more as that something that enhances you is largely your own creation. It is not an illusion. It is more than an impression. It is a reality but a reality which exists only for you, for it is the result of the fusion of two selves.

So I cannot conceivably be to any one else what I am to you, nor can you in turn be to any one else what you are to me. Clotilde is mine and nobody else can own her, let alone claim her, for she exists only for me. And so it is for you. I often wonder whether a day will come when we shall be sufficiently self-aware to realize that, except for bestial or utilitarian reasons, there is no place for jealousy in human relations. Except in the most grossly material sense, nobody can possess the person that we love except ourselves. I fear we still are far from that state of enlightenment. But what a joy it is to have someone to dwell in the innermost recesses of one's heart, where one can always find him, always appeal to him, hold converse there with him as with an indwelling God! All that you are to me, Love.

The Lippmanns[15] got here yesterday morning and as they can stay in Italy only till the 18th and as I know that they enjoy I Tatti as much as ourselves, we are leaving them there Thursday and going straight through. How I ached for your physical presence yesterday on the Via Appia. It was supreme and, but for your presence, complete.

Write to I Tatti from Wednesday on, and write often. You cannot write too often if only a line.

Yours,

B.B.

15. Berenson and Walter Lippmann, the American political columnist, first met in Paris, during World War I.

I Tatti
Settignano
June 28, 1931
Darling,

I ache for you and want so much to be with you and close to you and enjoy the dumb ecstasy of being with you. I feel no need of words, on the contrary, as if one uttered them out of bad habit, or perhaps conversation demands it. It is different when I am not with you. Then the written word, the paper your hand has touched, the sign that you have been concentrating your attention upon you-me, becomes all-important. So write, dearest mine, write about your sorrows and ennuis and *miseriuole* [little problems]. They bring to me nearer. And life would not be life but ecstasy were it not for obstacles and difficulties.

Today you are already at La Cava,[16] I hope in fresher and even cooler air. How I look back to those hours spent in the house where you are now. I remember saying to myself: "This is where she will be. These spaces, this furniture, these garden chairs, this view, these approaches. Now I shall be able to place her when she returns and I can waft my spirit toward her so much more easily and know just where to find her."

You must encourage Gino[17] to see us every time he can. We could send the car for him so he would lose no time. He could lunch or dine. Not only do I like him, but I want to make him feel, if possible, that I am not a hostile element likely to disturb him. Then, if he frequents us, he may end by seeing that certain *usi e costumi* are far from universal, and indeed belong to a cave-dwelling, rather than a polished, contemporary society.

16. Cava dei Tirreni, site of Villa Marghieri, the Marghieris' summer residence near Salerno.
17. Gino Marghieri, Clotilde's husband.

We went to San Cresci, Pellegrinchen, Morra[18] and I. Pellegrina and I talked of you the whole time, and Morra was an enchanted listener. Pellegrina simply adores you and by adoration I mean love with a sort of respect and great admiration. I must tell you she always talks as if she worshipped you. Indeed she was not little of a *galeotto*[19] in preparing me to love you, the moment I could. Maria Teresa Rasponi is more calm in her expressions and besides she is a new acquaintance. Yet in her, too, I felt an immense affection for you.

So you need not feel that nobody loves you. Darling mine, know that whoever loves you, and many do, I love you most.

B.B.

La Consuma
Florence
September 5, 1931

No word from you this morning, my Darling, my joy, and I wanted it so much because I had a curious night. My sleep was constantly interrupted and sinking and waking, you were in my conscience and not only there. How I yearned for you, how I longed for you!

I hope it is only the freakiness of the post and no other reason that has delayed the letter which you must have written and posted. Perhaps it will reach me this evening.

The weather is almost cinematographically startling in its changes. Yesterday we had a moaning *scirocco,* hot and feverish, but as beautiful as what Ruysdael never lived to paint. Today is boisterous and pungently cool and autumnal.

18. Count Umberto Morra di Lavriano became a student of Berenson's in 1925. His *Colloqui con Berenson* (1966) chronicles his conversations with Berenson during frequent visits to Villa I Tatti.
19. Culprit, matchmaker; from Dante's *Divine Comedy,* "Inferno," canto V: "Galeotto fu il libro e chi lo scrisse."

The Maclagans[20] got here for dinner and their two boys, nice boys just like him the one, and like her the other. The talk at dinner fell on Joyce and to my amazement it turned out that Maclagan was a great admirer of *Ulysses*. We argued, of course, and I argued him down. That is not hard, but that a near contemporary of mine should find *Ulysses* worthwhile made me sit up. This morning I read Valéry's *La Jeune Parque* and *Le Cimetière au Bord de la Mer,* his two famous poems, and I glanced at pages of his prose. I have tried often enough and each time I am baffled. Too much sauce and too little fish for my appetite.

We can discuss the why and wherefore of my state of mind when we meet. How I look for you, how forward to that day! Don't forget me, not even for a minute.

B.B.

Cava dei Tirreni
Salerno
September 7, 1931

I could not write yesterday as Gino did not feel well and I did not have even half an hour to myself. When I could finally rest, I was tired and worried. He is better now, and so is Lucia.[21]

I have finished today the book you advised me to read, Chekhov's *Duel*. How different are Russian books! They create turbid and troubled atmospheres. It seems that this is what *all* Russian novels have in common. I feel disturbed by them; they give me a sort of *smania* [tension, impatience]. Sometimes, when this *smania* does not result in inner peace, I conclude that the book is not really good, that it simply recounts a disturbing story and is overwhelmed by it.

Now I will read *High Winds*.[22] Darling, reading what

---

20. Sir Eric Darlymple Maclagan (1897–1951), art historian, and his wife Hellen, née Lascelles.
21. Lucia, Marghieri's second child, born in 1926.
22. A novel by Arthur Cheney Train (1875–1949), published in 1927.

you want me to read seems the only way of being near at all times. I can recall the moments at La Consuma when I wanted to tell you about every thing I read. Your photo is now over the fireplace in the bedroom and I look at it when I write on my desk. But I also look at you with my "internal eyes" and talk to you every moment.

Beloved, all my love,
Clotilde

La Consuma
Florence
September 9, 1931

> *The days were sunless and the nights moonless*
> *Parched the pleasant April herbage*
> *And the lark's heart outburst tuneless*

if you loved me not. This is the way I felt at times and for hours together yesterday because there was no letter from you. To get through the evening I had to get Nicky to read me *Vingt Ans Après.*[23] I hoped it would make off missing you, longing for you and worrying for you. The result was not a success because the book was not exciting enough, or because nothing short of something tangible as a letter from you could lift me out of my mood. For I easily fall into moods, moods which do not submerge my reason but render it inoperative, impotent.

Perhaps more than you, more than any one, I have felt the Real Presence so that it does not suffice me to carry you in my heart, in my veins, in my pulse. I want more and I can't tell you how often I wake in the night and ache for you. You always are invisible to others like a Homeric deity, but always there although not perhaps in the sense quite in which I shall be present when you talk with Pane. I fear he might feel my presence only too much and become aggressive. Tell

23. Dumas's sequel to *The Three Musketeers* (1844), published in 1845.

me about him and what you said to each other. Dearest, I am sure you have never been loved so much as I love you.

Pellegrinchen was and is with us. They all make fun of me as the hero deserted by his nymph, Bacchus deserted by Arianna. I feel too stunned to write.

B.B.

La Consuma
Florence
September 15, 1931

No word from you. A hurricane is blowing icicles into my insides. The thermometer has sunk to 14C. The worst is that Mary, who is returning this forenoon, is bringing the most fashionable, the most elegant, the most spoiled of New York's "great ladies." I dread to think how she will feel in this Spartan house, in this Siberian weather. And that is not all. The friends who arrived yesterday are also from New York and nothing is more socially distressing to me than trying to entertain people of different "worlds" from the same town.

What a marvellous effect to be seen, the lower hills close by are literally capped by the top of a rainbow.

How abstract you are in your letters. You say nothing of a matter of endless concern to me: your health, your internal, your private weather. You say nothing of Lucia or of Gino. You do not tell me how your days go by, what is the varying color of your hours. I am a little enough of a gossip but you, to me at least, are even less. Loving and loved we remain the same or nearly the same instruments. But what different music each love draws out of us!

Between your love for me and your love for P[ane] there is in common only the impersonal psychological energy. And jealousy finds its pasture there. To make sure there is enough of that energy for himself, the lover wants to monopolize it all.

In the last *Pegaso* appear letters of Scarfoglio.[24] What a prodigious Italian, after Stendhal's own heart. What would not that sentimental Romantic have given to live and love like that! In the same No. are notes by Sibilla Aleramo,[25] surprisingly subtle and unexpected.

Yours,

B.B.

Cava dei Tirreni
Salerno
September 15, 1931

Dearest mine,

How strange not to get any letter from you till now! How soon we get used to happy things! I want to answer to yours of yesterday. No, dear, it is not that I want to make a statue of myself and present me to you in one determinate way. Far from it. I have been recollecting the impulse that pushed me to tear up a letter that I wrote you. It was mostly for this: I had been writing about my discussion with Pane and reported to you some of his own phrases. Well, I knew after I wrote under the impulse of my wish to communicate with you, that he would not have liked me to do so, that he

24. *Pegaso* was an influential monthly journal of arts and letters founded by the journalist and art critic Ugo Ojetti and published from 1929 to 1934. Among its contributors were members of the traditional modernist schools of Italian literature, such as Alberto Moravia, Curzio Malaparte, Eugenio Montale, and Elio Vittorini. Edoardo Scarfoglio (1860–1917), journalist, short story writer and critic of nineteenth-century literature, cofounded Naples's principal newspaper, *Il Mattino,* and remained its director until his death.

25. Sibilla Aleramo, pseudonym of Rina Faccio (1876–1960), whose autobiography *Una donna* (1906) described her quest for liberation from the oppressive bonds of marriage and social convention and her emergence as an embattled, independent writer. Widely reviewed and translated on publication, *Una donna* is considered a precursor of modern feminist thought in Italy.

would have suffered from it. And I simply could not, just before his eyes, post the letter without feeling guilty. I know, I knew I was wrong, but he was not just nuts. I could help neither writing the letter, nor tearing it up. Second, I had written the letter in haste, and I felt it was confused and not clear. And now, haven't I been doing now what seemed guilty three days ago?

And, my dearest, do you feel that I have not been loving you? No, please, do not feel that. I wish I were in your room, or on the yellow sofa, when the fire is creeping up the chimney and we could discuss all this *vive voix*. Look here, I know that I can't help feeling in a multiple way, and I know that I can't sacrifice any of the voices of my spirit without lying to myself, but this makes my relationships hard and complicated, and to be trusted is such a heavy charge to endure. Because we are generally trusted not for what we are, but for what others want us to be. And the worst is that we want to be how the people we love shape us in their loving imagination, their interpretations of us. Is all this clear to you? I wonder: have you ever felt like this, or have you accepted this ordinary *equivoco* [misunderstanding] which always exists at the bottom of most relations? Dearest, do answer. I pine for your answer,

Clotilde

La Consuma
Florence
September 16, 1931

Yours of the 14th has just reached me. Did you write the 15th? A letter of that date has not reached me.

Thanks for the photo. It is very, very good, but I want just another one with an expression that is more permanent and representative than this photo, where you are showing your teeth and laughing. Lucia, on the other hand, comes out well, but I shall be glad to have one of her alone as well.

You ask me to write about Chekhov's *Duel* and Leskov's

Enchanted Wanderer. I don't feel happy talking from memory of things thereof only the impression remains, but no clear recollection of details or even plots. That is the case with most books and that is why I dislike talking about most of them, unless it is to the person with whom I am reading it together. My impression of both these stories is remembered with such pleasure that I am eager to read them again, if only I could afford the time. I am so familiar with the Russian spirit, feel so much at home in it, such acquired as well as instinctive sympathy with it, that it is hard for me to believe that your distaste for both these stories is absolute. Is it not due to the lack of familiarity? If it were positively exotic, you would unconsciously make allowances, but being merely unfamiliar takes the aspect of inadequateness or even formlessness.

Has it occurred to you that the first impressions are seldom more than the projection of one's whole past upon the present moment? To approach the new fact and be able to penetrate it instead of being merely taken about it, requires humility, patience, good will, all at the service of intelligence. Culture, in my sense of the word, consists of having so perfected one's approaches to all manifestations of the spirit that seldom one fails to get their own taste and not the taste of the palate we bring with us.

Love,

B.B.

La Consuma
Florence
September 17, 1931

The letter explaining why you had destroyed one written three days before reached me yesterday evening. The only part that made me happy was your wishing you were here to discuss *a viva voce.* The rest of your letter took several readings before I understood. And finally, when I did understand, I half wondered why it was addressed to me whose doctrines (what a big word!!) are so identical with what you seemed to say.

I want you to "feel in a multiple way" and I don't want you to, and would be horrified if you "sacrificed any voice of your spirit." And if you did, you would be lying to yourself. I am very eager to discover what that self is. Thus, far from having a pattern, or a mould into which I want you to satisfy my own private ideals, I have thus far felt toward you an intuitive reaching out toward an energy whose energy enhances me, but whose shape and mechanism is still a mystery.

And is it not that sense of mystery that makes the beloved fascinatingly obsessive? I believe I have never got over that sense of mystery with anybody I deeply loved. So I don't expect you to live up to any standards my "loving imagination" has set up for you. And I do not want you to give up anything or anybody for me. I truly want to enrich you with all you can take from me and my universe and assimilate. My utmost wish with regard to yourself is to make you into *Unsereiner.* This means that I want you most preciously to preserve every atom, every nuance of your own individuality but developed to the utmost, and then only to contribute all that you have become to the ideal society of kindred souls which for accidental but happy reasons centers about me.

You ask whether I have accepted this "ordinary *equivoco* that there is nearly always at the bottom of most relations." No, I don't accept it, but for better or for worse, I resign myself to it. My own individuality is a fairly crystalline substance and shaped to my own consciousness. I am however accustomed to its being distorted in the eyes of every person I approach by the kind of iridescence he subjectively draws out of me. And this is so inevitable that we are in human relations—when aesthetically and not merely polite-socially considered—a different person with each other individual.

I have resigned myself to the fact that others will take from me not what I *alone* can give, which, as I believe, they can get nowhere else. I have learned to see them finding in others what they suppose they had discovered and enjoyed in me. Very, very few go on finding in one individual a something that nothing can replace. Courage, my Darling. If you truly love whatever me or another, if you have a genius for love, all will be well.

B.B.

La Consuma
Florence
September 18, 1931

What should I not have given to be at Pompei with you! I dream of spending a month there at least and my dreams always include you, I wonder sometimes how much you feel drawn into the beauty of artifacts.

After days of uncertain weather, it is very radiant again this afternoon. Nicky and I have just returned from our morning stroll to the Belvedere and beyond, to see and smell our familiar sights and odors, to be caressed by the familiar breeze, to be warmed by the sun and shaded by the trees you know.

I wish you could see the marvellous object that is now on my desk. It is an Indian lotus with its pink petals deployed out of his canary yellow *cheline* [small petals]. Sustained by a long pliant green stem clustering into an exemplar of arrangement, vigor and softness. I have perhaps never seen before a flower with such matchless beauty. And its odor is the full equivalent of the visual impression.

Moravia[26] came to tea and dinner yesterday and was as frank and discursive and open-minded as a year ago. Again he seemed a promise and a presence. We talked of you. I told

---

26. Alberto Moravia (1907–) is best known for his realistic novels depicting the moral vacuity of conventional Italian middle-class and working-class life, including *Gli indifferenti* (1929), *Le ambizioni sbagliate* (1935), *La mascherata* (1941), and *Il conformista* (1951). Moravia actively opposed Mussolini's Fascist regime.

him I hoped you and he would get on. He said he asked nothing better but feared that Gino had been set against him.

Three weeks yesterday. Let us not many more pass before we meet.

Your loving,
B.B.

La Consuma
Florence
September 19, 1931

No letter, and it is as if out of the day a joy hath taken flight. I feel a depression and oppression during these inter-letter hours that is irrational, and like all real human irrationalities, both poignant and invincible.

A caval donato Dio manda le mosche.[27] So I have to put up with an attack of lumbago which makes my rising up and lying down tortuous and torturing. Hoping to dissipate it, I took last night a whole tabloid of aspirin. Wherefore I woke up early and have felt below par ever since.

I am going to tell you about two of Turgenev's stories we have read recently. In English they are called *The Duellist* and *Clara Militsch*. The second is a study of obsession and the first of a character. This one is as fine a bit of literature as there is in modern fiction. The Russians alone dare to display the contradictions, the unexpectedness that make characters as distinct from incarnate functions *à la* Hebbel, Kleist, Stendhal, or from types *à la* Molière or Maupassant. Most of our Western story-writing suffers from over-integration.

I wish, I wish so many things, and wishing is itself a state of mind.

With love and expectations,
B.B.

---

27. Old Italian proverb meaning "It's a hard life."

La Consuma
Florence
September 21, 1931

If you are, as I hope, my dearest, better and have the leisure of mind and calmness of heart, take up the little Wordsworth I sent you and turn to page 248 and read the "Lines Above Tintern Abbey." I cannot forgive myself for not having read them when you were here. It made me very sad when I realized that they did not come back to me along with the poems I was reading with you. For these lines of the "Tintern Abbey" were for my best years of youth and manhood most frequently in my mind, and of most constant murmur on my lips, like the murmur of the breeze in an Aeolian harp. How it applies again to the landscape in which I am now!

Top of page 249: "But oft, in lonely rooms and mid the din" down to [stanza] "break" and particularly the lines from "that blessed mood in which the burthen of the mystery." On page 250, from "when like a roe I bounded o'er the mountains" to "unborrowed from the eye." On page 251: "a sense sublime / of something far more deeply interfused / whose dwelling is the light of setting suns / and the round ocean and the living air." And the address to the friend, the sister, is one of which I can apply every word to you. Read this poem and ponder over it. Read it as if it were written for you and me.

No word from you yesterday, nor as yet today and considering the severe *settimana inglese* [28] of the posts, I may not hear from you till tomorrow. So I can only pray that all is well for you, that your headache is going or, better still, gone, and no other evils have come to annoy you.

Lovingly,

B.B.

---

28. English week, a reference to the five-day work week that, compared to Italy's six-day week, would further lengthen delivery time.

La Consuma
Florence
September 23, 1931
My darling,

You ask why is it that you don't have any feeling of strangeness toward Tolstoy or Dostoevsky, while you still do feel toward Leskov and Chekhov. It is for the same reason that the littlest children feel perfectly at home with the techniques of autos, of aeroplanes and of electricity. God knows, I don't. It is for the same reason that everybody, nowadays, grows up taking Wagner as a matter of fact, or Proust.

I remember when Wagner was regarded as absurd, and as of Proust, most of the contributors to the *Hommage à Proust* [29] that appeared after his death told me years before that his writing was in the first place not French, and then too boring and stupid and disgusting. I do not understand the mechanism but it is certain that one generation accepts almost unconsciously what the previous could understand only *in paucis* [by the few]. I remember no more than twenty years ago, not only Paul Bourget, [30] but even Mrs. Wharton being alarmed about my sanity of mind because I had such a love and admiration for Dostoevsky. I fear that even the greatest is not manifest at once. Very few get to being what I call "Freemen of the City of Art." And those few only and alone can recognize at sight the quality of a new acquaintance in art . . . or the overwhelming majority never gets farther than to crave for fresh bread, that is to say bread baked that day, but always the same bread.

29. The January 1923 issue of the *Nouvelle Revue Française,* dedicated to Marcel Proust.
30. Paul Bourget (1852–1935), French novelist and essayist, author of numerous novels about the high bourgeoisie in which he argued for the preservation of tradition, especially religion. As a literary critic, he produced innovative work on Stendhal, Taine, and Renan.

This must do for today. Love me as much as you can. I love your love, but I love you even more.

B.B.

I Tatti
Settignano
September 27, 1931

People all day long, and I am tired, tired, tired. At last I got too tired to want the Countess Serristori[31] to stay longer, although she is leaving tomorrow for New York. I dare say if I did not know it, I too should be eager to go and have a glimpse of it. Every day that passes I have less desire to travel for the sake of seeing vast agglomerations of bipeds, governed by other bipeds whose position compels me to accept their personalities although so disproportioned to their authority. So I want for the rest of my days to see places from which material civilization has withdrawn, leaving haunts for dreams, dreams romantic, intellectual, metaphysical, but mere dreams.

After the lodging-house furniture of Poggio allo Spino, I had last night and this morning moments of rapture in my surroundings here. They have an almost ritual beauty and sanctuary splendor. And now come then:

Complete incompletation, O come,
Pant through the blueness, perfect the Summer,
Breathe but one breath role beauty above,
And all that was death grows life, grows love.

B.B.

31. Countess Hortense Serristori, a close friend of the Berensons'.

Hotel Plaza
Rome
October 4, 1931

Dearest mine,

Here I am between two appalling distractions, the hard past and the chimeric future, measuring the feverish intensity of the *liberazione nel vuoto* [liberation in emptiness].[32] I was just sitting on the edge of the bed, unable to decide how to begin this new day, and looking vaguely at this horrible hotel room, fearing the very moment when I shall go and possess with my first look the degree of hostility that the new house will mean for me, when there was a knock on the door and you came.

The last moments were dreadful. I went into the room to say good-bye and, I noticed, my father-in-law did not get up to greet me and say *bonne chance*. The old aunt gave me a hand, and so *it was done*.

Gino was very good to me. He never said a word about it in these last days, but he saw and guessed everything. So many details, what a book Moravia could write! He was sorry for his family through his bones, I am sure.

Pelly is here; I am going to meet her in the new flat. So it is done now. I won't look back like Euridice in the bas-relief in the museum of Naples. If I look back I am lost, and I will not.

My dearest, all my love, and my love to Nicky and Mary. I feel they sympathize with me.

Clotilde

---

32. Criticized by the Marghieri family for her lifestyle and literary ambitions, Clotilde decided to move to Rome.

I Tatti
Settignano
October 4, 1931

I have just come back from my morning run around the garden, alone this time, for Mary is taking her day in bed and Nicky is week-ending with Alda.[33] It is a day of tender beauty like a fruit so mellow that at the least touch its exquisite envelope will break. My senses appreciated and valued what I saw but my heart was with you; for I kept waking up again and again the night wondering how you had stood the journey, and how you had reached the hotel, how you were feeling, were you sleeping, were you comfortless? And I am still so preoccupied that I can't give my mind to anything else. I can neither find distraction in anything, nor can I concentrate upon any problem. So my heart thumps and beats violently and I ache and ache, and all for you.

I did not dare to tell you how much I dreaded you leaving Naples. We are hearth-bubbles and shine in our true light only when we spring from the earth where the long, long years have rooted us. So I hope you will return to Naples some day, although for material reasons Rome is so much more accessible.

Darling, you cannot by any effort of imagination fathom my love for you.

B.B.

---

33. Baroness Alda von Anrep, née Mariano, Nicky Mariano's sister and wife of Egbert von Anrep, chief administrator of Villa I Tatti. She later assumed her sister's post as Berenson's librarian.

Via Barnaba Oriani[34]
Rome
October 8, 1931

Dearest Bibi,

I am deadly tired. I think in part must be the reaction of what I went through in the last weeks, and in part because the benefit of sleep seems to have been taken away from me. This is a small home, where from every room one hears the telephone ringing and the entrance door, and this is quite enough to prevent me from having my afternoon sleep without which I am altogether another human being. I seem to go raving about, not well knowing if I am alive or not. Everything seems so strange, as if happening to another self. I have lost my own consciousness. All my powers are reduced, even that of suffering. So I hardly noticed that Gino is very sad and avoids me.

Pellegrina gave the fireworks of her presence and then slid away, and I was left in contact with reality. And yet I know that this is the worst pain, the more humiliating one, this feeling of lowering our dignity. I feel like a poor, tired beast who wants to sleep and be well nourished and rested, so to be in condition to suffer or to take pleasure in life.

So many thoughts are still in the background of my consciousness. I know they will be drawn out some day, perhaps when I come in contact with you. In fact they are coming out right now. It seems to me that the experience of most of humanity becomes clear, as if I could hear a chorus singing in myself of all the poor people, just because I change [from] a house of twenty rooms to one of six. My whole being and nerves are *à la merci* of a ringing bell. I step into a new universe.

I can't say how and what you are for me, though so far, so inaccessible.

Clotilde

34. Pellegrina Rosselli del Turco's residence in Rome.

I Tatti
Settignano
October 9, 1931

Thou shouldst have been here today, Darling, for there was never a day more poisedly, more radiantly, yet more temperately summer-like. And I should have taken you to see a lotus just opening out in the garden. In the afternoon I should have made you walk in a landscape wherein every element as well as the whole was already a work of art.

You would have enjoyed Ojetti's[35] talk at luncheon. He was full of his visit to Mantua, his *éloge* of Mantegna and the people he met there, including Balbino Giuliano[36] of whom he has a great deal to say, all very friendly and creditable.

Even without you and without as much as a word from you, it has not been at all an unpleasant day. If only one were up to the beauty of the world and could grasp it. *Domine, non sum dignus!*

Humbly,
B.B.

I Tatti
Settignano
October 11, 1931

Darling Love, an hour does not go by without my asking myself how you are occupied, how you are feeling. I should give anything to know, and yet there is no touch of mere cognitive curiosity in it, still less an indiscreet desire to

---

35. Ugo Ojetti (1871–1946), influential journalist, novelist, and art critic. Ojetti wrote for the Milan daily *Il Corriere della Sera* and founded the literary journals *Dedalo* (1920–1933), *Pegaso* (1929–1934), and *Pan* (1933–1935). Throughout his life he remained a high, though decidedly conservative arbiter of cultural matters ranging from literature to music and architecture.

36. Balbino Giuliano (1879–1958), professor of philosophy in Florence and Rome and author of several books on idealist philosophy. Giuliano served as the Minister of Education under Mussolini from 1929 to 1932.

enter into your familiarity. As I have often told you, but as to familiarity, much has to be left out of sight. So my desire to know what you are doing every minute, every time I think of you, is not a hankering for information, but again a yearning, a longing for union, a mystic state in sober fact. And in the same way I want to suck you into my magnetic field and make you share my states of feelings and mind, my thoughts, my ideas, my questionings, my conclusions.

After a sleepless night I had a delicious morning. It was as mellow out of doors with a golden haze touching the landscape. The bells were ringing sweetly—we are lucky to have such musical bells in our parish church—the temperature was perfect. I lay propped up against the pillow which supported my shoulders so comfortably that it was a pleasure.

I read Spenser. I was enchanted with the *Epithalamion*. I used to read it forty years ago but never realized how sensuous, almost voluptuous it is. How is it that the more the merely sexual impulse fades, the more one becomes aware of its diffused presence? I certainly do not identify all sense-pleasure with libido, but sublimated sexuality does seem to pervade the human universe in ways little suspected by the young at the height of their sexual powers.

I do hope your microcosm is less hostile, less annoying. If only I could take you in my arms and comfort you, if only. I do it in the spirit. Does it reach you?

B.B.

I Tatti
Settignano
November 9, 1931

Thanks, dear one, for yours of yesterday. The case you put now is certainly a very subtle and very interesting one, and I don't think it was entirely my fault if I did not quite understand your first attempt to outline it.

An hour later. I was interrupted by the doctor. He came to tell me about the operation Mary has to undergo in a few days, and then she herself had me called to her bed. I sat there and tried to cheer her up. And now the dinner bell has rung, and I sent this so that you may not think that I sulk or that I blame you in any way for the great suffering I have been through and I am going through. You youngsters have no notion what an instrument we oldsters become for suffering as well as for enjoyment.

I shall write more at length tomorrow. This is a token of my love and longing.

B.B.

Via Barnaba Oriani, 9
Rome
November 21, 1931

Dearest mine,

Nicky will have told you a lot, I am sure, but I shall try and draw out my real impressions of Mrs. Wharton. I was, first of all, so expecting the worst that I was astonished to find her not at all cold and distant for a first approach. But Nicky tells me she remains always at this point, she does not give more than that. The first talks we had, I realized how things are seen by her on a plane of clear, neat, clean visuality. She seems to be moderate and secure. I wish I knew if she had anything to say about me.

Yesterday afternoon I went to have tea with Marilù Pavoncelli [37] and she did not seem to me as beautiful as she was. She has now accentuated her type and therefore falsified it. She is too much *à la mode,* whereas she had so much beauty in her to realize a form of her own, outside a series. She was crazy about New York. She saw it in a new light, the skyscrapers were a revelation, and the luxury of the high-class life seemed to incarnate her ideal of social rela-

---

37. Marilù Pavoncelli, wife of the Marquis Pavoncelli, a wealthy land-owner from the region of Puglia who lived in Naples and was a close friend of the Marghieris'.

tions: gold and money translated into beauty, comfort, ease and voluptuousness. I was enchanted to hear her talk, but I felt a sort of malaise in myself. Then she said: "I want to see you often. All my cerebral *côté* is asleep. I can't wake it up with the sort of life I am living. The other *côté* of life has devoured it. Will you try to help me?"

While I write, here is your letter, dearest that you are. The book of Amiel—I got only the second volume, the other was taken from the library—is the *Librairie Stock, 1927, Introduction Bernard Bouvier, nouvelle édition conforme au texte original et suivie d'un index, et contenant une réproduction inédite.*[38] I am just about in the middle of the book, where it speaks of a French writer unknown to me, Dondan, and a book of his called *Mélanges.* Amiel speaks of this writer with enchanting words. Do you have him in the library? He speaks of him with terms that I would use for you, only in part of course. If you have the book in French, read it at page 162.

Nicky will have told you that I saw Balbino Giuliano and he was radiant when I told him that Nicky had said that he looked like a picture of El Greco. That made him aware that I had been in Florence. He did not say it openly, but he kept repeating things like: "I don't like *esteti* [aesthetes], I don't like *raffinati . . . mondani*" [refined, worldly people]. At the end I told him: "My dear, I dislike them so much more than you do, so it is no use saying it. And a real friend of mine is nothing like an *esteta* and especially *mondano,* and the reason why *you* are not a real friend is because *you* are *mondano,* you really are." He laughed and laughed, *quasi felice* [almost happy] . . . strange man. I was telling him the truth, but he could not catch it.

38. The book is the second edition of *Journal intime* by French-Swiss poet and professor of philosophy and aesthetics Henri-Frédérik Amiel (1821–1881), translated as *The Private Journal of Henri-Frédérik Amiel.* Written between 1847 and 1881 and first published in 1923, it records the author's wide-ranging literary opinions and analyses.

Darling, I must leave you and go to see an apartment. With all my love, all my youth and my *richesse de coeur,*

Clotilde

I Tatti
Settignano
November 25, 1931

I am so sorry that you were still in the dumps this morning and I want you to know that I am aware of it so tenderly, and so deeply sympathize with you. Besides all the love I bear you that makes one so understanding, I seem to myself to have for a male a fair insight into your nervous system. Do you smile? Perhaps, perhaps the gulf which I feel so wide and deep and full of storm and stress that stretches between man and woman is one I bridge as little as anyone, even between you and me. "In the sea of life enisled, we mortal millions live alone." But I stretch toward you with all the fibres of my being when I suspect you of being in distress. And worse when I add to it or deepen it.

Mary makes me unhappy again. We hope it is not serious this time, but she has fever and is very sorry for herself.

Nicky and I have just returned from Vittoria De Vecchi's. We chatted pleasantly but not as when we were alone. Then Luisa Malvezzi[39] joined us. If you have met her and remember her, tell me what impressions she made on you. I count so much on your appreciation. Vittoria showed me a photo of yourself with Lucy about two years old in your arms. If you still have a copy, send it. She also has shown me a photo of Balbino Giuliano. It is a face as beautiful as a Giorgione. How perilous to its owner!

November 26. No word from you today by either post and I am unhappy. I am so afraid that you are not only too weary and sad to write, but even to read me. So I want you

---

39. Luisa Malvezzi, a friend of Marghieri's and member of a noble Florentine family.

to know that I love you very much and I hope it makes some difference and does help a bit to pull you out of the dumps.

Yours,
B.B.

Via Barnaba Oriani, 9
Rome
November 26, 1931

I did not write yesterday as I had Pellegrina's visit the whole of the day. Raniero came, too, and apart from the nonsense he said about Fascism he was not so disagreeable. Strange that every time that I happen to utter too definitive, too extreme a judgement, I am brought by new experience to correct it.

We did not talk intimately with Pelly. Yesterday I was in a lazy mood and she was preoccupied with the business of the mines. All the better, perhaps, as I can't help feeling that she suffers a little about you, me and I Tatti. I got your two books. Thank you, my dear.

I made acquaintance in these last weeks with a very strange biped, as you would say. She seemed to me so interesting at the beginning, a beautiful Baudelairean being, but now I have found the needle in the haystack. Or better, there is no needle, only a haystack. I feel so interested in exploring a *fuoriserie* [unique] creature. I get through it a better understanding of myself. It is the first time I have come in contact with a woman of that kind. No, perhaps the second, I am sorry I never told you about her. It would be hard to describe my feelings toward her: curiosity, pain, a strange malaise, a sort of satisfaction with myself through the feeling of being at another level, but not all a sense of disgust as I might have had years ago. And strangest of all, if I try to remember what first attracted me toward her, I must admit that it was a sort of physical, mysterious attraction, as I realized in the first conversation that she was not intelligent, but only vivacious; not serious, but only superficial and dissipated by mundane life, idiotic entourage and so on.

Aren't we strange? When we meet I will tell you more. But why are we so far away? And I am afraid I shall not be able to come. And why must Edith Wharton have you and not I? Why not come to Naples or Capri for Christmas? How much we miss of each other!

Darling, I write in the room where I have always your *Crocifissione* under my eyes. I look at it and I love it more and more. The beauty of it is now all revealed to me. How I love to have it!

All, all yours,
Clotilde

I Tatti
Settignano
November 27, 1931

It is hard to know how to answer your letter of yesterday wherein you tell me of the friend you have been seeing. The case as you put it has little mystery for us males. We have experienced it not once, not twice, but again and again. You have yourself read innumerable novels on the same theme and Catullus sang it two thousand years ago when he shouted *Odi et Amo* to Lesbia.

Yes, attraction and repulsion, physical attraction and spiritual repulsion, equal as a rule sexual fascination and end as much as impulse ends. We males, we give way to these feelings constantly and we seldom like when we in-love, and do not often dare to ask what we do or what we don't. The more self-aware of us know that we can in-love a woman and dislike, even loathe her and execrate her for fascinating us into courting her. And when we do it, it is like tasting the apples of Sodoma, bitter ashes the reek of which we cannot get out of our mouth.

That of course is the extreme, and between it and the

bliss of in-loving and loving and liking and approving alto-gether in one, there are numberless graduations. On one of them occurs your relation to the friend who is now in Rome. I fear that to one of my experience of nearly fifty years of man and woman, there is nothing either abnormal or even unusual in the feelings you describe and certainly nothing mysterious. I dare say you find me *antipatico* and lacking in all subtlety. Perhaps I do in writing and perhaps I should even in speaking, and yet I believe I understand. The truth is that you women who mean to be free sexually as men, will end either by ruining yourself or by being as a matter of fact about it as experienced men are.

There are a few exceptions, a few bipeds like myself who through seven ages drag their adolescence with them and never get used to taking in-love as *geste quelconque* [a ges-ture of no importance], no matter how arduously attained, nor with amorous wooing, BUT take it always as a spiritual illumination, as a Burning Bush, as a promotion in the hier-archy of the soul. Not that we too are not capable of the most animal lust, but we know lust and and recognize it, no matter how coated, how sugared, how scented.

Now, if I were courting you, I should not send you what I have just written. I do, although it but grossly and vaguely tells you my meaning. You are intelligent enough to believe that there is meaning in what I say, and you will not readily write me down for either a fool or even an *innocente,* al-though the last must be a great temptation.

Yours,
B.B.

I Tatti
Settignano
December 8, 1931

Your letter of yesterday was very dear and if it really is true that I started you on new channels of thought and feeling, everything will ultimately turn out well, even if I do suffer a great deal first.

You ask me why I want to be truthful about the kind of love I feel for you now. How can I answer in a few words and not still distort, misrepresent and stultify my meaning? Let me try, and you in your turn be intelligent and sympathetic and indulgent. It is something like this: when you left me at La Consuma and the lyric rapture of your presence had evaporated, I became aware of a terrible obsession. It took at first the aspect of an imperative need, a headstrong impulse to rejoin you, to be with you no matter under what circumstances. I mastered myself as best as I could, childishly counting on your coming to I Tatti about the fifteenth of October. When you failed to appear, I was stunned. Reviving, I began to realize that my lyric had been a key, a golden one; it seemed at first that it had been turned to iron and I was opening a door behind which yawned infinities of emptiness. I knew these infinities of emptiness were within myself and I understood that what I expected of you was to fill that hollowness and reunite me to myself.

I became painfully aware that I had been over this calvary again and again, that hitherto passion had always taken that way with me and that there was no reason to suppose that even if you were ready to play the part of Quintus Curtius to my inner abyss, it was not likely that, more than any predecessors, you could fill it. Or if you gave me the illusion of filling it, that the illusion would last long.

So what I want to get rid of is not loving you either morally or physically, but the obsessive yearning for you as a sacrifice to the unappeasable feeling of hollowness, of loneliness, a sacrifice to all the chimerae with many heads each craving a distinct and different unrealizability.

There would be a cure that I cannot take. It would consist in seeing you all I wanted of you in my own atmosphere. As that is not practical, I shall have to get over it with pa-

tience, prayers and fasting. If at the end I find myself loving
you as an individual and not as a sacrifice, loving you as
Clotilde and not as an impersonal, or merely physical attraction, loving you as a companion of body and soul, then I
shall be happy. But "Ah prince, what labour!"

I have spent more than half an hour with Mary. She
asked me to come and rub her hands which she felt were
dead and only to be brought to life by my loving caress. I
was touched. Then she insisted on talking about you and so
sympathetically, so fondly. Poor, dear Mary. She has been
pretty near the brink and has not yet recovered from the
shock.

In thy hands I lay my spirit,

B.B.

I Tatti
Settignano
December 12, 1931
Dear,

I was in despair yesterday to have no word from you,
and felt so frightened that my last letter had hurt you. Today
I received yours of two days ago and you confess that I have
hurt you. Then perhaps you don't realize how very much I
love you. My love has nothing of a lyric intermezzo about it.
It is not a relief for more serious affections, nor an escape
from the mediocrity and the dullness and weariness of ordinary life. In truth I do not need such an escape, for excepted
when ill I scarcely know what it is to be without zest for the
passing moments that could embrace and hold back when
they pass.

Your failing to come in October and your categorical
announcement after your last visit that you would not be
able to return in December, but instead rather banteringly
teasing me to chuck Mrs. Wharton and join you in Naples or
Capri, brought it home to me that you were not house-free.
And I wanted so much to love you that I was silly enough to

let myself believe that you were free to come and go as you liked. The final realization that you were not heart-free either, while only flaming the flame of love for you, tore away all veils from the tragic reality that, for me at least, passion means nothing else than the headlong urges to complete interpenetration.

And how can I answer the question at the end of your letter: "Why suffer? Except by our isolation?" Yes, it is just that. I need your physical presence, I need to breathe the air that you breathe, I need to be close enough to your body so that words cease to have purpose and become pure music. I need all that, and if I do not get it I perish.

If Mary takes a turn for the better, I shall be going Monday the 21st to Hyères. For a month I will be for letters three days distant and I shall ache and yearn more and more and more. You cannot love me as I love you, if you can be so philosophical about separation. You cannot measure the pain, the gnawing pain I feel. I dare say if you felt it you would understand wanting to diminish it, if you could not wholly get rid of it. Dear One, do not think I am making you reproaches. Far from it. I congratulate you if you can love me with so much more joy than sorrow. I cannot even conceive this desire, but I want to love you less wildly, less rebelliously, less agonizingly. I want to love you more serenely, more on the plane of spirit and less on the marble of matter and material presence and contact. I want to be able to love you in absence and not ache like a cruelly amputated creature the moment you are out of my sight. I want to love you so that the hours we do spend together shall not be poisoned by the dread of their ending.

How darling of you to wish to be my last love. Will you be? You can, that is to say you could. But do you mean it, or is [it] merely a happy thought? If you mean it, do you realize what a burden you are taking upon yourself? Your frail body, your delicate spirit, can they undertake such a responsibility? I have no doubts they could, but is it worth your while, am I worthy of all you have to give and take and suffer to remain my last love? What nonsense am I talking, mere records of the mental disk buzzing.

Yet, Darling of Loves, I do want to love you so integrally, so really, so free from humbug and rhetoric, yet so tenderly, so passionately, so joyfully. But you in your turn must let me say *nearly* everything that passes through my mind, and try to understand so as never to be hurt *for long,* and never fail to tell me when I do hurt. We are sensitive in different spots, so to speak, and like children we have not learned each other's weak spots.

And when can I hope to see you again? Is there a chance of your coming here in February, if only I could look forward to some such light at the end of the tunnel?

Dear, I must stop.

B.B.

Sainte-Claire Le Château
Hyères (Var)
December 25, 1931

Can you imagine one of my chief reasons for coming here just now? You won't be able to guess, so I'll tell you. It is that here just about a year ago I had a letter from you which made me realize for the first time that you were going to be a great deal to me, to mean very much to me, count greatly in my life. I from that moment felt an *amour curiosité* for you, mingled if you like with a touch of *amour aventure.* What never occurred to me was how far it would carry me.

And dear to me for so many reasons as this place had been before, because of so many memories of the affections and recollections of beauty and of holiday life, this one reason, your letter of a year ago, has made it dearer to me than all other reasons put together.

Reasons, but what an unreasonable philosopher I am, and your friend Signora Gigli, in the letter you showed to me, spoke of *il savio* [a wise man], save the mark!

And now, where do I stand toward you and where do you stand toward me? Where I stand I know, and you? What do I really know? What do I know about your depths, your nooks and crannies, your hidden caverns? Or is all this vain imagining? Is it all simple and subtilizing and filing away facts to make them more palatable? At this point I feel tempted to *à vous cracher tout mon coeur* [open my heart]. But now you must have troubles enough of your own and of a nature so serious that I have no heart to bother you with my bobos. These can go aching till I can whisper them into your ear with your hand that I love so much in my hand. Then perhaps I can pour out all that has welled up in me. By that time it may have settled and got cleared.

B.B.

Sainte-Claire Le Château
Hyères (Var)
December 26, 1931

Yesterday the Noailles[40] lunched here. The moment I laid eyes on Marie Laure I asked Edith whether she still saw the resemblance between this woman and yourself. This led to Edith's giving a very appreciative account of you which I enjoyed. As for me, Marie Laure's full face seemed so much broader, more mask-like, more *primitif,* or if you like more archaic than yours. But her profile did have a vague resemblance to yours, harder, more archaic again, but still, still the likeness was there.

And would you believe that it started in me a new interest in this person whom I have seen so often and I talked with her with a warmth I had never felt before? She responded in the same way, and thus far my love for Clotilde has made me see in a vague counterpart of her, namely Marie Laure, qualities that previously had escaped me!

---

40. Viscount Charles de Noailles and his wife, Marie Laure de Noailles, née de Sade.

She had her lips and nails lacquered with sealing-wax red and her hair was done in flat ringlets plastered against her temples. I told her I wanted a photo to send you showing off these ringlets.

Your last letter from Rome has just reached me, four days. There is no photo in it and you say nothing of having received the binding sent ten days ago. As for all you say in your letter, it is so beautiful that I find it hard to take it myself. And yet I want to. I yearn to believe that I mean all that to you. Let it be, let it last, let it last for ever.

Your own,

B.B.

Sainte-Claire Le Château
Hyères (Var)
January 5, 1932

Nor this morning either! No letter. I do so hope that the new self-insertion into a strange world was not too painful and that when this reaches you a homey feeling toward your new shelter will have overcome you.

Edith and Norton[41] and I tense with expecting Nicky who arrives this afternoon. Lapsley[42] would perhaps dispense with her society, for I do not get the impression that they were made for each other, being one so insularly Anglo-Saxon and donnish, and the other so cosmopolitan and unpedantic. What would she not be if she did not give up the world to be Martha for me!

You and I who are Marys should be grateful to our Marthas, so grateful that we never lose patience with them.

41. Robert Norton, British diplomat and painter who lived in France and Italy, and a close friend of Edith Wharton's.
42. Gaillard Lapsley, an American scholar of medieval English history, professor at Trinity College, Cambridge, and a close friend of Edith Wharton's.

Without them we should not remain Marys very long. It is because they toil and moil that we keep free for being Marys, and following the winds of the spirit-age and our impulse too. What privileged parasites you and I are! I am old enough to know and to love you all the more for it.

B.B.

Sainte-Claire Le Château
Hyères (Var)
January 11, 1932
Dear Clotilde,

After twelve or thirteen days without a single word from you, I got a short letter at last. You tell me your boy had high fever and this prevented you from writing. And you make me feel silly to have worried so much, but at the same time relieved that it was nothing worse.

And in compensation you entertain me with the hope that you will come to I Tatti in a month or so. I hope you will. I am quite sure you can manage it if you want to— enough.

I have little to tell you about myself. News from Mary has been more reassuring, but on the other hand Mrs. Wharton's doctor opened up prospects of further trouble that made me quake with fear. At the same time, something in wind and weather upset me and then I had to go to bed, where I am writing to you now.

Nicky complains that Norton is too absorbed in his painting to be attentive to her as he used to be. On the other hand, she has finally subdued the severe and cold Lapsley. Evening before last I heard him say to Edith: "Have you seen how beautiful and distinguished Nicky was looking just now as she bent over the music?"

I am anxious to get back, so I shall not make any other visit on this side of the frontier, but stop over at Genoa to see

Laura Gropallo and the Lubbocks[43] at Lerici. Why do I tell you all this? It is only senile garrulity.

B.B.

I Tatti
Settignano
January 21, 1932

Listen, you Dear. Mary sends you the particular message that she wants you to come to us for as long as you can stay. At her present rate of very slow progress she ought in a week to be, we dare hope, out of danger, so that we could enjoy your society with a free heart. Will you now try to come in about a week?

I think it would be better to talk to you rather than attempt to write in answer to your letter of yesterday. I could not write it all in a nutshell. I cannot get over your twelve days at Naples of neither writing to me or even taking the trouble to get my letters forwarded from Rome. I know there are attenuating circumstances. But I did put and pour my heart and soul in those letters. At least I thought I did.

And you have encouraged me. You had begged me to think of you at the minute when the New Year began. I did. I wrote at length. No response. It was worse—no, it was not worse than death. But it did make [me] unhappy as I had perhaps never been in my soul. And did it not occur to you that you had a certain responsibility toward my integration of spirit? Don't you realize that you should consider my idiosyncrasies, as I most genuinely try to consider yours?

---

43. Laura Gropallo was a close friend of the Berensons'; she spent several months each year at her villa in Nervi, a small town near Genoa. Lord Percy Lubbock and his wife, Lady Sybil Lubbock Scott Cutting, née Cuffe, lived in the town of Lerici, near La Spezia. She had previously been married to Geoffrey Scott, Berenson's private secretary for twelve years. Percy Lubbock was a friend of Edith Wharton's and wrote a biography of her, *Portrait of Edith Wharton* (1947).

But, no. I shall not go on. For every syllable carries with it a full-fledged swarm of misunderstanding. And I do want to love you not because I must, but because it is a joy, because it is enhanced life, because it is radiant. Not because the *bacillus amandi* is coursing thro' my veins.

And never let yourself think for a moment that any one has ever said a word against you. Nor would any word have any effect, except to disgust me with the person who said it. So, if you love me, come.

B. B.

I Tatti
Settignano
January 23, 1932

I am sending this to Naples but shall not say much for fear of your having meanwhile gone to Rome and the danger that *nella confusione* this will fail to reach you. I enclose some Kodak prints that will amuse you for a minute. Edith has come out well.

Mary has given us a great fright and yesterday a consultant came to see with fresh eyes into Mary's case. He was not alarming in his report, not to me at least, but on our walk later in the day Nicky burst out with pent-up fears. I really do not know what to think. I find it difficult to entertain the idea that Mary may not recover. Perhaps it is only animal optimism that leads to me expect those very near to be immortal. Nobody linked up to me can die while I remain alive: "Vie de rose, pas de jardinier mort." But Nicky did succeed in frightening me. Mary speaks sympathetically of you and affectionately and every day asks for your news.

Benedetto Croce[44] has just spent two hours here. He

44. Benedetto Croce is, of course, best known for his philosophical and historiographical work, particularly his use of the concept of historicism, the belief that history is a creation of the present and not merely a neutral record of the past. He also wrote on aesthet-

told us all about your father-in-law's[45] career. He talked of others, including acquaintances of your own. Then we launched into more general topics, chiefly literary and historical. What a memory he has. I have always maintained that to really get anywhere you must have a retentive memory. I have a very bad verbal one, and not too good in other respects.

This is not a letter but a interim report. I forgot to say that Maria Teresa walked me Thursday.

Für die Ewigkeit dein
[Eternally yours],
B.B.

I Tatti
Settignano
February 21, 1932

Darling, dearly beloved, you threaten to withdraw your confidence, your faith in my sympathy; you will not pour out your heart anymore to me. If only I could get you to believe that my great unhappiness about you is due to the fact that you don't pour out your whole soul. You keep back so much. You give at the most half thoughts. Only once at La Consuma, when you talked so torrentially about your troubles at Naples, you suddenly burst into the cry: "But I am not telling you all. I am telling you half truths only." It was that cry that made me hope I had found a woman who had the integrity of mind to open her heart to me and leave it wide open.

But it closed up, almost at once. I believe I know why,

---

ics and founded *La Critica,* an important journal of cultural criticism launched in 1903. A conservative at heart, Croce was a leader of Italy's Liberal forces. Although initially uncritical of Fascism, he later repudiated Mussolini's regime.
45. Alberto Marghieri, senator and chairman of the University of Naples.

and would not hesitate to tell you, provided you were real and genuine enough to listen to me. As it is, I itch to sit down and write it all out. But I have no time and probably no talent to write it out in such a way that it would purge and liberate me. So for your own sake no less than for mine, I would love you to help me create a relationship between yourself and myself that will permit you to be perfectly and wholly frank and outspoken, without any half-admissions, without any ominous silences, without reserves of any kind or any sort of reticence.

What you would tell me might have a great deal of passing pain, but nevertheless make me supremely happy. For I want to be your friend. I want to sympathize with all that goes on in you, no matter what it is: *Clotildae nihil a me alienum puto*.[46] No matter even if it reveals how much more and earnestly and spiritually you care for another than me. Believe me, it is the imperative need of integrity and no desire to monopolize you that torments me in your case and makes me so miserable.

Give me your whole soul to love and cherish as you are free to give all the other and such marvellous parts of yourself to whom you will. Not that I don't desire them. I want them only too passionately, but I am ready to sacrifice them for a completely integrated friendship with you. From you to me as it is from me to you.

Perhaps I am asking what is impossible "and alone live for ever only the kings of the sea." I think you are intelligent enough about others to understand what I mean. Understanding you may yawn, and conclude that it is more than you bargained for. You wanted an exotic diversion, and this diversion turned out to be gravely, almost puritanically serious, and painfully in earnest. In that case, the sooner the

---

46. Nothing that concerns Clotilde is alien to me—clearly a play on Terence's "humani nil a me alienum puto" (nothing human is alien to me).

misunderstanding is cleared up, the better for both of us. Can you, and will you be a friend as I tried to define, or is it a thing for which you have no need, not as yet at least?

Whatever you decide, let me urge you for all the deep love that I have for you, to re-integrate yourself and live from and for that central self. But I see that I am losing my sense of humour, for the last sentence, although I mean it with the whole of me, might come out of a lay lenten sermon.

So, my much loved, much desired, much yearned for Darling, I end wishing you so well, and if only you had them, on your own terms.

B.B.

Piazza dei Martiri, 30
Naples
February 23, 1932
Dearest Bibi,

Here is your letter. It makes me wonder and wonder. It makes me hesitate in answering. To talk would be so much more natural, whereas writing seems so sententious. I wish a good angel inspired my words never to hurt you. You seem to be so *possédé* by a fixed idea, more than an idea, by an instinct of possession. You want to possess my spirit, my soul, my brain, so that you might have me. I can't find the words, but I know this feeling. It is almost as ferocious, allow me the word, as the other; at least they participate of the same essence. If you deny it, there is no use going on, and that is why talking would be so much easier. But I am sure. And you are terribly spoilt by the life you have led, and your extraordinarily charming nature has made all experience easy. And if you will it, you rage for it.

I understand you, my dear, for I am nearly as bad as you. Whenever I wanted something, I should have it at any price. But I know what it means not to get hold of a soul. It can make me crazy, but the best way is not to break it into pieces like a children's toy. I have the impression you were doing that with me. I sympathize with you, dear. I recognize myself in your devouring curiosity—no use changing its name: this is it—and male instinct of possession.

You may hide it in words, amiable and mystical. The fact is: you have to face it. I would rather see you so than discover you under a milder language. But I don't want you to suffer for me and I must tell you, my dearest, listen: I am quite true to you; that is, I don't justify your doubts, your suffering. I have talked to you twice very, very openly, once in La Consuma, but once at I Tatti, too, while having our tea the first or second day when I was there in November. And my cry at La Consuma, I remember so well even the *sfumature* [subtleties] of my feeling. I could feel that through my talking, you ended by having a sketch of me that was false, a picture of me that was incomplete.

I felt miserable for having condescended to "describe" life instead of synthesize it, and I felt that I had delivered to you a false image of myself and of someone I had loved in the past, and I cried out to you. But this is only half the truth. I had sinned in my *superbia* [pride] trying to revive a past life and make it alive without treachery. We cannot possess one another's past; hardly one another's present. We can only love and give. Giving makes us rich in return. I have not yet learned this, not at all, but I know that all other love is sorrow and bitterness and unchains too powerful desires with no reason. Love is only a spontaneous offer. This is my vision of it in a state of grace. I know we must get to this, but I am far from it. And you? Are we at the same point?

What is sure is that I am entertaining in my daily thoughts this loving correspondence with you, and no other affection can shadow it. I won't destroy anything vital in me, so I won't destroy one atom of my feeling for you as I won't destroy other affections. Because everything can be destroyed and you know this, my dearest, *far better than I do,* and your life gives evidence of this truth. I remember that at the very beginning of our acquaintance I thought that I could have never loved you just because I felt you belonged to many, that you were not a monad. I myself was just like you because I never found harmony in my way. But then you gave me a wider and richer vision of love unchained. You know that I am very fond of him. We are friends, but he has not monopolized me. His being your opposite torments me, not in my heart but theoretically, if I may say so. I have found it, I should say, like the incarnation of the two principles of life: seeing and conception of amorous feeling.

And I? I am myself a mystery to myself between you two. But I have no greater joy than to dissect myself with you. I can't bear it that you should not recognize it. Ask me anything, openly, but anything. Get free, *do, do*. Anything I will answer.

All my love
Clotilde

I Tatti
Settignano
February 28, 1932

My dearest love,

I have not been myself since your long letter of five days ago. I don't know what is the matter. I don't think it is merely that some utterances in that letter had a kind of paralyzing effect. I dare say it coincided with some grossly physiological upset. But I cannot deny that your letter did upset me. I have studied it and I remain unable to meet it, particularly as you warn me that you know you are right despite of what protestations I may make and the refuge I may take in petty phrases. So I should not write just as yet, for my mind is void and empty and null.

I write, nevertheless, because I do love you so tenderly, so devotedly, that I do not want you to think for a day or longer that I am in any way put out by you or cross with you, or that I am sulking. No, darling mine, it is none of these things. The whole truth, as I see it in my own mind and heart is that I love you in every way, that I want to love you just as you are, that I have no desire to interfere with you and still less to change you, but that I am consumed for those very reasons with the longing to know just what you are. My curiosity is not so much about your material and social and emotional connections, although they interest me, but about your reactions toward them, about what goes on in your mind and heart. Just because I love you so tenderly, so devotedly, so affectionately, and so little in cannibal fash- ion—at least so it seems to me—I am like a religious mystic who cannot ever be satisfied by comprehension, by penetra- tion, by union with the object of his love and desire. *Ist das so niedrig was ich dachte?* [Is what I thought so lowly?]

Thirty years hence, when you are my present age, if you remember with enough vividness and warmth the infini- tesimal vortex known for some years as Bibi, you may think it was not so mean that I felt that way toward you.

Love

B.B.

[I Tatti, Settignano, February 29, 1932][47]

You want me as a diversion, a relaxation, a safety valve for the great passion you have for another. And if I were hero- ically magnanimous, I should be happy to serve you in this role. But I am still too animally selfish for such saintliness.

[B.B.]

47. This note was written in Berenson's handwriting on the reverse side of Marghieri's letter of February 23. It was never sent.

I Tatti
Settignano
[February 29, 1932][48]
Dearest,

You could have started the discussion while you were here and we could have got somewhere. Writing, well, from what point of view shall I answer? A number present themselves to me each demanding wheels of elaboration. If I had the literary gifts to give the adequate forms to each of the answers, I should have achieved a masterpiece beggaring Proust and his likes. Obviously, gift apart, this is out of the question and I shall attempt, feebly I fear, to answer in a way suitable to the present case. I wish, by the way, you had not torn up your "tumultuous" letter, even if it was, as you say, "indiscreet." As a matter of fact, what do you expect me to say? Shall I tell you heroically and melodramatically: "No, I can brook no rival. Choose between us"? Why?

If you love two, and two so opposite to each other, I can only approve. Get all you can out of each of them and when you have extracted both, look about for more. I should however like you to draw your attention to the fact that much that seems so opposite in your two friends is due to differences in age, experience and ambience. When your friend, who is now 66, was the age of your other friend who is not half that age, he was also monistic and full of purpose. He was rigidly puritanical still and monogamous. He has now life behind him of necessity, no matter how others, you for example, may give him the hope that more is coming. The younger friend no doubt sees life spreading out before him as the fair fields of Lombardy did through the ages of Northern conquerors. The vital difference between the two is perhaps not exactly where you place it. It is not rather that the younger man bends his bow and shoots his arrow to the

48. This date is written on the letter in Clotilde Marghieri's handwriting.

target of achievement, whereas the other never cared very much for that, except as a means, but strove with such powers as nature gave him and circumstances did not thwart—strove, I say, to attain a certain state of grace, a certain delicacy of insight, a power of appreciation, of ecstasy, of sympathy, of identifying himself with all that is vital in nature and man. He wanted to become an instrument, and to him life was lived for the improvement of that instrument.

Therefore, the older friend has always disliked competition, rivalry, aggressiveness, deliberate self-assertion, acts of authority etc. etc. He has never sought honors or places of power. Your younger friend, no doubt *ad majora dei gloriam,* if you have not misinformed me, wants all these. I most cordially wish him success and the more so as his successes could not compete with anything I want

EXCEPT YOURSELF

If he could convince you that you must be his alone and leave me, I should be sorry indeed but I should not join battle with him, nor plead for you. "My service is one of perfect freedom," Jesus is reported to have said. I can do no better than try ever so humbly to imitate Him.

My darling Clotilde, who occupies such a splendid lodging in my spirit and in my heart. You know how much I make of the Real Presence and how I should miss that, and ache for you. Yet I will not fight for it. Come to me free.

I hear the car. I must stop.

B.B.

Via Reno, 22[49]
Rome
March 7, 1932
Dearest Bibi,

I feel I am going through a tunnel and can't get to the end of it. From time to time an opening reminds me of free

49. The new residence of the Marghieris' in Rome.

53

air and sunlight, but soon all gets dark again. I am like one who is pursued by what is to be done, a sort of *imperativo categorico*.

Things are now even more difficult. My husband is in Naples for some new business and does not even come on Sundays. In the meantime, I had to take the boy out of school because his second grade report was so bad that he would have had to repeat the year. So now he studies at home. I had to take two professors, and for the rest of the day he is at home with me. I can't have two governesses, and this one I have is so good for the girl, but won't have two children. Oh, dear me! What vampires are sons . . . I don't know why it comes back to me the title of a book, *Sons and Lovers*. But children *are* terrible. I dare say you understand me entirely. I think it is my mother's blood that works in me in such a way that I have to let all my blood be sucked. I feel a dreadful responsibility.

And yet it wouldn't surprise me at all if all of a sudden I had to say good-bye to everyone and enter a rest house. I Tatti seems so far off, a kind of realm of luxury where I am not prepared to enter yet. I feel I should be *rimessa a nuovo* [like new], first, before I can come back to you. Pelly told me you may be coming to Rome for Easter. Is that possible? We are going to Naples for five days, but if you came, my God, I think I would stay here just to be free and stay with you. If only it were true!

Yours,
Clotilde

I Tatti
Settignano
March 10, 1932

My poor tormented darling, what a time you are having, in a way almost as enigmatical as Mary's dreadful pains which the doctors do not understand at all. And yet I do understand, for I have from earliest times had a sacred hor-

ror of children and the *will* not to have any of my own. I did
not trust my stock, in a biloquial sense, and I certainly could
not trust my nerves. And the idea of a tie with anybody that
is not elective is so repugnant to me that I cannot be fair to
my own brothers and sisters. They are charming, cultivated
people much above the average, but I am always on my
guard against claims as a brother.

And children would be worse. Nor are they ours. They
are descendants from savage ancestors, and not only one's
own, but of the accomplice in begetting them. No, generation should be left to people who still can perform the highest as well as the lowest physiological functions with the
same thoughtlessness.

However, your children are there and you have to bring
them up, and I am very sorry for you and deeply sympathize
with your moods of rebellion. So much that you might
resent it!

Is there anybody among your Neapolitan acquaintances
who knows German well enough to read Werfel's *Die Geschwister von Neapel*[50] and tell you, who will pass it to me,
what they think of it? As a novel I do not think much of it,
but I find it interesting as anthropology. I wonder how true
it is. Can such a patriarchal isolated household still exist?

If you had written a few days before this last letter to tell
me you could manage to send your family off to Naples for
Easter, and be in Rome by yourself for five whole days, I
certainly should have come. I already made arrangements to
spend the holiday with Mrs. Wharton. Nicky and I will
leave the night of the 24th and stay away a fortnight. I cannot
disappoint Mrs. Wharton for she really counts on me and
does care about my society with heart and mind. And I cannot and would not disappoint her.

---

50. Franz Werfel (1890–1945), Prague-born playwright and novelist.
Published in 1931, the book was translated into Italian as *I Pascarella,* and into English as *The Pascarella Family.*

But Nicky will be away from April 15 for ten days or more. Could you not come then for as long a visit as possible? Mary would be enchanted for she asks every day why you are not coming and when you are expected. By the way, if Nicky and I go, it is because Mary's daughter will be here to replace us. So, if you could manage to come in April it would be wonderful. It would be "the time, the place, and the loved one altogether." Try to arrange it. I shall not storm and fret if you don't, but do try.

Dear Clotilde, I am so much with you but I fear it is not of much help. Darling, Darling . . .

B.B.

I Tatti
Settignano
May 6, 1932

Your little letter finds me in the depths. If only you had come yourself, you might have pulled me up. Yes, I shall probably reach Rome the evening of the 16th, that is to say a week from Monday. But there will be no end of people to see—sins of the past—and there will be Mrs. Wharton commanding my time. I shall see you deemly and converse with you as according to descriptions I have read. Tolstoy once used to talk above the din and shout to prisoners behind bars. I so dread the prospect, that if I could get out of going to Rome I should. And it is because of you and you only. The fact that I shall see you and yet not see you gives me every kind of anticipated discomfort. Perhaps the reality will not be so bad.

Besides being in the dumps, I have been in a painful condition of nerves. It has taken all the energy I had not to burst out and bark at people. And this is the Florentine season, when we have to see so many people all day long and most of them so indifferent and some hateful. My insides have come back on me and I have wretched nights and worse mornings faint and sick. And worse and worse anxieties about money. I had about one million of your money in Kreuger and Toll Co. Every penny of that lost.[51] And that is far from the worst. So I do not know how much longer I shall be able to carry on this very costly establishment. It makes me doubly regret that you have not been able to come here, for who knows whether I shall ever be here another spring.

B.B.

Via Reno, 22
Rome
June 29, 1932: Monday morning
Dearest Bibi,

Your letter of Sunday tells me the reason of your being worried and low-spirited. I perfectly understand and sympathize and I like the way you have faced in yourself the dilemma between being the slave of the standards of life you have been enjoying hitherto, and having your freedom of soul. I still hope and hope that you won't have to give up I Tatti. I am sure so many solutions can be found to prevent it. I can't think of you going through the awful detachment.

Excuse my writing about myself. I hadn't realized you had so concrete worryings and I thought you were feeling tepid and I complained for that. But I know too well what a transition means and I sympathize with all my heart. If only one could do something. I know we can. We can give all the richness of our love, company, mind, thought, and so reward largely for all that has been taken away in ease of life.

51. This letter misled Meryle Secrest to suggest that Bernard Berenson lost one million lire of Clotilde Marghieri's money in Kreuger's bankruptcy; see Secrest, *Being Bernard Berenson* (London and New York 1981). However, what Berenson means is that he lost one million of his own money in Italian currency—"your [Italian] money."

You have meant so much to me, you can hardly imagine. It is through you, more than any one else, that I have not felt the transition so bitterly.

I am still reading Aksakov.[52] See how slowly I read? I let myself be *enveloppée* by the subject by reading little by little. I have begun to write my impressions about it. I thought of translating the book, if that could have made me earn something, even little. It should be a great relief for me to feel free to realize my wishes, considered that I have had to renounce them sometimes for lack of money.

Darling, to talk with you without inhibitions, so freely and openly, is such a joy. Your spirit blows into mine and brings it to new life.

All my love,
Clotilde

La Consuma
Florence
July 19, 1932

Yes, by all means come with Vittoria, August 10. I have the greatest confidence in her as a friend of yours as well as a friend of mine. I am sure she takes us each separately. It is quite likely that every one *vingt ans aprés* will be here: Pellegrina and Vittoria at La Gocciola, the idyllic villino below us, and Maria Teresa Rasponi at Vallombrosa.

Day before yesterday the Ojettis came to tea and dinner. We talked of Alvaro and Pancrazi[53] and *Pegaso* and Nicky be-

---

52. Russian novelist Sergei T. Aksakov (1791–1859).
53. Corrado Alvaro (1895–1956), author and journalist best known for his compassionate accounts of the hardship of peasant life in southern Italy, particularly in his native Calabria. His books include *Gente in Aspromonte* (1930), *Vent'anni* (1930), and *L'uomo è forte* (1938). Pietro Pancrazi (1893–1952), journalist, novelist, literary critic, and Ojetti's co-editor at *Pegaso*. Pancrazi was a follower of Croce's philosophical and aesthetic doctrines and wrote numerous scholarly volumes on twentieth-century literature as well as *Donne e buoi dei paesi tuoi* (1934), a novel.

gan to speak of your article and Mary chimed in. Both sang so high that there was no room for my voice. Ojetti got interested and asked to see the article. Then he said he himself would write and ask you for it, and took your address. But like other great men he may forget. So, if you don't hear from him in a few days, send him the article all the same (*Il Salviatino, San Gervasio, Firenze*).

I must stop

B.B.

Cava dei Tirreni
Salerno
July 26, 1932

I got a letter from Pane telling me about his visit to Gillet[54] and he tells me about you in these terms: that he wishes to write to you long letters, but he is held back by a sort of inhibition. I told him not to feel like that towards you and I encouraged him to write any time he wishes it. He was glad to meet Gillet, but I know he wrote to you about it.

I have read Julie Talma's letters.[55] I devoured them. They are *crocquantes* and very refined *petit bonbons*. They do reveal a very feminine being together with a maturity of mind clear and master of itself. What really struck me was the might of her mind. There is no fluttering in her. She is quick and exact. And she knows herself. She is not a liar, is she? She speaks of herself with a lovely candour. And do tell me if you are of the same opinion.

Balbino Giuliano wrote yesterday saying that he has returned to private life and would be glad to come here for a couple of days. I answered saying that I would be glad of it,

54. Louis Gillet (1876–1943), French literary critic and a close friend of Berenson's. He translated into French four of Berenson's books on Renaissance painters. His own works include *Dante* (1929) and *Correspondance entre Louis Gillet et Romain Rolland* (1949).
55. Julie Talma Carreau (1756–1805), author of *Lettres de Julie Talma à Benjamin Constant* (1933).

───────

59

but perhaps a little perplexed, as I always am when I have to meet him, as our conversations usually end in storms. I told him this time I hope it would not happen, and that it would be better to renounce political discussions. And so now I am waiting for him. A word of Julie Talma just seems appropriate: "peut-être cherche-t-il des orages pour oublier ses dégoûts" [Perhaps he seeks storms to forget his disgust].

Dearest, don't say that you are more loving than loved. Shall I tell you that I have been feeling the contrary since we left Rome, I mean in this new phase of our correspondence? My girl, thank God, is well again, and if nothing prevents it I will leave the 9th or the 10th. I long for it.

Clotilde

La Consuma
Florence
July 27, 1932

I feel exactly as you do about Julie Talma and her letters but with the difference perhaps that you regard her, I feel, but perhaps I am mistaken, as the best for her kind. Surely, I wouldn't have humanity made up of Julie Talmas only. On the other hand, a civilization that has not and cannot produce her is, whatever its qualities of mental and moral storm and stress, not a civilization but a dynamic barbarism.

As for your friend Giuliano, do tell me in detail about his visit, whether he can control his secretions and whether he turns out nothing of your quotation from Julie Talma: "Perhaps cherche-t-il des orages pour oublier ses degoûts."

If you had been through what I have since I left Rome! In the first place my health got worse and worse and when I came up here I had one of the worse fortnights in the way of physical debility, discomfort and nerves that I have ever had. In the midst of this and on top of my palpitating anxiety about Mary's health, fell the bombshell of my income. Can you believe it? I have suffered not so much from the possibility of losing nine tenths of my income as from the annoyance of the transition from one scale of leaving to another, and equally from the distaste for seeing lawyers etc. What made things worse was the likelihood of having to move to Paris or London, or even New York almost at once, and thus miss your visits here altogether.

This last fear as I learned yesterday is over. I need not leave till September 2 or 3. So you must come directly, there is room for you and you must try to arrive the day Mary leaves, so that the car which takes her down can bring you up. *Quanto siamo ridotti!* [How low we've sunk!] As for loving, you are so young and may live to learn what it is.

B.B.

La Consuma
Florence
August 5, 1932
Dearest,

You must try your best to come Wednesday the 10th. Mary is going down that day and will see you either at the station or at I Tatti on your way here. So be sure you let me know in good time when your train reaches Florence.

Alas! I have to go September 1 to London straight. I cannot begin to tell you how much I dread it. Not only do I hate business and I shall have to do nothing else, but I have a horror of attempting to do on the cheap what I have been accustomed to do without extravagance but also without anxiousness. I expect I shall have to stay away till about October 20. Try to direct your plans toward coming to us for a few days toward the end of October or early in November.

Dear, you must arm yourself with patience and for the nonce become yourself an extrovert, or you will be very much disappointed with me this time.

At all events, you are likely to have it cool here.

With dear love
B.B.

Cava dei Tirreni
Salerno
September 7, 1932
Dearest Bibi,

I will send you the *Corriere della Sera* with the article of Ojetti on the book *Three Pairs of Silk Stockings*.[56] It appeared two days ago and I haven't read it yet, but a friend of ours who came here yesterday, a business friend of Gino, said he read it. I made him read mine and he said he could hardly recognize that it was the same book. He must have spoken of the style and the Russian temperament and nature. I am so anxious to read it and I shall send it on to you as soon as I can.

I am expecting Curzio Malaparte[57] for a visit. He wants to go with Gino and buy a *torre sul mare* [towerhouse on the sea] and on this occasion I will give him my article for the *Fiera Letteraria*. While I am writing, your tea arrives . . . Darling, I thank you. It was finished when I came home and all these days I felt a great difference and longed for our tea

56. A novel by Panteleimon Romanov (1884–1938), published in Russian in 1930 as *Comrade Kislyakov* and translated in 1931 as *Three Pairs of Silk Stockings*. Romanov's satirical portrayal of post-revolutionary society includes graphic descriptions of the promiscuity and indifference of young people who have come to regard sex as merely a biological function.

57. Curzio Malaparte, pseudonym of Kurt Erich Suckert (1898–1957), novelist, playwright, and journalist. Associated with the Futurist movement, Malaparte in 1922 became an adherent of Fascism. He founded several journals and magazines, including *La Conquista dello Stato* (1924) and the literary review *Prospettive* (1937–43), coedited the prestigious *Fiera Letteraria* from 1928 to 1932, and served briefly as editor of both the Naples and Turin dailies *Il Mattino* and *La Stampa*. In 1933 he was arrested by the Fascist regime and internally exiled for five years, largely due to personal jealousies and to his controversial writings and associations with opposition intellectuals while traveling abroad. His novels include *Kaputt* (1945) and *La pelle* (1949), a description of Naples in the aftermath of the Italian defeat in World War II.

that reminds me of the sweet obsession of perfume and taste of I Tatti and La Consuma. Thank you, Bibi.

I had another letter from Pane who, coming back to Naples, has plunged again in his worst mood. His mother made him find his sister's portrait on his desk with a coloured cloth wrapped around and a garland of orange blossom on the head. Just think . . . he was disgusted. I will see him next week.

Things go so badly for us that it seems we shall not be able to afford to stay in Cava, to have, I mean, two houses open at all times, and I can hardly believe it. I wake at night and can't sleep anymore. I am not a heroine and yet, Bibi, I shall have to do it. I shall go to Rome as frequently as possible and come to Florence too. This is what I look for in the most intense and passionate mood.

And now I must tell you that you must not think that I am going to be depressed and diminished by this new trial. I shall write and write to you, and write my articles and read Mommsen[58] and just look at my particular ill fortune as at an infinitesimal grain of sand in the universe. My dearest Bibi, you will never know what you mean for me.

Yours lovingly
Clotilde

Piazza dei Martiri, 30
Naples
September 30, 1932

Dearest Bibi,

I am writing from Naples one hour before I leave for Cava. I came here yesterday morning to see my mother who was not well. She is better today and I can go back to Cava.

58. Theodor Mommsen (1817–1903), German historian and expert on Roman history and law. Mommsen's *Römische Geschichte* (1854–1856) introduced a new, realistic approach to the study of

The day before yesterday we received the visit of Curzio Malaparte and Signora Borgogne, his friend . . . they say, and her husband. He was not at his best, he was feverish and just out of his bed after a throat infection. He spoke very little about politics. We drove to Positano where we took a sea bath. Mrs. Borgogne was dainty to look at, but silly, and so was her husband. He would only talk about the success of his *bonhomme,* Lenin. I gave Malaparte my article.

I also saw Pane briefly yesterday. He is spending the weekend with us at Cava and I shall write to you about everything we discuss. In the few words we exchanged yesterday you were often mentioned. And you are in all my thoughts. I have to compare you with any one I meet. The pleasure, the perfect pleasure that I have when I am with you makes it so much difficult to have any intellectual relationship with anybody else.

Your loving,
Clotilde

31, Tite Street
London
September 11, 1932

What hard news! But I am proud enough of the way you are determined to take it. And even if under the circumstances of your case I can do so little materially, my admiration for your pluck, my deep affection, my eagerness to give all that you can use of me may be of some comfort.

And as I must always blurt out first what weighs on me to say, I fear that my vexations to my Embassy are of a kind to preclude my making any suggestion of the kind you propose. *A voce* I could explain simply and in detail why it is so, but it would take long, and it might be indiscreet to have it down in writing. Please tell Gino how very sorry I am. I sus-

---

Roman history. He was awarded the Nobel Prize for literature in 1902.

pect however that he is mistaken in supposing that our Con-
sulates let themselves be dictated by our Embassy. They are
pretty independent and use their own local knowledge or
bend to local politics in all questions concerning them.

If you move, you must let me know when you do. Is the
address to be Piazza dei Martiri, what number? I have
forgotten.

I hope you will get away often and to Settignano as
often as possible. Of my welcome you can be sure enough,
but of Mary's and Nicky's no less. Give my greetings to
Pane and tell him that I shall write to him soon. And if you
see Malaparte, tell him I should like to know him, here till
October, and afterwards at Settignano. I am just finishing
his book which I find stimulating as well as informing.

Yesterday afternoon we drove out to Trevy's and left
Nicky there. It is an enchanting country with a tropical lux-
uriance of trees. All the same I did not envy Nicky. In the
evening we had people to dinner but Fry[59] really claimed all
my attention. Roger Fry is a bastard of my mind in its earlier
phases but has a much greater interest in techniques than I
have ever had. He has long been at the head of everything
artistic in England and longer still forgotten that he owes me
anything.

Gusty November weather, no end of people to see, no
end of things to see, very little inclination to the first and
very little energy for the second. I sigh for you and the van-
ished moments at La Consuma.

No end of love

B.B.

---

59. Roger Fry (1886–1934), English scholar, art historian and collector, and former student of Berenson's. His books include *The Artist and Psychoanalysis* (1922) and *The Arts of Painting and Sculpture*
(1932).

Cava dei Tirreni
Salerno
September 12, 1932
Bibi dearest,

I am writing from my bed at 7 o'clock in the morning, so that nobody will disturb me. I should tell you about yesterday. Pane came to see me and we spent the whole day chatting. He read my article and what he had to say about it was that there was not enough "critical judgement." It was too much of a *compte rendu* [summary] and a presentation of the book, well done yes, but no criticism. He also said it was written *da un angolo di visuale etico* [from an ethical viewpoint], with the sacrifice of the artistic evaluation. And I think he is right.

Despite all the pleasure it gave me to read the book, a pleasure of style and situations, I am now painfully aware that I hardly said anything. The article lacks something very important.

Pane also told me he is writing on Piranesi, Rodin and Manet. He will show you his works as soon as they are completed. Your name came up after ten minutes of conversation and in fact we spent the whole time talking about art. We read aloud some of Baudelaire's *Curiosités Estétiques,* and we went around and around the eternal question that I also discussed with you: "Why do I like this, and why do I dislike that."

He told me of his Parisian life, the paintings he most loved. But the artist he most talked about was Tintoretto, just seen again in Venice. By the way, I asked him why he did not like Watteau . . . and he jumped out of his chair: he *loves* Watteau. He said he believes he is the most *malinconico* and *sensuale,* with an infinite grace and so on. We talked again of Katherine Mansfield and what you and me had been saying about her. He admires her a great deal, and everybody is reading her.

Dearest, I am so happy of your better news.

Clotilde

Cava dei Tirreni
Salerno
September 15, 1932

Dearest Bibi,

I showed your letter with the *compte rendu* of one of your London days with people of your world. I read your letter aloud to Pane and Gino. We soon began to discuss why we all have the habit of taking ideas so passionately that we create *lotte atroci* [bitter struggles] between human beings of the same society.

Pane said you have such a particular and personal way of expressing yourself, so much "yours." For instance he will never forget that you said he would enjoy to be Rockefeller so that he could establish an Institution for the "Absolutely Intransitive People."

Pane left yesterday in the morning, and so did Gino. My sister went to Naples to see my mother who, again, does not feel well, and I remained in solitude to finish my reading of Pauline Leader.[60] Now I will try to write about it.

A few days ago I had a long talk with a young man who is very interested in Communism and with whom I couldn't help talking about you, as I had just returned from La Consuma and had such bright memories. I was interested in him and I could feel he was overwhelmed in his turn. But I suddenly realized that I had spoken too much. He was like a southern man who is not yet free; coming in contact with a woman like me he was at the same time enchanted and surprised, but also shocked. He became silent and I felt sorry. You see, I wanted an ear where I could cry how wonderful life can be within the ray of some superior beings. Perhaps it was not a worthy ear. For the first time I wrote down my impressions of such an apparently unimportant event. I shall send it on to you.

60. American writer Pauline Leader's autobiography *And No Birds Sing* (1932).

I got a letter from Signora Torraca.[61] She and her husband are coming here on Wednesday after visiting Corrado Alvaro in Positano. She will remain a few days. I am glad; I like her and she will be good company in Rome, as she already was last year. I will tell Malaparte to come and see you. I enclose a photograph of him. Doesn't he look like Carnera?[62] There is something brutal in him. The other person in the photo is the young, let us say, philo-communist. But for goodness sake, don't think that I told him about us. We only discussed arts and life, nothing more. I know how to preserve my intimacy.

Good-bye, dearest Bibi mine,

Clotilde

Piazza dei Martiri

Naples

September 19, 1932

Dearest Bibi,

I can hardly tell you how dreadful it was to be with my mother during her operation. Poor soul. How she has suffered, and how we all suffered with her. Her face seemed to get older at sight. Bibi mine.

And, do you know? At night, while she rested, I wrote an article on Pauline Leader and sent it on to *La Stampa* where a friend offered to introduce it. If it gets published, I will send it on to you. It will *belong* to you, dearest.

Clotilde

61. Jolanda Torraca, née Vesely, wife of Vincenzo Torraca (1887–1979), journalist, literary critic, director of the Eliseo Theatre in Rome and a close friend of Marghieri's.
62. Primo Carnera, international boxing champion.

31, Tite Street
London
September 22, 1932

What have you not been through! No, there is little more wretched than to see our dearly loved suffering physical pain! And one feels so baffled, so helpless, so humiliated! It is hard to put up with it and unhappily one has to put up with more and more of it as one's age increases. And in the midst of all this you received my egotistical letter! How often it seems to me to think of the difference of mood between the writer and the recipient of a letter! There, too, if one was too considerate, one would do nothing.

And where I love you most is not for your heart alone and your natural love for your mother, but for finding relief in writing. You must send your article on Pauline even if not appearing in print. And now you must go on with Aksakov!

It would be indeed an adventure to go to Pernambuco[63] and if you are a goodish sailor you might enjoy it. Of course I should be desolate to think of you getting farther and farther away from me in space. One cannot help giving to more space more than length and distance. One gives it *éloignement* [remoteness] and that tends to wind out one's heart strings to the breaking point. And besides, Italy would seem to lose what gives it soul if you left it. And I should return thither with reluctance and not with alacrity. As it is, pleasant or unpleasant, I greet each day with the thought: "You are bringing me nearer to Clotilde."

It has turned very cold, but it is bright in a sort of septemptrionic crepuscular fashion. Mary remains in bed, bored and unhappy. That skims off any cream of the pleasure the day might bring. And yet for a moment, when I conquer the

---

63. Gastone Guidotti, the husband of Clotilde Marghieri's sister Raffaella, was appointed Ambassador at Pernambuco, Brazil, where he lived until the close of 1933.

panic at the thought of all the things and the people to see, I enjoy both very much. The last two days I have been seeing an old love affair after thirteen years. She remains at nearly seventy glowing, radiant, caressing, enchanting, a living demonstration that a woman's sex-charm has the body for its seat, but is independent of it. And this woman has lots of brains which unhappily she has not used except unconsciously. Therein so different from you, my Beloved.

I adore you

B.B.

31, Tite Street
London
September 26, 1932

I am so glad to hear that your mother is better. Now I want to hear that you are not going to Pernambuco. It would hurt me to the quick and I am selfish and I hate pain that is not transfiguring. And I want to see you as soon as possible and talk about your writing and keeping you supplied with subjects. I have already told Mary about it and she is enthusiastic and eager, and as she reads most novels she will be able to help.

I should not be writing to you this morning for I have endless engagements, but I send you my love. To give you an idea of what it is like, you must believe that every day I am having a better and more interesting time, recovering more and more of the past and making it present and vital again. Old and young "make a noise as if" they were delighted with my society, and I constantly enjoy theirs. I see wonderful things and every cabinet and every hidden treasure is open to me. And I'd chuck it all to see you, to be with you. This is no Victor Hugo exaggeration, for at night I wake after two or three hours of sleep and I toss about in a fever of longing and yearning and lusting for you. Body and mind ache for you. I compose long and long letters which I should not write, not that I should not dare, but that the

written word might fall into profane hands and that furthermore it is always too definite.

My affairs, well they are not brilliant but we shall be
able to remain at I Tatti and to afford you hospitality. I only
wish I could have enough of it. Oh, I must thank you for
having written to Nicky.

Yours,

B.B.

31, Tite Street
London
September 29, 1932

Do not fail to write at once whether to address you in
Rome. Remember, I do not receive your letters till the third
day after you have written them.

Now as to Werfel, it is surely a book for you to write
about and so much so that it is for the reason that I have sent
it to you. He has great power of observation and no small
talent for construction. Only it is autobiographical and ethical and only at spots literary. And how far he can stray the
moment he has left to imagination, you will see in this pre-
posterous British hero. But as a highly gifted foreigner's attempt to present and interpret Neapolitan life, it should interest you immensely. In its time, Reboux's *Petite Papacoda*[64]
seemed to all of us an extraordinary picture of Naples. That
however was distinctly of the lowest layers or even the un-
derworld. Werfel on the contrary gives us something like the
class you yourself suffer from.

Of course, it is possible that Italians in general, Neapolitans in particular, are not yet interested in the foreigner's
attempt to present you as he believes you are. I who am interested, who am eager to understand, have found the book
informing, illuminating, suggestive, at times grimly amus-

---

64. French author Paul Reboux's *La petite Papacoda, romain napolitain*
(1924).

71

ing. Nicky was even more interested and she has the advantage of remembering Naples not unlike the one described by Werfel, and being at the same time so detached from it that it no longer offends her.

Yesterday I received most unexpectedly a letter from Pellegrina. It is so beautiful, so delicate, so sincere that one wonders why she does not more often express herself, her real deepest self. She asks after you and says she has no word from you since seeing you at La Consuma.

I am so glad that your mother is better. I hope she will recover quickly. Mary is perhaps better, too, but her case is complicated by psychological factors. Yesterday evening she actually dined and sat up afterwards as if there was nothing the matter with her because Norman Angell[65] came and she wanted particularly to see him and hear him.

It is autumnal. I sit by the fire and outside is grey and the foliage is tossing wildly in the wind. It has its own charm, as if only you too were here to feel it.

B.B.

Cava dei Tirreni
Salerno
September 30, 1932
Bibi dearest,

I am packing and I only have the time for a few words. I shall be in Naples tomorrow if the whirlwind does not dispose otherwise. I will then spend a week in Rome, guest of the Torracas who kindly asked me to go there. And when are *you* coming back? I am planning that my second visit to Massimo[66] could be followed by a week at I Tatti.

65. Sir Norman Angell (1873–1967), prolific English economist, journalist, and international peace activist. Angell is best known for his widely translated *The Great Illusion* (1909), an argument against the economic benefits of war. He was awarded the Nobel Peace Prize in 1933.
66. Marghieri's oldest child, born in 1921.

Meanwhile, I must work. I have nearly finished *The Pascarella Family,* a good book, I should say, on the whole a little *voulu,* don't you think? One wonders whether it gives a faithful image of the *usi e costumi,* but the question itself is an implicit criticism. I feel something picturesque, *a uso e consumo dei forestieri* [for the benefit of foreigners], *a colore locale* that is *outré.* Do tell me if you think that I am right, but don't say too much or I will eat you like a cannibal.

Darling, I must go now.

Clotilde

Piazza dei Martiri
Naples
October 3, 1932

I finished *Pascarella*'s book. But there is so much about Fascism that it will be rather difficult to avoid mentioning it or discuss it.[67] If not that, what am I to review next? Do tell me, please at once. If a contract is signed, I shall have no time to wait. I shall be so grateful to Mary if she tells me what is worthwhile reviewing, especially just up to date, before everybody else talks about it. You know how this is very important.

Darling, all my love to you. I feel your love and trust it.

Clotilde

31, Tite Street
London
October 5, 1932

No Dear One. You can write about Werfel without touching Fascism. I did not find that episode important, al-

---

67. The Fascist government prohibited the review or circulation of publications blacklisted for containing politically sensitive commentaries or criticisms of the government. In the case of books not specifically banned, editors and reviewers often censored themselves, discussing the work's literary merits without any reference to political matters.

though amusing. But eternal Naples comprises rather than suffers Fascism. We are all thinking what to propose you. So many current interests here are too specifically local to be made intelligible to your public. It is rare that a piece of pure *belles lettres* is at once fit for British and continental admiration and enjoyment except perhaps after a long interval of preparation.

I have already suggested the criticism of Desmond MacCarthy.[68] I find that a long article on Shakespeare by Logan Pearsall Smith[69] that appeared in the last *Life and Letters* has attracted as much attention as any novel. I am sending it to you on the chance that it may kindle your interest and excite your ink to flow. And if you like the *tour d'esprit* of the writer, I shall send other things of his. He is a composer of delicately ironic and just barely wistful aphorisms which have been highly appreciated in *Anglo Sassonia.*

Now darling, one thing must be getting clear to you as it is to me, that you must come very often to I Tatti if you want to lap me. The stream will flow to your mind's desire at your touch. It is not only that I talk better than I write, alas, how much better! But that I lack the time to write at anything of the length required to say what I have to say. And what I have to say is not due to superior wisdom inspired by some holy ghost, but by fifty years of reflective, assimilated experience. It is all at your disposal and I shall do my best not to resent it if you prefer in me and out of me what I myself should not.

London is enchanting with almost a Summer splendour and gladly would I stay to enjoy place and people. I fear I shall not see Morra again, nor Wells.[70] Friday night, before leaving Saturday for Paris, I hope to see a woman I have

68. Desmond MacCarthy (1877–1952), English novelist, scholar, and literary critic for *The New Statesman* and *The Sunday Times.*
69. Mary Berenson's brother. He introduced Desmond MacCarthy to Berenson.
70. Probably a reference to H. G. Wells.

most admired of all English women. It is thirteen years since I saw her. She is now old and very decrepit, but I hear she is as wonderful as ever.

Mary, alas, is still in great pain and I hate to leave her. All, my beloved, that is mine to give is yours. Yes, all. Do not hesitate to ask. I shall be frank and what I cannot I will say and what I can I will rejoice to give you, my Darling.

B.B.

Hotel Vouillemont
Paris
October 14, 1932
My poor Darling,

Where are you? At Naples, and are you to remain there, or returning to Cava, or what?

Mary writes that she is getting better, so that I hope she will join us before long and that by November 2 or a day or two later we can leave straight for Florence. I will not attempt to tell you about the people I see here. Mrs. Wharton nearly, and Norton every day. Both love Nicky, and Norton cares for her more than for me. Then another great friend of our group has appeared, Mrs. Daisy, the sister of the Marian Crawford who wrote so many books and novels about Rome and southern Italy. She is an intellectual rather than a clever woman, but as good as gold, but *tout ce qu'il y a de plus comme il faut* [in every way respectable].

The person of persons, however, is Philomène.[71] I have mentioned her to you again and again and even shown you a very tiny snapshot of her walking away from the sea. Of all my acquaintances, she has the richest nature and the largest

---

71. Philomène Lévis-Mirepoix (1887–1956), French writer and wife of Count Jules de la Forest d'Yvonne. A good friend and sometimes fellow traveler of the Berensons. She was introduced to them by Edith Wharton, upon whose urgings she later settled in the town of Hyères.

or at least biggest soul and in some ways the least confined intelligence. Being with her is unadulterated joy. There is no sex feeling between us except what is inevitable and diffusedly life-enhancing. She now has a daughter who may be no more than fourteen but looks and behaves grown up. You should have watched her listen the other day to Mrs. Wharton!

Yesterday we went to Rouart's[72] to see his collection. If you see Pane, tell him I thought of him and wished he be there with us. Rouart's father was a great friend and patron of Degas, Renoir, etc. whom I frequented a great deal forty-five years ago. The present Rouart married the daughter of Berthe Morisot[73] and with a cousin who married Paul Valéry shares the house they now live in. The Rouarts still own Manets, Degas, and live in the tradition of these heroes of our personal, I mean private life.

And last night with Mrs. Wharton and Norton we went to see the last play by the author of *Le Sexe Faible*.[74] It was even better than all his former ones. It was as detached and witty as founded on sound sense as the very best work of the ancient Greeks. It was as Greek in essence as Julie Talma's letters. The really perfect revival of Hellenism has nothing to do with Greek stage properties, of course. What interesting faces in the audience! But whatever and wherever I do or am, you too are there, unfailingly.

B.B.

72. Denis Rouart, French art collector and friend of Edgar Degas's.
73. Berthe Morisot (1841–1895), French impressionist painter, sister-in-law and preferred model of Edouard Manet's.
74. A three-act satirical comedy by French dramatist Edouard Bourdet (1887–1945). First performed in 1931, the play caricatures post–World War I society, as a growing breed of spoiled and ineffectual young men and strong enterprising young women threaten to overthrow traditional sexual roles.

Piazza dei Martiri, 30
Naples
October 17, 1931

I wish I knew Philomène! There are so many things about her that seduce me! I remember what you told me about her. I am attracted to any rich nature, more so than to intelligence; and something in her life attracts me so much. The way she has braved a worldly situation . . . that is the sign of a free individuality and of a strong one. I should love to meet her some day.

I saw Pane yesterday morning and he was in better condition than the other day, when I saw him at the cinema. Perhaps because we were not alone, he did not feel at ease. We spoke of Lawrence; he had just finished *Lady Chatterley* and inquired why I had been so little indulgent with that book. I explained that I could not consider it a work of art, as the author claimed. Pane had read the book with the greatest interest and had found many qualities in it. First of all the courage to unveil the hypocrisy of society and individuals regarding sexual love. He thinks there is in Lawrence the antithesis of all various perversions of mind, such as Gide etc., the coming back to sane, simple nature. And he found most penetrating the criticism to Anglo-Saxon society and the excess of celebration. He spoke a great deal about that. I wondered I had paid so little attention, in spite of every one's great interest, to Lawrence's new verb. He bored me and I left him behind.

I got the letters, thank you my darling. I have not had the time to read them yet because I have been working very hard on my article. I am so glad Mary is better. Do enjoy your life in Paris, your friends and everything, dearest. But don't forget me.

Clotilde

Hotel Vouillemont
Paris
October 18, 1932

I hope to be starting for Florence in about a fortnight. We expect Mary in a few days. She will be horrified by the vertiginous life I am living here. As she doesn't care for most of my Paris friends and occupations, I fear she will be bored and I expect to have no little difficulty of keeping her from being too bored. You cannot have an idea of how much asphyxiating *scirocco* a bad mood of Mary's can be.

Yesterday I went to Chartres with Philomène. We talked on the way out with the freshness of the morning in our brains and we struck sparks out of one another's mind and kindled a flame of mutual delight that was simply perfect. Then we had hours of that complete creation of the Middle Ages, as much their flower as the Parthenon was of the Greek world. And yet how imperfect! Man seems unable to do any great thing perfect in design and detail.

The evening before I spent with another of my loves. She has been one of America's greatest beauties and with it intelligent and cultivated. She was full of gratitude because five years ago, when everybody was advising her to leave her husband, I urged her to stick with him and to be willing to pay something for continuity.

If you knew how much it costs me to snatch the minutes for writing to *you,* you would know how much I care for you.

B.B.

Hotel Vouillemont
Paris
October 20, 1932

I spent yesterday afternoon with Gillet. He looked in broad-brimmed black hat and black overcoat like a Merovingian turned Protestant person. I gave him an introduction to you which he will present if he finds time. I dine with him this evening before his departure. Last night we dined with a very Catholic American maiden lady, the flower of respectability, but much travelled and when at rest residing here or in California. And what an apartment she has in the heart of Paris, but with a court separating it from the street and looking on endless gardens! She talked of *Lady Chatterley's Lover* in the exact terms you quote as Pane's. Only she went further and assured me that the Pope in a recent evangelical went far along the same road with Lawrence!!

As for me, I fear I am concluding that he is but a more vehement and expletive manifestation of the flight from our painfully and exquisitely constructed House of Life, in which people of my kind had been full free men. He represents the flight from civilization on the part of all, whatever their birth, who could not participate in it. Let them seek satisfaction on their own level! I may be impressed by their yells and screams. I may even sympathize with their writing and sweating, but they find satisfaction on a neolithic level which my ancestors in Judea and Hellas emerged from three thousand years ago.

No doubt we can admire the candor and sincerity of people who know that they are fit only for cave life, and if they express their minds with vitality and brilliance, we may be excused for being momentarily carried away by them. But it must not last. We must quickly get back to our own House of Life.

I took Philomène yesterday to see Charlie Du Bos,[75] whom she also knows well. While she was conversing with

───────

75. Charles Du Bos (1889–1939), French essayist and literary critic whose published letters and journals chronicled his association with French literary society, as well as his reflections on the works of such authors as Byron, Goethe, Mauriac, and Bernanos. His wife Zezette translated Berenson's studies on Venetian painters into French.

───────

them, I talked with Daniel Halévy.[76] You may remember that he wrote *La Décadence de la Liberté,* which I got you to read. He began of his own accord to speak of Malaparte and was very interesting. If you remind me when we meet, I may still recall. He too is going to Italy presently, and if he goes as far as Naples I will give him a letter for you.

How I should like you to meet Philomène! I see her all day long and the more we are together, the more alive we both feel. And so would you with us.

B.B.

Hotel Vouillemont
Paris
October 21, 1932

I like your article on Pauline Leader. It tells with tact and zest all that the reader can want to know if he is not going to read for himself, and enough to encourage him to read for himself, and to direct him in the way he is to penetrate it. Your style is still a bit archaic and I like it. I shall regret when you have lost it, as you surely will in the course of writing. Night before last I dined at Gillet's with Valéry. I asked whether he knew the writings of Lawrence. He had read *Lady Chatterley* only and thought little of it, and thought the taste for it was merely pornographic.

Last night the Daniel Halévys dined with me. I gave him a note to you. We talked a great deal and I noticed that his ultimate criterion was sincerity. It isn't mine. I ask in the first place whether really the person cannot possibly help thinking or feeling as he does. And then whether such a person can live harmoniously in my House of Life. If he does not pass these tests, I will not have him.

I am having what others might call a wonderful time

---

76. A prominent French intellectual, Halévy (1872–1962) wrote numerous studies on contemporary social and political problems, and was active in support of Alfred Dreyfus.

here, but I'd rather be with you. I should like a month here with you alone, and then launch you among my friends.

B.B.

Hotel Vouillemont
Paris
October 28, 1932

It is sunny and inviting outside but I don't dare to go because I have such a cold and such a cold.

October 29. I could not go on, feeling too dizzy and too sick, and later in the day I got your word telling me you too were down with the flu. Poor darling! If only we could be together, flu or no flu it would have been, it would be bliss! Instead I had yesterday to get up, wretched as I felt, and go to a big lunch party and in the evening to a dinner party. I could not get out of either because they were arranged for me. After the dinner I looked at the Greek, Egyptian and Medieval collection in the house. It was Mme. de Béhagues', and I forgot my woes.

At the dinner was my old friend Abel Bonnard,[77] just back from the country, and other people who discussed Lawrence. By the way, I shall want his *Letters* returned to the library. Read only the personal ones, and particularly those to women: Ottolina, Cynthia, Catherine, etc.

Last night, the beautiful Russian I was chatting with said: "Quel charme que vous avez, vous qui êtes un si grand savant!" [How charming you are, and such a great scholar!] I heard myself answering: "Je ne suis pas un savant, je suis un amant" [I am not a scholar, I am a lover].

It is true. I am above all things a lover of beauty, of

---

77. Abel Bonnard (1883–1968), French journalist, poet, and novelist. Bonnard served as the Minister of Education under the collaborationist Vichy regime (1940–1944). He was later condemned to death, reduced to ten years' exile, by the French High Court of Justice and stripped of his membership in the Académie Française.

quality, of women, of friends, of nature. I love and most of all YOU. What could I not give for a fortnight with you at Capri next Xmas. Would there really be no obstacles on your side?

We expect Mary and Johnnie[78] this evening.

B.B.

Hotel Vouillemont
Paris
October 31, 1932

It is dreary here and tomorrow is All Saints and the following day All Souls, and both days are dreadful in Paris. And it always drizzles and makes me long for the South, for Wadi Halfa,[79] if only I could fly there and take you along. And besides I am beginning to feel not that I have exhausted Paris, far from it, but that I have had enough of all I can enjoy and hold. Furthermore, Philomène leaves tomorrow for Bizerta and I shall miss her much more staying on than if I, too, left. However, we are staying till Sunday. For one thing, Mary arrived only two nights ago and although she is free of her troubles she is very weak and I want her to recover from the London journey which was fatiguing! Then I must wind up, see things I've got still to see and certain people. So we shall, if God is good, be again at I Tatti Monday evening, the 7th.

Now about your visit. I will not attempt to tell you how eager I am to see you, how Mary will welcome you and Nicky of course. Mary speaks of you constantly and with the keenest interest, now that you are going to join the ranks, to her sacred, of writers. There is a complication. It is that Mrs. Wharton will in all probabilities come for a ten-day visit five or six days after we arrive. So if you were in-

---

78. John Walker, a close friend of the Berensons', lived in Florence until 1935 and worked at the American Academy in Rome.
79. Wadi-Halfa, an oasis on the Nile in northern Sudan.

tending to come for a short visit of five or six days, come any day, say even Tuesday the 8th, and stay till the day Mrs. Wharton arrives. I don't ask you to stay with her because she is as bad a fellow-guest in anybody's house as she is a perfect host in her own. Or if, as Vittoria hinted, you mean to make a long stay in Florence, you might go down to Vittoria's during Mrs. Wharton's visit and then come back to us for just as long as you can remain. The third alternative, but that would cost me dearly, would be to wait till Mrs. Wharton has gone.

I have blurted all this without attempts at diplomacy, for you understand the situation in all its implications well enough to take it as I give it. If you write no later than Thursday, address to Settignano.

My cold is still troublesome and I am eager to know you are getting over the flu. Mary read me a charming letter she received from you but I had none for these whole days. Next time I write I will give you a list of the passages I have found most significant in Lawrence. You can look them up and see what you think.

At all events, nearer and nearer to thee.

B.B.

I Tatti
Settignano
November 10, 1932

I don't know how this day has passed but at the end I have but a minute left for writing. Need I write? I dare say you would not mind not hearing as I should. But do unto others as you wish them to do unto you.

Mrs. Wharton, if her cold is cured and she has done with her dentist, should be here in three or four days. She will remain about ten days, say till the 25th at the latest. Then you would be free to stay here as long as you liked: the longer the better. For I enjoy your society very little at first. It takes me some time to tear through veils, worse still to melt down walls of ice that tend to come between me and you during absence. So the longer you stay the more I enjoy it.

Of course I hope you will come to Vittoria's just as soon as you can, and she together and you by yourself will come up as often as you can and I may even meet you both or you alone in Florence. I am so glad that the meeting between you and Gillet came off as well as I hoped. He is a very dear person, almost a saint *a spasso* [out for a stroll] from the cathedral portals of Rheims or Amiens. He is infinitely *chantable* and therefore gets on with everybody. At his house you will meet everybody you are likely to wish to meet in Paris, and indeed you could not have a better *entrée* than he could procure for you.

I am sorry to hear that Croce attacks Valéry. Valéry has told me again and again that he knew it was so, and I denied it again and again because I should like them to be friends and I don't see why Croce should attack Valéry. You may say that the attack was only in the approach. Yes, but human nature and poets' being what it is!

Soon?!?

B.B.

I Tatti
Settignano
November 11, 1932

Mrs. Wharton is not coming before the sixteenth and I have my doubts whether she is coming at all. She will scarcely stay later than the 26th, so you can surely count on coming to us that day if it suits you. Of course if Mrs. Wharton decides, as we should know in a few days, not to come, you will be free to come as soon as you are ready and for as long as convenient. I always want you, but not for a moment when you would rather be elsewhere. Yes, it makes me unhappy when the people I want to be with to be my peers and companions betray that they are neither ready nor inclined to prepare themselves for companionship.

All art exists in relation to the ego. When it tends to temper, to fortify, to refine, to enlarge the scope of the ego as an instrument, it is humanistic, heroic, classical. When, on the other hand, it treats the ego like an idol to flatter and worship, or when it deals with it as with a spoiled and perhaps sickly child that has to be humoured, dandled and caressed, then it is not ever first rate, may even be a symptom of Narcissism or Onanism. Katherine Mansfield, for all her qualities, belongs to the last category. And Lawrence, for all his faults, to the first.

Talking of Lawrence, I have not yet had the time to tell you that I have read Mabel Dodge's book.[80] It is prodigious and almost makes me regret that I have never moved a hand to know Lawrence, and makes me ashamed that twenty-five years ago I was so over-refined and over-brahminical that I treated Mabel Dodge very standoffishly when she made very decided advances. What a narrow minded, exclusivistic culture-Puritan I have been the greater part of my life. I suppose that it could not have been otherwise, brought up as I was in Boston; and with a father whose one and only religion was humanistic culture.

Hope I am getting into shape. May be a trifle better. Interesting people are passing through. I feel my mind working once more and my tongue loose. By the time you arrive you will find me at my average, but toothless. I have lost two, and while the bridge is prepared I shall not be an attractive sight. Luckily I am old enough to know that it is not

80. *Lorenzo in Taos* (1932), by American poet, essayist, and social critic Mabel Dodge Luhan (1879–1962). Dodge was instrumental in building the artists' colony in Taos, New Mexico, of which Lawrence was a part, and wrote several books recounting her friendship with him, including *Winter in Taos* (1935) and *L'Amica di Lawrence* (1948).

looks in a man that attract and least of all in a man of my years. I fear attraction is more chemical than aesthetic, let alone rational. How fun a symposium would be on the elements that attract men and women to each other!!!

What a sunset we had just now. Symbolizing what? Impossible it should symbolize nothing.

B.B.

Piazza dei Martiri, 30
Naples
November 14, 1932

Yes, I think the time is ripe for us to meet. I feel that some clouds have gathered over us and the sooner will be the better if we can disperse them. I shall be Saturday in Rome at the Torracas' and Monday in Florence. If I can come straight to you I shall be happy; no matter for Vittoria who will not mind even if I told her at the very last moment. Otherwise, if Mrs. Wharton is with you, I shall go to her and wait.

I shall see you as often as possible, I hope. It seems that I have so much to say and till a few days ago I was full of joyful expectation. But after your last letter my mood has changed. I feel that there is something hurting in yourself concerning me which takes the form of a literary disagreement. So the only thing I can say is that we must meet as soon as possible.

I loved the *finale* of your letter about the sunset. I adore your letters as fragments of a Greek temple. Once I am with you, I shall miss your letters . . .

Your loving,
Clotilde

I Tatti
Settignano
November 16, 1932

No word from Mrs. Wharton, although this is the day when she should have been here. If she does not come, you will of course come straight here Monday. We shall wire to you when we hear differently from Mrs. Wharton.

I wish you were here already to profit by the weather which is simply marvellous. One wishes to cling to every moment as it passes! If only one were worthy of it! I am not. I suppose I am paying for two months of over-social activity and ensuing accumulation of fatigue. It has to be paid for with compound interest, with feeling of collapse and ferment of bad temper.

Your *boutade* about missing my letters when with me reminds me of what I read somewhere of the 18th-century couple who so enjoyed writing that, as they were never separated, they put a paravent between them and threw the sheets over to each other as they got them written. No matter how I look and talk, my heart will dance with joy to see you.

B.B.

I Tatti
Settignano
December 11, 1932
Beloved Darling,

I had hoped to get a word from you this morning to tell me how you got to Rome and what it felt like out of this simile-ivory tower. My thoughts have been with you and something more, I felt and feel as if most of the radium left in me rushed in particles but in steady stream toward you.

Nothing has happened here since you left. The first evening passed quietly between Morra and myself talking of common friends and common interests. Yesterday we had the Doro Levis[81] and Nesta De Roubeck to lunch. Levi is perhaps the soundest classical archaeologist now living in Italy and an angelic person to boot. He is starting soon for

---

81. Doro Levi, Italian archaeologist and specialist in Cretan and Mycenean art.

Mesopotamia. In the evening Barbara[82] in white and very tall and slender looked really distinguished. Johnnie was there and our architect Pinsent,[83] a great figure in the past of I Tatti, and Morra. It was pleasant, or would have been had you been there.

There was a wonderful sunrise in the morning. I welcomed it doubly because I have slept little or nothing since you left. I long for you too much.

Your *bereft,*

B.B.

Piazza dei Martiri
Naples
December 18, 1932

Dearest Bibi,

The days are running like water through hands with no concentration. I read but feel absent-minded. Your letters are the real point when I come in contact with my real self.

I read the first chapter of *Moby Dick*. It is fascinating, so full of open, fresh air, breeze. On the contrary, I am fighting, excuse the word Darling, with *Brave New World*. It bores me. Besides, there are words that I don't understand and it makes me feel uncomfortable to go through a book as in a mist. But I am savouring Arnold's essay very much. I felt at home with it.

Just think, Bibi, that since I left you I saw Pane and Torraca in Rome, but afterwards I have not had a single day with some touch of intellectual quality.

Is Nicky with you? Give her my love, dearest Bibi, and write to me. My love for you is very real in my present fluctuant state of mind.

Clotilde

82. Probably Barbara Strachey, daughter of Rachel ("Ray") Strachey, Mary Berenson's eldest daughter by her first marriage.
83. English architect Cecil Pinsent.

Sainte-Claire Le Château
Hyères (Var)
December 21, 1932

Darling Clotilde,

I have just read your first letter to reach me here. I hoped
to find it when I got here at 8 in the evening, but was almost
too tired to feel disappointed. Driving in the dark for nearly
three hours, after six passed in the train was benumbing.
And in the train I had an awful tummy-ache which doubled
me up with pain. And yet nothing could have been more
luxuriously comfy. The disagreeable note was the strident
jabber of some Milanese overwhelmed by their money.

Before starting I had an hour of Laura Gropallo. How it
would interest me and amuse me to see you together. You
already have a common ground in your antipathy for Huxley's *Brave New World.* By the way, the words you don't
understand must be of Greco-Latin origin and therefore to
be unravelled if you applied your mind. Perhaps you cannot
give concentrated attention to what should be obvious.
Well, Laura is the quaintest thing imaginable, small, bird-
like with bird-like tosses of the head, dividing her gestures
between caresses and withdrawals of indignation, disdain
and despair. She is painfully flattering out of affection, for is
not flattery a caress and, even if abused as Judas did, it more
frequently is as sincere at least.

You infer that we, for Nicky is with me and returns day
after tomorrow for Christmas on her own, spent a night in
Genoa. What a noisy night! I scarcely slept; good reason
why I felt so tired yesterday and the train journey there had
been so tedious—three mortal hours from Florence to Pisa,
bumping, never really going and as if the locomotive were
looking out for new stoppings.

Well, tired as I was, it was enchanting to be received by
Edith's embrace and the brawny hand-shakes of Norton and
Lapsley. We chatted, we gossiped chiefly about books and

their writers, about the Noailles who have just got back, and the Al. Huxleys who are near. I felt so sleepy and finally at 11 when I got into bed Nicky came and read me the end of *Hidle*.

I am truly sorry, which is truly magnanimous in a pasha with nine tails like myself, with a fierce animal tendency to keep females strictly immured in his own harem, I nevertheless truly regret that you have seen neither Pane nor Gaeta,[84] and I sincerely hope that the one or the other will by the time you read this be stimulating your mind, but not your heart so much.

You see I love you quite foolishly and youthfully, nakedly and unashamed. And love me as much as you can, the more the better for both of us. And so Merry Christmas to you and yours.

B.B.

84. Oscar Gaeta, Neapolitan lawyer, friend and business partner of Gino Marghieri's.

PART TWO

1933–1934

Sainte-Claire Le Château
Hyères (Var)
New Year's Day, 1933: 9:30 a.m.

Did you receive my message at the stroke of your midnight which ushered in the New Year? And what did it tell you? And did you send me one? Why did I not receive it? Were my senses and my soul too gross to receive it?

It is stormy and as the sheets of rain break from the South they strike against the window as waves against the portholes of a ship at sea. And the wind roars. I love the sounds of that commotion. I love myself in them and get the ideated sweep of a life large enough to suit a spirit which feels so cramped in a puny and helpless little body like mine. *Cuccia cuccia* [lie down] I have been saying for nearly sixty-five years to the mad dogs within me. And they seemed to obey. But what is the cost? I often think the cost is a thwarted nature, one that has never found the largest satisfaction, one that has never given adequate expression, one in short that has almost always had to put up with a second or third best. Only when one falls in love does one enjoy the precarious illusion that is commensurate with oneself and fulfilling destiny. How uncertain that state is, how momentary, you probably know fully as well as I do, despite my double length of experience. Can you not, will you not join me in trying to find a rock of security in the flux of illusion? I long to return from every flight to tell you all that adventure has brought that was new, and renewed that was old. Would you care to hear, would you understand? You could, but would you?

There is nobody alive today so much to me as you are, and I want it to be for ever and ever.

B.B.

Sainte-Claire Le Château
Hyères (Var)
January 2, 1933

No dearest, you had not told me Gillet had invited you to stay with him. I hope you will and very soon. I am eager to have you measure yourself against people in a world as high in standards as you will encounter in Paris.

Of course a woman of your years and kind has both advantages and drawbacks. S.A., sex attraction, gives an immense advantage, and who so wise as to discount it mentally and spiritually and not to delight in it naively? On the other hand, it prevents a woman from coming into real touch with her male equals; for no matter how advanced we are spiritually and intellectually, as males and females we are likely, when it comes to realities, to ignore in the opposite sex everything that is not sexual, and to use our own spiritual and intellectual qualities as pimps as panders, to use Shakesperean language—as *galeotti,* to use Dante's—for our sex attractiveness.

So it seems to have been, as Aldous Huxley told me yesterday, with Katherine Mansfield. She could not resist trying her sex attractiveness on every male she heard as being at all out of the ordinary, or of whom she heard or whom she on meeting found sexually attractive. It led her into extraordinary adventures, most of them disastrous, and none satisfactory. She was in short the *femme inassouvie* [frustrated woman] who seems from male to male always expecting a satisfaction that the last male, although the xth, has not given her. Strange that with all her intelligence—but when sex vanity is concerned what good is intelligence! She never came to the conclusion that there were other realities than trying one's sexual attractiveness to attain TRUTH through a series of make-beliefs!

They, the Huxleys, told me lots of anecdotes about K.M. and I shall tell you some when we meet.

Delighted you are reading Cellini.[1] I have several times and I am always ready to re-read him.

I love you "for keeps," as they say . . .

B.B.

Piazza dei Martiri, 30
Naples
January 7, 1933
My beloved Bibi,

I thought we had found our rock of security in the flux of illusion! Your two letters, the two last ones, keep my boiling pot full of alarming questions. I wish we were near to talk things over. But let us all the same in the distance.

Have I well understood that you wish to tell me "to return from every flight to tell me all that adventure has brought that was new, and renewed that was old?" At which sort of flight and adventure did you hint? Since you were speaking of love feelings that give the precarious illusion that one is fulfilling one's own destiny, it seems that you alluded to that. Anyhow, since you asked me whether I would care to hear, and would I understand, I tell you my dearest that whatever you tell me I am willing to understand and to share; anything, as long as I would feel that from any flight, any adventure, you return to me as to a rock of security.

---

1. Benvenuto Cellini's *Vita,* a picaresque autobiography of the artist's stormy life under such patrons as Pope Clement VII, King François I of France, and duke Cosimo de Medici of Florence.

No matter how something in me would bitterly ache as long as I felt that you cannot do without my affection, I would be willing to share everything you might tell me.

So in your letter you tell me that there "is nobody alive so much to you as I am." I believe in what you say.

My letter has stopped and recommenced twice. Then your second letter arrived on Katherine Mansfield and what the Huxleys told you. How astonished I was! How much to say about it. What are "facts" and anecdotes that people can tell us second hand. What she has given of herself through letters and journals is her real self, what does the etiquette so commonly used, *la femme inassouvie,* mean? She was not a *femme vicieuse,* then her *inassouvissement* was . . . well, aren't we all *inassouvis?* All the truth is in the interpretation of those easy etiquettes. I can't absolutely believe that—it isn't a matter of mistrusting Huxley's words since they report "facts." She is to me what she is through the expression of herself which she fully gives in some of her letters. Her spirit is so high, so noble . . . But what a long talk it would be! Her *civetteria* [coquetry], if we may call so her will of power through sexual attraction, was certainly not of a vulgar sort. Some of us have the instrument innately at our disposal. We use it badly or wisely; this depends on how we direct it. She can't have used it badly. And how can *you* say that she had no other realities than trying her S.A.? She loved art beyond everything, Bibi! How can you say that? To think that when I read her, I was thinking: "what a pity, this woman has not gone through love joys and miseries. I wish she had been more of a female." And now . . . dear me.

By the way, I will ask you for a present this time. Dare I? I must tell you. I have read Katherine Mansfield's letters neither in English, nor completely, but only a selection translated in French. And now especially that you have read them all, I realize how inadequate was my reading of her in just a selection. I must say that I should love to have her correspondence in English. I am asking you something, see Bibi? You can't say that I don't feel brotherly toward you, too.

Luigi Scaravelli[2] has come here *in grande incognito* for three days to work, but I dare say I shall see him. What a strange, nervous, excited and sensitive creature he is. I will tell you more when I have seen him.

Gillet told me he will give me his daughter's apartment near his, so that I will not have to stay with his family.

My darling, answer the first part of my letter. To all, please, answer.

Clotilde

Sainte-Claire Le Château
Hyères (Var)
January 9, 1933

I fear, my darling, I can't answer yours posted the 7th at all adequately, for this is our last day here and besides having the last letters to write, things to do, papers to arrange, Mrs. Wharton is snatching us away for a last whole day of exploration.

So let us at once come to what I wrote about Katherine Mansfield. What I said was not my own—for I knew nothing whatever about her as a person, less than nothing in fact. I repeated what the Huxleys told me, both of them together.

My own experience of women inclines me to believe that both the K.M.s, the one of the Huxleys and the one of the letters, may be the same person. Look at Colette. She is in her descriptive and subjective pages at least as delicate, at least as subtle as Katherine Mansfield, more refined, really, vastly more cultured, even so much more of an artist, BUT, being French and not accustomed to put back out of sight the actualities of animality in herself, she lets you infer in herself all that she so arduously ignores.

2. Luigi Scaravelli, Florentine philosopher, writer, and literary critic.

And besides, writing as all other art has but tangential relation to the personality. I have known mediocre souls and dull minds write incommensurably beyond what their speech or action promised.

However, be that as it may, I am sending you her letters. To me it matters not the least what kind of pen wrote them, whether one be signing acts of grace or keeping the accounts of a brothel, whether of gold or brass or rusty iron; all that concerns me is the letters themselves. The rest is besides the mark and mere gossip. But I am startled to learn that you know Katherine Mansfield's letters from the French selection and translation only. What will you say when you have the originals, providing of course that your English is adequate? I wish you knew how happy it made me that you asked me to do something for you, if only something so trifling as these letters.

Do you own a Racine? When you find time, read the plays I have just read, *Phèdre* and *Andromaque* and *Britannicus* and *Bérénice*. What music, what serenity, what light!

I have given you more time than I should. I shall be late and get scolded.

B.B.

Hotel Savoy
Genoa
January 15, 1933
Dearest Clotilde,

The last days were filled with picnics for the weather was as of Paradise. Norton read out a great favorite of Edith's and Lapsley's, a story of Thyra Winslow called *A Cycle in Manhattan*. It treats of a family that arrives in the steerage, attains to wealth and ends with the youngest son, an artist, discovering a marvelously picturesque and romantic studio which turns out to be the first tenement in a slum where his parents found refuge on landing in New York.

By the way, what has become of your issue on *Giobbe?*[3] And have you not written lately? Or am I not to be told? We all left Hyères Tuesday morning. Edith and Morra and I in a car and Nicky and Lapsley in Norton's. The landscape with its grey olives, its Aleppo pines, suave rhythms and jagged outlines is one of the most attractive I know. We talked all day of books and people and all car loads met for luncheon at Nice. Afterwards, we went on beyond Mentone to a great friend of Edith's named Lawrence Johnston, a man of nearly my own age who lives for gardening. So he has one above Mentone and another in England and he divides his time between them. I was not a little surprised to discover that the layout of the more designed part of the grounds suggested ours at I Tatti. I did not dare to ask, for people easily get huffy when you question the absolute originality of their ideas.

We found staying with him a well-known figure of Anglo-Riviera society, Lewis Mallet, another man of about my own age who has been ambassador and whom I have known for forty years. We have never made friends. I believe he was born to be an upholsterer and would have had a more successful career, more satisfactory to himself, had he pursued through life that instead of the diplomatic profession. If one could only discover in time what one best could do, and do it regardless of consequences!

We dined there and it was full moon. Its lights rained down like an influence and the stillness was almost as between the stars. Yesterday we left Edith and Norton and Lapsley and got into the car of the Beaumonts who sent for

---

3. Italian translation of *Hiob: Roman Eines Einfachen Mannes* (1930) by Austrian novelist Joseph Roth (1894–1939). Roth's novels focus on the theme of the wandering Jew living in a state of exclusion from society, plagued by anxiety and spiritual torment. His own life reflects this theme: Roth committed suicide while in exile in Paris from Nazi-controlled Austria.

us to lunch with them in Mentone. The frontier road on the Italian side was flowered like the alleys of a public garden.

The Beaumonts are society people; he English and she German. They are over seventy now but she still has a great deal of attractiveness and reminiscences of everybody in Germany, as he of many in England and in America.

I love living chronicles, always since my youth. And I love you!

B.B.

I Tatti
Settignano
February 7, 1933
Dearest Clotilde,

I am sorry to hear that Rosanna[4] is having a bad attack of asthma. I am more and more in sympathy with illness as I myself get feebler and feebler, and more and more subject to attacks. Thus, the world ever remains a reflex of what goes on within me. We are the living torch wherewith we light up all that is not ourselves. We furnish the music, we give the pace to the dance, yes even the dance of the Lucretian atoms. In vain we stand aside and try to become mere observers. In vain, for our only instrument is our own sensibility and that is in the first place not entirely in our own control. And then even if it were docile and obedient, it constantly changes not only in kind but character. Is objectivity then hopeless? Only as all else, if you measure by results. But if I measured the joy of making the efforts and the illusions of success, the satisfaction accrued is worth while and not without a certain effect upon our permanent, I mean abiding House of Life.

I look forward to seeing what you have to say about Roth's *Giobbe*. Send it directly. If Ojetti is no inferior to the

4. Clotilde Marghieri's sister.

task, why don't you try to give yourself the challenge of doing it better? "The criteria assumed by Bernard Berenson in his *Italian Painters of the Renaissance*" could be the title for an essay that might turn out "interesting." And I should not expect it to be more than "objective," although I don't know whether I should have the coolness to say as Louis XIV is supposed to have said to Racine: "Je vous louerais plus si vous m'aviez loué moins." [I would praise you more if you had praised me less.]

We have finished *Genji*,[5] alas! It ends with the most effective "stop-short" I have ever encountered that I can scarcely believe that it was intended. Perhaps Murasaki died just then and would have gone on had she lived.

How glad I am that you are reading Racine. Nicky is reading Jules Lemaître's delightful book on him. Would you like to see it when she is finished?

Love to Maria Teresa and to yourself. What news of Pane and your Bolshevik?

B.B.

Piazza dei Martiri, 30
Naples
February 9, 1933
Dearest Bibi,

What a letter yours that I have just received! Yes, we are the living torch wherewith we light all that is not ourselves, and what a flame, yet smooth light, comes from you!

It is a pity I haven't read Murasaki. I have not the leisure for it. I must read it when I am in the country. What a task it would be to write about you, even in the most objective

---

5. *Genji Monogatari* [The Tale of Genji] (1004), the classic fifty-four-book narrative of love and adventure in medieval Japan, by Lady Murasaki Shikibu (c. 978–1030), foremost writer of the Heian period. The book has long been considered to be Japan's first novel.

way. I wish I had the capacity! Pane should do it, and he would be better than me. I should love to do it but I couldn't help making a portrait of you in your whole, and this would be so difficult. What a temptation . . . I know I will do it someday. I will pour my heart and soul into it, but first I must work at my instruments.

I had a glimpse of Pane a few days ago, then he went to Rome and came back yesterday. I hope to see him tomorrow.

The Bolshevik is like an affectionate dog and I see him, give him a good pat, but our relation does not go further. He is tenderly life-diminishing, as you guessed, so I am dear to him but I don't seek him. He has been and still is such a help for Gino and all his business.

Oh Bibi, I had such a pathetic adventure these last two days! I met again, after years and years of absence, an old school friend of my brother, the first young boy of 16 that I met when I came back from England to Naples. Of course we loved each other. I was not even fifteen but to me it did not last six months. To him it lasted for years and he went through incredible sufferings, as he was my brother's bosom friend and was obliged to follow my life and my flirtations. I had a glimpse of him from time to time. I called him Otello and tried to escape from him; his love annoyed me, and now to meet him again and recall to life a world that seemed to be dead . . . This was worse even than Joyce's story. He could remember infinite details of me, and a strange creature emerged before my eyes: all tenderness and cruelty, such a strange composition of hell and heaven, and that was me. Then he went to war with my souvenir, a little book, on his heart and when he was made prisoner he destroyed it for fear it might be touched by a soldier. And I never knew about this continuation of the first love. Oh, Bibi. When he left last night I cried such a silly *enfantine* cry, over what?

Well, I recovered my first youth, that is for me close to childhood. What a poignant feeling. Yet, when I feel like that, I become so troubled. Life becomes unreal. Do you understand? To whom better than you could I tell this adventure? It was nothing and it shook me deeply.

Your loving,

Clotilde

I Tatti

Settignano

April 12, 1933

Dearest Clotilde,

I am glad you have accepted to go to Siracusa.[6] Get your dear head full of Theocritus and Virgil's *Bucolics*. Read in Thucydides the part about the Athenian invasion of Syracuse and its tragic ending. At Siracusa get Orsi[7] to show you some of the coins. Let all this simmer your mind and heart and serve hot through your pen.

There is a book by Fritz Weege, *Die Tänze in der Antike* (Halle 1926), which is full of reproductions. If you can get hold of it, and there is sure to be a copy in the library of the Sovraintendenza per le Antichità,[8] look through it.

I am sending you two novels by Morgan[9] that have been so much talked about in England, and Mrs. Sinclair Lewis's book about herself and her husband, the very famous novelist. Nicky insists upon it, but I have a notion that once you tried it here and did not find it to your taste.

We are having our ambassadress on a visit. She is a dear, dear person, but as remote from our real inner world as if she were a Yakut,[10] and it is like an irruption from another world.

6. Siracusa, Sicily, site of an archaeological dig directed by the Società Magna Grecia, founded by Umberto Zanotti-Bianco.
7. Count Paolo Orsi (1849–1937), Italian archaeologist and historian of eastern Sicily.
8. Italian government office charged with the oversight of antiquities.
9. English writer Charles Morgan (1894–1958). His *Portrait in a Mirror* (1930) was well received, and *The Fountain* (1932) was a bestseller in Europe and America.
10. A people of northern Siberia.

I fear Mary is not likely to be able to get away at all in the near future and that we shall be overwhelmed by visitors. I have seen both Maria Teresa and Vittoria, both so dear and both so talking about you chiefly.

So much love and sympathy,
you Dear
B.B.

I Tatti
Settignano
May 2, 1933
Dearest,

I hope it is not *scirocco*-ful for you to enjoy your outing in Siracusa. Were I with you to enjoy your enjoyment, for I am debarred from all pleasure of communal and gregarious kind. Unless indeed I succeed in isolating myself completely, which seldom occurs. On the contrary, I count it as an infirmity, as is every sensitiveness that unfits one for the rough and tumble of life and for extracting what pleasure and even happiness ordinary social conditions offer. I am eager to know how you are faring in Syracuse and I hope you will find time after your return to tell me what you experienced there, and even what you thought and perhaps, to relax, what contacts you made there.

Yesterday we all went to the funeral of Iris Origo's[11] little boy. He was such a wonderful little creature in himself, and was to have all that good birth, splendid connections and fabulous wealth could give. Yes, it has been well arranged that the trees should not pierce through the firmament. Poor Sybil Lubbock, his grandmother was there of

---

11. Iris Origo, Italian-American novelist and literary critic, author of *War in Val D'Orcia* (1947), a diary recounting the experiences of an Italian family in the Tuscan countryside in 1943. She is Lady Sybil Lubbock's daughter by her first marriage, and the wife of marquis Antonio Origo.

course. The Braccis[12] and Morra came and dined here before returning to Montepulciano. Margherita spoke of you so nicely, let me say. I feel so at home, so entirely at peace with her, that I never see her without realizing the pity it is that she and I don't live in the same town.

The garden and the countryside have never been so beautiful, but I am too worried and have too many people to see; so many have a trick of telephoning that they are here only for a day or two and that they must see me. Impossible to refuse. And as most of them are too old for trams and too poor for taxis, we have to send up and down all day long. And so I fear it will be until the middle of June. But we mean to try to get away June 1, if meanwhile things have not got much worse.

And what about yourself, and where will you be now till you come here?

Love
B.B.

Hotel Villa Politi
Syracuse
May 3, 1933
Dearest Bibi,

I have been here two days and I am overwhelmed by beauty, heat and work. I have already sent my article and a copy I will send on to you as soon as it comes out.

I went to see Orsi but he was very tired and ill and not very talkable. I tried to go to Pantalica this morning but I got so exhausted, it was so hot, that I had to give up.

My second article will be about the dances. Pizzetti's[13]

12. Countess Margherita Bracci, née Papafava, and her husband, Count Lucangelo Bracci.
13. Ildebrando Pizzetti (1880–1968), composer, director, and musical critic. Pizzetti gained a broad fame with his opera *Fedra,* which opened at the Scala Theater in Milan in 1915.

music was enchanting. I did go to Palazzolo Acreide, and the small theater was beautiful, but I could not see the *Santoni*.[14] Oh, I have become a poor globe-trotter, and I am not, absolutely not, a good archaeologist!! I am sure you laugh at me; I wish I could hear you and Nicky laughing at my failures. But I like to be teased by you.

All my best love,
Clotilde

I Tatti
Settignano
May 5, 1933
Darling,

It was a sweet surprise to get your note from Siracusa. I did not expect it and receiving it made me happy. Yes, I wish I had been in Siracusa with you, but not on an occasion like this. Places like Siracusa, Rome, Athens are haunts for dreams and not scenes for routes and kermesses. I am speaking for myself of course. And that is why we hate killing the thing we love and we hate the killers. And yet it is inevitable. The more we love a place, the more people go to it, and finally through their concourse, they entirely change the character of the place, viz. contemporary Rome.

Here is incredibly beautiful. Our garden is a dream of Paradise and I enjoy it with all the training that fifty years of conscious looking has given me. I wish you were here already before the freshness has passed from the rose.

No end o' love
B.B.

14. The remains of an ancient Roman villa at Palazzolo Acreide. The *Santoni* are the villa's mosaics, which had only just been discovered.

Cava dei Tirreni
Salerno
June 29, 1933
Dearest Bibi,

I got yesterday Mary's book[15] and my favorite and fla-
vored tea. Thanks immensely for the exquisite present, a
tasteful link between us. At the same time I got a letter from
Gillet, answering to the one I sent nearly one month ago. He
said that, *pour ménager mes sentiments,* he is only putting my
initials on his *bouquins.* Then he hopes to come to Italy for
the *Mostra Cattolica.* Did you know about it? He wants me to
arrange a few lectures for him in Naples and in Palermo during the Autumn, which is by the way a very difficult moment, unless he means December.

The work has begun in my future nut-shell in Torre[16]
and I shall have to look after it. It seems that it will be ready
at the end of August and I intend to settle there as soon as the
house is ready. My brother is unwillingly doing the work—
as the house is absolutely inhabitable—and I know that I
shall pay very dearly. Gino is now uncertain whether it represents a good solution or not. In the meantime, I let the
work begin, assuming all the responsibility for it. I must
have if only a nutshell near the town, and not a reclusion like
Cava, where I can live and possibly die. So, against everything and everybody, and if only for two weeks, I shall come
to you. We need a good deal of talking.

I am writing an article on Céline. Do you know it also
appeared translated into Italian? How unexpected! Of course
it is only 420 pages, which means the best was suppressed. I
am sorry I don't have here the letter where you first told me

15. Mary Berenson's *A Modern Pilgrimage* (1933), an account of her
    travels in the Middle East.
16. Torre del Greco, site of Villa La Quiete, on the slopes of Mount
    Vesuvius, near Naples. This remained Marghieri's permanent resi-
    dence until 1937.

about the book. I remember you said precious things about it. You probably think that I have chosen a difficult book to review, but it attracted me so much, even with its difficulties. Besides, I know what I think of the book. Literary merits apart, it is extremely "healthy," against all general opinions and disgusted impressions. First of all, it is sharp, and even if brutal, it provokes a reaction. Furthermore, every ill or ugliness when so described, with such a brilliance and grandeur, has a beauty of itself which transforms evil into spectacle. Life is like that, when seen from the point of view of the author, and it is better to report it courageously.

But there are two things I am not sure of. Perhaps you can help me. Do you feel there is in Céline more pity for this human sordidness, considering how the wretched rich let the poor decay, or more the unsatisfied love for life and pleasure that revolts for its being *refoulé*? He hates with voluptuousness, didn't *you* say that? The article will be ready in a week.

I am anxiously waiting for your letter. And it doesn't cost me anything to write first to deserve a reply . . .

Your teasing,
Clotilde

La Consuma
Florence
August 14, 1933

Whatever your journey, you are I hope rested after a cool night's sleep and waking to a pleasant sense of relaxation of calm. I wish I were with you, although it remains so Elysian here. The same temperature, the same freshness, the same opalescent distances.

You should have heard what Mary and Morra have been saying about you. Morra particularly, with a finality in the setting of his mouth, said again and again: "She will write."

Letter from Alda full of praise of Pane who captivated her with his exposition of knowledge about Roman ruins and how they were built. Then he seemed to hold me up as the *pagano per eccellenza. Non me lo sento* [archetypal pagan. I don't feel it].

The *die* is cast. I am going to Vienna the 2nd of September. I hate in general to move and particularly from a spot as enchanting as this. But once in Austria I shall, I believe, enjoy it—the works of art and a long stay with the Thurn und Taxis[17] etc. Of course much depends on the meeting with my *homme d'affaires.*

I am sending this off with Parry[18] who is just going to market at Consuma. So take lots of the cream, my love,

B.B.

Cava dei Tirreni
Salerno
August 21, 1933

I haven't had a moment for myself these two days. I feel so tired, not having had some time to concentrate and be with my own self. Nicky and Alda came on Saturday and I was so happy to see them. But they were tired after the long excursion on such a hot day. It is very hot now, and Cava is particularly damp.

Pane spent the day here yesterday and was in a miserable mood and made me and Iolanda depressed, as if life was all in black and white. How mysterious is each human being! Our chief subject of conversation was personality as a necessary limit and the fact that each of us has to *prendere partito,* judge and choose. He complained that I was "undetermined." He is inclined to see human beings as an expression of society, of an institution, in other words *un'espressione storica del suo tempo e del suo ambiente* [a historical expression

---

17. Austrian prince Alexander von Thurn und Taxis and his wife Mary, née Hohenlohe, close friends of the Berensons' and visitors at I Tatti.
18. Hugh Parry, Berenson's English chauffeur at Villa I Tatti.

of his time and milieu]. I tend to see in a human being mainly a human being, which makes it so much difficult to love and hate. He insisted he would accept a few exceptions, but that in general every one is an "expression" and not a "personality."

The article is finished and I hope it will come out soon. I am now reading Racine with great interest and I have begun *Trivia*[19] as well. I found some of the sketches very fine and subtle.

Dearest, all my love,

Clotilde

La Consuma

Florence

August 23, 1933

Dearest,

Your report of the themes discussed between you and Pane brings home for me the very *tedesco-Neapolitan* [German-Neapolitan] he, Pane, is. What a pity to be so tangle-footed, like a fly on fly-paper, by this Vico-Hegel-De Sanctis-Croce fallacy. It is a variant of the eternal problem of the freedom of the will. Everything is preceded by the entities that generated or produced it. That does not mean that this thing, whatever it may be, Pane, you or I, was at any moment entirely predetermined.

We must not judge results as an aesthetic-ethic activity, with the ticklishly uncertain and fallible intermittent knowledge of origins. Only God could give such a chain of factors which necessarily summed up into a result that was Pane, you or me. Historical determinism seems akin to Cubism and other leanings toward appreciating in the work of art the skeleton in action or, if you must be more precise, the skeleton with the minimum of muscles and arteries and veins and glands to make it work. But I must not go on. To write

19. Logan Pearsall Smith's *Trivia* (1929).

about such questions is a serious and endless business. If you can receive me and I can come for Christmas and Pane will not feel inhibitions in my presence, we can discuss them at our pleasure.

The *die* is cast. I leave for Vienna the 31st and possibly I shall be joined there by Adèle Khan if she cares enough about me to come all the way from Biarritz. Then we go to Biba's[20] for a fortnight and finally to the Thurn und Taxis.

I have at last read Lawrence's *Sons and Lovers*. It is marvelously written and he does grope therein so sincerely after the truth of the man and the woman business.

I do so long for you,

B.B.

Cava dei Tirreni
Salerno
August 24, 1933
Dearest Bibi mine,

I am about to go to Torre and see my new home. I think my article will appear today and I will send it at once to Mary. In a way I am sorry that it appears today because I wanted to make a few changes, in particular I wanted to mention the Palmyra desert and the watering camels.

You see, I did see you sitting on the fine desert sand with the camels slowly appearing in the distance . . . No, this is silly perhaps. I felt like that, though. Do tell me what you think of it; I made it much lighter and I hope Mary will be pleased.

We had a change in the newspaper: Barzini[21] has left, and I don't know who will replace him. Don't fail to give me

---

20. Countess Byba Belasi Khuen, née Lutzow, wife of count Carol Khuen Belasi. Berenson occasionally visited them at their house in Czechoslovakia.
21. Luigi Barzini (1874–1947), journalist, foreign correspondent for *Il Corriere della Sera* from Argentina, Japan, Libya, Spain, Mexico, Russia, and the United States. In 1923 Barzini founded the New

your new address. By now Nicky will be with you: please give her my love. May I ask who is this Adèle coming from Biarritz?

Clotilde

La Consuma
Florence
August 28, 1933

Dearest Clotilde,

We are all delighted with *Saper Viaggiare,* and Mary most of all. She is writing herself. Some of the phrases are admirable and would look well in an anthology of travel accounts. Nicky's return brings a curious sense of reality into life. She is so very much at the heart and center of all my activities. She comes back full of enthusiasm about the Ruffinos and Giuliana[22] and a great appreciation of Pane. She says the three former have noticed a great improvement in the last named, and I told Nicky I thought it was your influence.

SCHEMATA are always indispensable as spoons for ladling up, as moulds for shaping salvages from chaos. They also are like skins without which no living thing can thrive or mature. But when you have sucked the juice of the grape, its skin is worthless. So with schemata, woe to the people who use them any more than juice. They should be like postage stamps.

Adèle is a beloved and charming and highly placed

York–based newspaper *Corriere d'America,* which he edited for ten years. Marghieri here comments on his departure from the editorship of the Neapolitan newspaper *Il Mattino.*

22. Carlo and Titina Ruffino, née Martini-Marescotti, and her daughter Giuliana Benzoni. Their villa was located at Capo di Sorrento, along the Tyrrhenian Sea just south of Naples. Titina was the daughter of the Italian novelist and literary critic Fernando Martini.

woman between you and me in age, wife of the famous New York financier Otto H. Khan.

I shall look forward to your article on *Lorenzo in Taos*. Lawrence was one of those rare artists who cannot be detached from what they have created—like Goethe, like Byron, like Nietzsche—and must therefore be studied in their letters and through the people who have known them as well as through their own published masterpieces. Make this idea the theme of your article, and love me.

B.B.

La Consuma
Florence
August 31, 1933
Dear Clotilde,

Be sure to send everything you print, only cut out the article and enclose it in a letter. Papers may not arrive.

It has turned chilly here, 16 degrees, and I begin to feel it at once in my insides. All the same I wish I could stay on as I am quite full of zest for work and could now go on with Michelangelo. I have, after finishing a further study of Signorelli, found time to look only at the photos of the Michelangelo drawings. They have not frightened me. What terrifies me is in all the masses piled up by Aryo-Teutonic-Hegelo-Mystico-Catholic-Nonsensical Germans. Their stench would overpower me and like the coward that I am I mean to let Nicky clear the way for me.

Nicky has read out to us a very remarkable small book on youth under the Soviets by Manhert. You can get it in French or in English. It is very much worth while.

Do write every other day at least and tell me whom you see, what you suffer and what you enjoy.

B.B.

Cava dei Tirreni
Salerno
September 8, 1933
Dearest Bibi,

I feel weak and depressed. Things around me are getting worse and worse. What I had feared about Gino making a tragedy about Torre is just happening and bitterness sometimes becomes overwhelming. As long as one can talk his sorrows over to others there is hope, the worst is when you can't.

The 30th of September I will go with my mother to Torre to see the last few touches at my house, "La Quiete." Don't worry, dear, no chance to have *quiete* as long as I live . . . My new address will be Villa La Quiete, Santa Maria La Bruna, Napoli. Remember to add my maiden name, Betocchi, as there I am more well known under that name.

My article on Lawrence has not appeared yet. When it will, you will see how well I remember everything we discussed about him.

My love to you and Nicky,
Clotilde

Grusbach
Czechoslovakia
September 9, 1933
Dearest Clotilde,

Here it is paradise and in the sense that Nicky and I deserve after the six tormenting days in Vienna. The countryside is farmstead and forest and lake and river with the view stretching to distant hills. Their house is in a charming park furnished with pre-Ritzonian comfort. My hosts you already know something about. Biba, her husband, the darling little boy and besides Biba's father, now over eighty but dressed to kill and very interesting to me. He was ambassador of Austria in Rome for many years and understands international affairs as few. There is besides Dorothy Pahlfy,

the youngest sister of Gladys Deacon, the duchess of Marl-
borough, of whom you must have heard me speak often.

The hours go by too quickly. In the forenoon I sit with
Biba watching the others play tennis or croquet and chatting. In the afternoon we drive with horses through the forest. And we chat all the time.

I forgot to say there is a prodigiously learned young
Prussian who knows everything and seems to have thought
deeply. We have endless talks. *Per contra,* I have in the last
two days read a remarkable book. It is an English translation
of all the passages in Amiel's journals bearing upon his love-
life. At last I have the account of what women mean in the
life of a sensitive, cultivated, intellectual male. Will it interest
you, I wonder? To me, it seems like one of the rarest revela-
tions ever made.

Write here before the 14th and then again to Hotel Bristol, Vienna, till the 21st. I hope this will find you more
cheerful. Don't forget about our tryst next month.

B.B.

Grusbach
Czechoslovakia
September 11, 1933
Dearest Clotilde,

I am glad you are going to call your little place at Torre
"La Quiete." May it be a happy omen and give you peace of
mind. But do you really want it? Look into your heart. I
don't ask you to tell me what you find there. Perhaps you
can't, perhaps you won't tell.

I have not heard from Gillet since you were with us at
Consuma. He and I do not carry on a *correspondance suivie.* I
am not surprised, therefore, at long intervals between letters. Poor devil, he is so driven that I marvel at his finding
time for a private life of any kind.

You ask whether he would resent irony. Coming to think

of it, I do not remember Gillet laughing or in any other way wasting energy of that sort. In my presence at least. Again I say, the poor dear is so driven and harassed. You can scarcely conceive what his life is like. I admire beyond measure the quality of his existence considering the multiplicity and time-consuming absorption of his occupations.

Write after this to Hotel Bristol and converge your plans on a visit to I Tatti in October.

With so much love

B.B.

Cava dei Tirreni
Salerno
September 13, 1933
Dearest Bibi,

I am again in bed, this time not well at all. I don't know what happened to me.

I must tell you something. I have been reading these past few days *Sons and Lovers* and I think it is a beautiful book. I "felt" the book intensely and as a critic I could not help remembering you talking about it with no admiration at all. I do not understand why you did not find the book good in its own *Weltanschauung,* and expressive and vigorous, yet with the calmness and fluency of a masterpiece. I want to know what you think of it. And what an unforgettable mother!!

Write to me, dearest Bibi, as soon as you can.

Clotilde

Hotel Bristol
Vienna
September 17, 1933
Dearest Clotilde,

I have just got here and found yours of the 13th in which you speak of being so ill. Need I tell you how anxious it makes me! It may have been brought on by doing too much, but there must be something, I hope not too serious, that fatigue brings out. I wish you were writing oftener so that I might have a letter tomorrow instead of waiting for an answer to this.

My opinion on Lawrence's *Sons and Lovers* is entirely your own. Not only the mother but the husband of the married one were charged with interesting vitality. The sex problem is treated as perhaps nowhere else and without the hysterical mysticization that annoys me in most of his work. It certainly is a book that is important and almost great, certainly beyond any other of his that I have read.

All this objectively. Subjectively, Amiel's *Philine* is endlessly more to my taste, although it is by comparison thin, very thin.

The ten days spent with the Khuens were an unalloyed delight. I can't remember regretting so much the end of a visit. The country had a northern charm, a sort of piety and humility that you know nothing of in Italy. Then the people were the sort with whom one could never disagree except in opinion. Strange! Biba's husband, an angel on earth, is out of nationalistic fever a Nazi and Biba splutters after him. Today we nearly quarreled but not really. Biba has such a delicacy and intelligence of heart. Then her parents were there and the father is of the best company. He has been behind so many international scenes and knows so many interesting historical personages.

I am going through the whole of Baudelaire's criticism. With pleasure but not with profit. His phrasing apart, he has nothing to tell me. Then, too, I am reading Lemaître's *Chateaubriand* which is amusing always, and at times illuminating.

If you write no later than Tuesday, address here. So much love, my dearest, and do your best to keep well.

B.B.

Hotel Bristol
Vienna
September 24, 1933
Dearest Clotilde,

As the luggage is going down and being packed into the car which is taking us to lunch at Werfel's, I have time to send a few words about the Guidottis.[23] They appeared yesterday morning and we went together to the Arts Museum. They lunched with us here and in the evening they went with us to the *Nozze di Figaro* at the Opera. They leave for Prague this morning.

Neither of them has any sign of the cold they had brought here from the trip, during which they encountered nothing but bad weather. Guidotti was very much impressed by the *puszta* and told me he preferred the great stretches of plain and vast horizons to any mountain landscapes. I had more talk with him than with your sister. She told me of what it was like in South America and what a patriarchal primitiveness Pellegrina's sister was likely to encounter in Chile. I loved your sister's voice, forehead and eyes, chiefly because they reminded me of you.

Guidotti was interesting on the situation in this part of the world and I felt him eager for more. His mind is inquiring and free. He talks suggestively and knows how to ask stimulating questions. I got the impression that they were happy. Raffaella was satisfied with the way things had gone during her absence with her own little girl.

We lunch with Werfel at the Semmering and then take the train for Graz where we spend the night and tomorrow forenoon. There may be nothing worth seeing at Graz, but names of towns tend to become "motor ideas" demanding

---

23. Gastone Guidotti, Italian diplomat and his wife Raffaellina Guidotti, née Betocchi, Marghieri's sister. Gastone Guidotti was appointed to several countries in Europe and Latin America.

realization. I shall be an infinitesimal shade less dissatisfied with myself when Graz shall be more than a mere name.

The week here would have been pleasant but for the anxiety about the immediate future which kept mounting all the time.

I have seen again and again the pictures I most enjoy and the other works of art as well. The only interesting new person I have met is Count Costi, who has written the book on the Rothschilds and on Montecarlo etc. He was disappointing.

I wish I could look forward to seeing you soon. I shall write once again to Cava and then to Torre.

With love

B.B.

La Quiete
Santa Maria La Bruna
October 4, 1933

I am here at last! It seems so untrue. My house will be ready in a fortnight but Gino has made such a tragedy of my moving here that my family finally lost patience, especially my father who is rather a violent and impulsive man. To speak of synthetically, life is not easy, and I am trying to get free of my own surroundings with no great results.

I got your letter from the *tappe* [stops] of your journey. I am happy you enjoyed it and I hope that coming home will not be disappointing.

About my article, I should tell you that the newspaper notified me that it is strictly illegal to mention Lawrence.[24] What do you think of it? They asked me to send something else, that they would publish willingly. I sent a piece on Eleo-

---

24. *Lady Chatterley's Lover* was banned throughout Europe and Lawrence was among the writers blacklisted in Fascist Italy.

nora Duse.[25] Did I ever tell you I met her once, before she left for America? After ten minutes of conversation she told me she lived "nel paradiso dei miei ricordi" [in the paradise of my memories]. She seemed to me a poor suffering being, and I almost felt sorry for her.

I got Julie Talma's letters. I will write on them and I thank you for sending the book. I will bring it back with me when I come to I Tatti. When? Let me hope it is going to be at the end of October.

Love,
Clotilde

I Tatti
Settignano
October 10, 1933

I was in bed all day yesterday with high fever and could not write. I am now better and just well enough to wish you were here to enjoy with me the incredible beauty of the sky, the light, the foliage and the flowers. It is too beautiful to last. Perhaps it is providential that I cannot smell anything. On top of it all the odor of the *olea fragrans* would drive me crazy.

But I read your article on the Duse and liked it immensely. It is well composed and well written. Was she a *poseuse*? Perhaps not. But she certainly made no effort to keep down in herself, tame and transfigure the demonic in her—as all the greatest people do. Like the showy, the *cabots,* the exhibitionists, she on the contrary fed the demonic in herself, exploited it and marketed it. You may grant all I say and ask how can one be an actress in any other way. Perhaps one cannot. In which case acting is a dubious pursuit.

Nor was the Duse an actress at all. She was only a per-

---

25. Eleonora Duse (1858–1924), celebrated Italian actress who toured widely in Italy, England, and the United States, and partner in a ten-year legendary love affair with Gabriele D'Annunzio.

sonator, as great as you please, but not an actress. Perhaps there never again will be acting in the sense of the Reston, Rachel, Salvini, etc. Sarah Bernhardt is still in the tradition.

Cheer up, dear, the worst is yet to be, but will always find me loving you.

B.B.

La Quiete
Santa Maria La Bruna
October 13, 1933
Dearest Bibi,

Your letter enchanted me. I am not so worn out by my sorrow and worries that I cannot feel happy at your sudden touch. To think that I worked so hard at my article just to make that one point! the central point about the Duse which you made in a few words, in a few lines with a complete psychological portrait. It is good you did not send me that letter earlier. I couldn't have resisted the temptation of using it, and now I would be tormented by it . . . All the same the article was successful, and now I will write about Julie Talma.

I am reading the book with intense emotion. This woman really had a pagan simplicity, a free mind and absence of moral troubles. She cannot have had any social resentfulness in the fairly unprejudiced society of her time. Apart from her freedom of mind, this makes her genuine. I like the way she "tames her demonic," to use your splendid expression, and transfigures her love into an exquisite tenderness.

Dearest, I am *sous le charme* of your letter. And thank you for reminding me of the olea fragrans. The school I was brought up in was pervaded by it, a perfume I am crazy for!

All my love, Bibi dear,
and don't sneeze too much!
Clotilde

I Tatti
Settignano
October 16, 1933

I am writing to tell you that Nicky and I are going to Montepulciano tomorrow and mean to return on Thursday the 19th. After I do not expect to move again until toward the end of December. Mrs. Wharton writes that she will be here November 8 or 10.

Mary seems a little better but yesterday we had a cable to say that my sister Rachel Perry is very ill.

Here I try to avoid worrying over Mary and my finances, and little by little to insert myself into work. It does not come easy. I have had a *débauche* of review reading. When I feel listless I enjoy anecdotes, information and comment on today's life.

Nicky is reading aloud a novel by Roth much better than his *Hiob* but nothing so good as Werfel's *Martha*. By the way, Werfel told me that his *Geschwister von Neapel* was the only one of his books that was burned and forbidden in Germany.

What do you say of Malaparte's arrest?[26] Tell me if you know anything. Let me find letters from you Thursday on my return and tell me when you are coming.

Yours,
B.B.

I Tatti
Settignano
October 19, 1933
Dearest Clotilde,

We got back last night bringing Morra to stay with us. I found your letter of the 16th and it made me very sad, not so

---

26. An early supporter of Fascism, Curzio Malaparte had fallen out of favor with the authorities and was confined to internal exile on the island of Ischia, off the coast of Naples, near Capri. See also n. 57, p. 62.

much that you had to put off coming here, although I mind that a great deal, as that you are so ill, so down and so full of bothers big and little.

At Montepulciano I should have been happy except that it was cold. So I am worse than when I started. The first evening Morra brought Pancrazi who was at his warmest solidest and most genial. A good dose of Pancrazi would be the making of Pane. Why doesn't he write any more, Pane I mean? Bracci told me about the furniture you were getting and how precise and clear your orders were. *Corre voce* [there's a rumor] at Naples that he, Bracci, thought that your mother was rich and that the Marghieris had not suffered greatly in reputation.

On the way home we stopped over for lunch and tea at Barbialla. Maria Teresa had her mother who was ever so much nicer than I would have been led to expect. She must have been a beauty!

A nice note from Raffaellina. I hope for better news soon and my heart broken at the delay of your visit.

> With love,
> B.B.

I Tatti
Settignano
October 31, 1933

I am getting very anxious about you, my dear, for days have gone by without a single word from you. It makes me fear that you have been too ill to write. Is that so? In that case, let me hope that this will find you in much better state. My sister's death makes me far more anxious than ever about my loves and I was always anxious enough.

Here nothing interesting happened. I believe I wrote about Albertini's[27] visit and how much we talked, literature

---

27. Luigi Albertini (1871–1941), influential journalist, founder of the weekly *La Domenica del Corriere,* and editor of *Il Corriere della Sera*

chiefly. He is outgrowing his London culture-snobbery and becoming a real mind.

I have seen more of my resumed friendship after a lapse of thirty years with Elizabeth Ellis, the sister of Alice Garrett. Elizabeth is a free and large spirit who seems to understand everything and to have no barriers or fences in her mind. So it is a joy to be with her.

There always are people passing through chiefly from America, old, old acquaintances as a rule.

I am reading *Les Liaisons Dangereuses*. Foolishly I read it when I was not twenty perhaps. Then it bored me and for that reason I have never seriously looked at it in all the intervening years. How subtle and refined and rapier-like it is! What makes it so interesting is the triumph of human nature over all elaborate artifices. That makes it so much more interesting as well as more alive than De Sade's writings.

I had to change a large sum of dollars today at a loss of forty percent!!! And Mary's health troubles me still more. So please try to become an isle in a sea of misery.

Lovingly

B.B.

I Tatti
Settignano
November 21, 1933

Whose child, my Darling was this poor little Giorgio who has just died? Was it of the dear *incontranda* whose *incontro* led to so little that at this minute I cannot recall her name? If it is, give her my real condolences and if you will let me have her present address and I will write to her.

---

from 1920 to 1925, where he was replaced by Ugo Ojetti in 1925 for his opposition to the Fascist government. Albertini and his daughter, Elena, were close friends of Berenson's, as was his brother Alberto Albertini (1879–1954), also a journalist at *Il Corriere della Sera,* and a novelist and literary critic.

I am very sorry for you and for little Massimo. When I see you, you must tell me about this little Giorgio who was not allowed to grow old enough to lose glamour for actuality. Enviable little creature!

I cannot help it. I feel more envy than grief when I hear of a death, and yet I love life. But, oh the burden of it and the sordidness. Every day I feel less able to cope with it. I hang on passively until a wind blows me away. And yet, as said, the spectacle fascinates me and I still get *voluttà* [sensual pleasure] out of it. So I am most inclined to say: "Happy Giorgio" and "Unhappy those who survive him."

Don't let me survive you!

B.B.

I Tatti
Settignano
January 7, 1934

Darling Clotilde,

What I want to tell you is that my last letter may have sounded a little brusque and almost harsh. I confess your *état civil* [legal status] exasperates me and a certain hard indignation possesses me when I think of it, that easily finds vent when I write to you, just as a mother will seem violent to a child that has no matter how innocently run some dangers.

Behind it I love you more than ever but it is true that my love tends to abstract and alembicate itself into something too remotely ideal the longer I am away from its object. For which reason I do wish I could see you oftener, for I want to keep a live love for you and not a transfigured one.

How gifted people waste themselves, you on being a mother and a wife, tasks that any other females can accomplish at least as well, and my step-daughter Karin[28] on this stercoraceous business of psychoanalysis.

28. Karin Costelloe Stephen, younger daughter of Mary Berenson and her first husband, Benjamin Francis Costelloe, and wife of Adrian Stephen, Virginia Woolf's younger brother.

Yesterday a couple of Americans was here, he a professor at Yale University, a youth of 31. He seems full of brains, will and accomplishment, but he devotes them all to looking for manuscripts on the use of colors in the miniature painting in the early Middle Ages. He published dreary booklets and martyrizes himself, he and his wife, living on 240 Italian liras a week. I talked in vain. He told me he could not see wherein my work was more useful or interesting than his own.

It is hard to argue with one's juniors, not only because they have lived so much less, but also because they are so much more impelled by forces they are unaware of that victimize them.

Be a dear and write me from your heart and your life, and write often,

Lovingly,
B.B.

I Tatti
Settignano
February 16, 1934
Dear Clotilde,

Thanks for your last letter and for the two *novelle* that came a day later. Their atmosphere is light and charming. The transitions were excellent. The whole rhythm is excellent. They are slight, of course, but not too slight. They lead me to believe what I already hoped, that you would some day write short stories, novels and even romances.

Do not neglect any opportunity of publishing. And the more you write the better. Only I want you to attempt longer stories with more characters and content as you advance. All very slowly. Up to the present what you have published is a trifle too linear. It is time you thought of modelling. And send me everything you publish. I am not a harsh critic, not of you certainly.

I am so glad that you find consolation, comfort and

some happiness in nature. Stuart Mill felt as if reading Words-worth and loving nature as that poet did, might serve as a religion for people who could no longer entertain dogmas or believe in myths. I for my part have since boyhood got out of nature more than I ever got previously out of religions. And when later I again and again felt the lure of the church, I never failed to return to nature.

The Amiel is for you to keep. I should like you to read it some time. I wonder what Pane will say to it. Perhaps he will write and tell me.

Vittoria has been here all day with Placci[29] and the Cos-tas and Trevy of course. She spoke of you so lovingly. But the person who loves you most glowingly and most deeply of all our common friends is Pellegrina. Her Raniero is here, so I don't see too much of her. She sends up Cosimino al-most every day to play here.

And so we nudge along although on the edge of a precipice.

Yours,
B.B.

La Quiete
Santa Maria La Bruna
March 16, 1934
Dearest Bibi,

Elena Croce,[30] Gillet and I sent you a postcard from Ca-pua. We went there for the day on an excursion. I rejoice thinking that I shall make Nicky laugh when I describe my dreadful fatigue with Gillet's inexorability in sightseeing. And with my sleep in the car, so tired I was! All this while he and Elena kept visiting museums. We wanted to hide from

---

29. Carlo Placci, Italian philosopher and literary critic whose long-term correspondence with Italian economist Vilfredo Pareto (1848–1923) was published in Italy in 1957. Placci was a close friend of Berenson's.
30. Elena Croce, daughter of Benedetto Croce.

him that there was a *S. Angelo in Formis,* but no use . . . he knew quite well.

Benedetto Croce was very nice to Gillet. He came yesterday to the lecture as did Ojetti who, by the way, is coming here today for tea.

I spent the night together with Gillet, Ojetti and two young men, one of them a writer whom Ojetti knows from Il Teatro dei Pupi,[31] the Puppet Theater, a disgusting little place. Yet, Ojetti was as bright and jolly as ever. He was also very nice and kind to me and made many flattering remarks about my literary activity in the presence of many people at the club where Gillet gave the lecture. I must say I was red in the face and proud inside. I dare say that now my literary reputation has increased among my compatriots. I wonder if I should speak to him about my work. Not if he does not ask, and if he wants to laugh and be gay like yesterday. He was bored to death at the ceremony . . .

Gillet and I will go to see Croce tomorrow. After such a long time it is a good chance for me to see Elena, whom I find very mature and intelligent. She is like a woman of thirty; one can talk to her without feeling any difference in age. She was awfully nice with me and inviting. I feel again like re-joining the society of human beings and escaping from my solitary fairyland, which is by the way all like a coral submarine explosion, just wonderful. Around here I have only almond, peach and plum trees, and they have all burst out at the same time.

Gillet is about to go to Sicily for three lectures. He is happy the plan is now finally settled. We have not had a real talk so far, he is very *fuyant* and hard to catch. But I have an intoxicating feeling of enjoyment with my independence and with a guest in my own house, far from the atmosphere of drama and *comoedia.*

---

31. Traditional Sicilian puppet theater, known for its reenactments of epic tales of medieval chivalry.

Tell Mary how very happy I am for her anticipated welcome. She is so dear. And you? I wonder . . .

All my love,
Clotilde

La Quiete
Santa Maria La Bruna
March 21, 1934

The spring is here at last! Gillet was at Montecassino yesterday and will leave tomorrow. I did not feel well enough to accompany him, so I just went back to work and my quiet life.

Ojetti came yesterday and was enthusiastic about the view and liked my house. He said that I should really try to write something for *Pan,* and my heart was filled with gratitude for him and for you. Because I know you made all this possible.

We went to Croce's the day before yesterday and signora Piccoli was there and a good deal was said about you. I was astonished at the remarks that Elena made about you. I should like to know what you think of her. She is a fine observer but she is too intelligent for her age. She seems unable to develop further, which makes her admirable and poor at the same time. One asks oneself: where is she going to? She seems to have no force driving her into any direction. She is firm and clear, at that age! We talked a lot about I Tatti, you, and charming Nicky, and all your common friends in Florence.

Gillet is now writing an article on Croce. I believe he would do anything to be "purified" from his two previous articles of last year. Pane did not even want to see him and I was in constant embarrassment. Then Anna Gigli came and she told him that Pane was in Naples, so Gillet understood. We did talk *entre nous* very clearly about those two articles that had fallen like bombs and astonished us all. In fact I spoke so much that afterwards I felt sorry for him.

I just got a letter in the mail from *Il Mattino* asking me to work for a *giornaletto per bambini* where I should keep a weekly *rubrica* of letters from children who may ask questions such as "why is the ocean salted?" And I should answer to them in the next issue. I don't dislike the idea; it would put me in contact with children; I would find the way to amuse them with a short answer, as long as they don't ask me about the Duce and so on . . .

Now I must confess something to the I Tatti Library. I have found here, coming back from, slipped behind other books, the volume of MacCarthy's *Portraits*. I will send it on to Alda if you would rather have it before I come. I must beg your pardon and you must grant it on the account of the courage it took to confess it.

Well, I have to say good-bye. I shall write next to Florence. Write soon and answer to everything; don't leave any of the touches untouched.

Love,
Clotilde

I Tatti
Settignano
March 22, 1934

Dearest Clotilde,

That was a delightful, amusing and cheery letter I received a couple of days ago. I am so glad that you are getting out of your despondency and enjoying contact with people again, with people who have hearts and minds and tongues as well. I am glad too that you are making friends with Elena Croce and I fervently hope she may lead you into her father's intimacy. He is human of course, in little as well as in big ways, but all in all he is the most interesting Italian now alive. I mean for us who believe, nay not believe merely in the life of the spirit but have no other life open to us, or indeed desire.

You must try to see more of the right people without

enlarging your circle too much and without departing far from your center in the midst of the Pompeian landscape with the Odysseian view.

Yesterday I had an enchanting letter from Gillet speaking of you I need not tell you in which terms. If he is still with you, please thank him and give him my love.

Here Nicky and I are working hard to master our disgust with the meanness, disloyalty, pretence and incompetence of the Germans who have been befouling what I wrote thirty-three years ago about Michelangelo.

Pellegrina was here today after Rome, out of sorts. Vittoria is coming tomorrow before leaving for Casa Nova. Maria Teresa was here two days ago. You are the *pièce de résistance* as subject for conversation when I see these three ladies. They all look forward to your coming here.

With love,

B.B.

I Tatti
Settignano
March 29, 1934
Dearest Clotilde,

Ojetti lunched here today and was very appreciative of your little house and yourself. Of the first he said that it was in perfect taste and in every way attractive, and all that he saw seemed to him cosy and comfy. For the second, he evidently is quite *épris,* for he asked eagerly when you were coming and begged me to let him know at once. He was amusing about Naples, about Maiuri,[32] about Croce, about

---

32. Amedeo Maiuri (1886–1963), classical archaeologist and historian of ancient art. Maiuri held several prominent posts, serving as director of the Italian Archaeological Mission in the Aegean, overseer of excavations and monuments in the Dodecanese, and director of the National Museum in Naples. Founder of the Archaeological Museum in Rhodes, he was also among the first archaeologists to begin excavations at Vesuvius.

Gillet. I suppose Gillet is now in Sicily and how sad to have left you!

And when may we expect to see you here? The sooner the better. Meanwhile I hope you are not too bored by writing. It would be fine exercise to write about Gillet's visit.

Florence is very musical just now. Last night we went to a concert of Casals, Cortot and Thibaud.[33] Everybody was there. In a pause a message came that Casals wanted very much to make my acquaintance and would I go to his room. I went and found a pleasant, plebeian-looking little man, smoking a short pipe and caressing his cello. I murmured some compliments but he broke in telling that he knew all about me from a Mrs. Gardner[34] of Boston—a woman who played a considerable part in my life—and had always wanted to know me. Then abruptly he said: "Do you know that I own the first version of Watteau's *Départ pour Cythère?*" I understood then why he was so eager to make my acquaintance. He too labored that I was the supreme go-between American millionaires and works of art that might be for sale. So I assured him that I adored Watteau but was not an expert on his works.

I take it for granted now that if people are eager for my acquaintance it is in the hope of placing something for sale. It makes me rather shy of going anywhere and eager to confine myself to people who know me as in a measure you know me. Not only am I annoyed that I am such a cheap myth, but I know people will insist on believing in my magical powers and resent it bitterly that I do not let them benefit from them.

33. In 1905 Spanish cellist Pablo Casals, French pianist Alfred Denis Cortot, and French violinist Jacques Thibaud formed a celebrated trio that toured Europe to high acclaim.
34. Isabella Stewart Gardner (1840–1924), wealthy American art collector and socialite who supported Berenson's studies in Europe. Berenson advised her in assembling a major collection of Italian art, housed in the Isabella Stewart Gardner Museum in Boston.

But why all this to you who never have and never will treat me in that way! One can't help talking about oneself, can one?

May I say *à bientôt?*

With love,

B.B.

Cava dei Tirreni
Salerno
April 2, 1934

Dearest Bibi,

Your letter with the *histoire* of Casals was amusing . . . But what a poor man this Casals must be, except for playing the cello! Of course you are an authority for the public, but what are you for an élite of people of all the world and for the friends of your House of Life? That is what counts, for in that circle there is more than anywhere else. What you give to those you love is of immense value. I find in myself so often the echo of your words and at the right time they reveal to me all their significance. Sometimes I even regret that I was not able to take out of you *all* the juice of experience that has given you the right nuance of things. And sometimes I regret to think that you might, in my regards, lose this measure and become, like me, partial and somehow no longer *veggente* [clairvoyant]. Yet I know that the moment always comes when we reach a real understanding and when your words reach the real tone, the transparency that helps me, and perhaps both of us, to penetrate our real selves.

It is for all this that I am coming to Florence. We have been phantom-like to each other for such a long time.

All my love,

Clotilde

I Tatti
Settignano
April 27, 1934
Darling Clotilde,

It was a great pity that you had to leave. It really stunned me and for two or three days left me dumb and numb. Then even the day I wrote my first letter after your return to Torre I got a distressing cable from New York. It upset me so much that I really was ill with it. The trouble is not so much a material as an aesthetic one. I was ready for the worse on the economic plane, but unprepared for such a revelation of meanness, pettiness, hypocrisy and moral turpitude. The ugliness of it all made me so sick that I could scarcely drag myself about.

And nevertheless I had to play the host and be agreeable to crowds of people, Americans, British, French, Belgians, Germans, etc., etc., not only for lunch but for tea as well. Only our evenings have been quiet and Nicky reads out Thackeray's *Esmond*. It is the fifth time in my life that I read it. I am not sorry to be reading it again but it will be the last time. Despite its beautiful prose, historical settings and good character study, it is too much the mere chronicle. The psychology is a little too adolescent for my aging years.

I am so glad you could talk to Giuliano [Balbino] as you did. I only wish it would bear fruits.

Mrs. Wharton arrives Tuesday or Wednesday. It is beginning to be uncertain whether we shall be able to come to Rome or elsewhere. In that case, I hope you will come here before May is over.

Write often and with the same frankness and discursiveness of your last, as I shall love you as I have never loved you before.

B.B.

La Quiete
Santa Maria La Bruna
May 10, 1934

Hurra!! Ojetti wrote back at once and said: "Queste pagine sulla Noailles sono tra le migliori che ho letto di Lei" [These pages on Noailles are the best I have ever read from you]. And he will publish them. Only he wants me to say something more about her last volume, *Derniers Vers,* just recently published.

I am anxiously waiting for a word from you. You seem particularly *avaro* of news lately.

Love and love,
Clotilde

La Quiete
Santa Maria La Bruna
May 13, 1934

I was getting anxious about your silence and I was happy to receive your little letter this morning. By the time you receive this, perhaps Gino will have called you. He is going to Florence with Gaeta and I wonder if he will come and see you. He intends to. You will tell me about the visit, if it happens, won't you?

My article is almost finished. I hope to send it on to you in a few days. Read it and tell me what you think of it. Before I finished it I wanted to read *Le Livre de Ma Vie,*[35] but I haven't been able to find it. What I wrote so far is in agreement with your opinion, I think, that is she belongs to the middle-class in a spiritual sense. If I didn't misunderstand your humorous sentence, she is bourgeois in her ready-made ideals, her poetry has too much temperament and too little style. What I appreciate is that she is true to herself,

35. By French-Rumanian poet Anne-Elisabeth de Noailles (1876–1933).

even to her narrow ideals, and what bores me is that she is condemned to intoxication. Tell me, please, if she died old or not, what was her family name, and whether she was Greek. I asked Gillet for some information but he must be busy now with the Academy.

And do you know what extravagant excursion I am going to take tomorrow? I am going to see Zanotti-Bianco and his lady friend Signora Zancani, *segretari della Magna Grecia,*[36] who both have put their hands in their dilettantish excavation on a temple of the IV Century at the mouth of the river Sele, thirty kms. from Paestum. You know how Zanotti-Bianco carries on this sort of business: he acts, and occasionally succeeds, like Schliemann who wanted to find Troy after reading Homer's directions. After reading Plinius and Strabo, Zanotti and his friend had the idea that the temple MUST be there. They brought with them a few diggers and tried. He did the same thing at Sibari but did not find anything. Here, however, after a few days of search they found the right spot and in one day got five hundred terracotta votive offerings. Gillet wants me to go and take some photos and send them on to him for an illustrated magazine.

It is apparently difficult to get there. One must go by boat for about three kms. on the Sele, or walk (ahi!!) over marshy country. But I will try, hoping it won't be too adventurous for such an anti-sportive biped like myself. I feel very excited at the idea of doing something so unusual.

My mother is with me for a few days and sends you her love.

Good-bye, darling Bibi,
Clotilde

36. Secretaries of the Magna Grecia archaeological society. Umberto Zanotti-Bianco was a journalist, archaeologist, and philanthropist concerned with the problems of southern Italy and of oppressed European nationalities. In 1910, he founded the paper *La voce dei*

I Tatti
Settignano
May 16, 1934

My last two days were so crowded that I had to give Gino a rendez-vous at Fontallerta. Maria Teresa and I began at once to tell him that you should come here often, for here alone could you come in touch with other writers who could be helpful. He agreed heartily, declared that he wanted you to write and told us with pride how Gillet had given you the commission to write up the just discovered temple of Juno. I could not stay long and Maria Teresa drove Gino back to town. I got him to talk but he said nothing unexpected. I felt perhaps, but I am not sure, that he was on his guard.

Mary left in high spirit for London yesterday. She livens up when returning to her blood, as a horse when he smells his stable.

Mme. de Noailles' name was Bibescu, if I am not mistaken. All Rumanian great families are supposed to be descended from Greeks of the Etheria, that is to say the Greek quarter of Constantinople after the Turkish conquest. In that way only can she, I mean Mme. de Noailles, be considered a Greek. To me she is more of a society rather than a literary personage. It was the bottomless naiveté and candid snobbishness of Barrès[37] that made her fame. Barrès who was

---

popoli, and in 1921 founded the archaeological group Società Magna Grecia, which was later outlawed by the Fascist regime. In 1922 he headed an international charity fund to aid Soviet Russia, and later reorganized and presided over the Italian Red Cross. As an archaeologist, he conducted some important excavations near the Sele River, near Paestum, in southern Italy. Paola Zancari was an archaeologist and author of *Herion alla foce del Sele* (1951).

37. Jean-Luis Barrès (1862–1923), French writer, literary critic, and politician. A friend of Stéphane Mallarmé's, Barrès criticized naturalism in his *Le culte de moi* (1888–1891). He was also a member of the conservative opposition in Parliament and participated in the campaign against Dreyfus.

worth several hundreds of her, was dazzled by the word "Princess," by her having married a Noailles, by her frequenting the smartest dress-makers, by her "culture" for he was as ignorant as a great man of letters can possibly be.

Encouraged, flattered, caressed, she got over all inhibitions and allowed herself in writing and still more in talking to say anything that occurred to her. That impressed her adorers but shuttered me with boredom when I met her or read her. This is my impression. I have no desire to impose it, but I shall never take the trouble to modify it. I have other fish to fry.

It is so beautiful here with all the flowers, the nightingales, the colors, the smells, that one wonders why one leaves it for a hotel in a noisy city.

Lovingly,

B.B.

Cava dei Tirreni
Salerno
June 11, 1934

This is the first evening in a long time that I feel inclined to rest and write. Till now I have been restless, both physically and inside, to the point I did not feel like looking into myself as I write to you. You don't seem to realize that a letter to you always represents that to me.

And now that I can rest and write, I realize that I scarcely saw you in Rome. We did not come in touch and when we did I nearly hurt you. I shall wait until I come to you at Consuma, before we have the leisure of long talking. To Consuma, if you want me.

Although you smiled when you said it, I was distressed to hear that you still think, after all this time, that there is a mystery in me. When you said it, I guessed you felt uneasy with me, and yet I try to be transparent, even when sometimes I have to hurt you. Couldn't it be that you call mystery what you should call with another name? If this mystery hurts you because it is . . . mysterious, we shall try to make it clear again and again, until we succeed. I need you to see clear in myself, perhaps more than I can even realize. But I am afraid you will hurt me. Perhaps you are not enough detached for such help.

Until when are you going to stay in Rome? Write soon, you naughty Bibolinchen.

Clotilde

Hotel de la Ville
Rome
June 12, 1934
Dearest,

Again your letter was worth waiting for because it does talk about yourself—all that between you and me really interests me. Of course you seem simple and transparent to yourself, for you act according to your nature, habits, settled attitude and convenience. Why should you find difficulty in understanding it? Besides, don't you know the whole water course of yourself, whereas I get, so to speak, only intermittent jets of spray from where the course is perforated? And thus you puzzle me, I seldom quite understand, I am never fully at peace. Is it that I am too subtle, that I know too much, expect too much and thus find it hard to follow you step by step, as for instance I find Shakespeare so hard to follow, whereas Paola has no difficulty whatever, not only in penetrating it but in translating it for others?

But this is the eternal problem of lovers who don't live together, for which reason it is only when together for a long time that perfect understanding is attained. Wherefore I always long for you at I Tatti, or better still at Consuma where we can be in the same atmosphere for sufficient time.

Of course I want you at Consuma and you must try to come as soon as after July 15, if possible, and stay as long as possible. You never will outstay your welcome, my Darling.

No, I cannot honestly say that I enjoyed my flitting

glimpses of you here. If you had been a friend only, they would have been delightful, but being what you are they rather upset me. I think I shall leave for I Tatti Sunday or at latest Monday, and I fear a nasty time awaits me with my lawyer from New York. God knows what he will tell me about my affairs.

Meanwhile we are jigging along, the sea, the mountains, the people all day long. Pane lunched with us today, looked stronger and more normal than I had ever seen him, and talked vigorously and brilliantly. Torraca too was entertaining. What fine conversable fellows these Southerners are! I feel such mental energy in them.

Write when the spirit moves you and love me when and how you can. I always love you, perhaps most when I am a bit cross.

B.B.

I Tatti
Settignano
June 21, 1934

I came last night and found your dear letter. I will not attempt to analyze further what it is that separates us. If you come to Consuma we may easily attempt to get at the stone of stumbling. And if not, well perhaps it is just that irreducible distance that keeps me your bondsman.

If only a creepy feeling did not possess me that I do not stimulate you, do not life-enhance you, do not liberate you, but perhaps on the contrary intimidate you and drive you to hide or at least to be on your guard. Perhaps it is Shakespeare's "Youth and crabbed age cannot live together."

It is very beautiful here and so luxurious, so delicately harmonized! But even a hotel in Rome is good enough and I enjoyed myself there, to the scandal of Father Confessor.

With love naked and unashamed,

B.B.

Cava dei Tirreni
Salerno
August 1, 1934

All that I can do is to come for a week, ten days at the most. It will not be a stay but a visit, far better than nothing. You can't imagine what would have been for me to renounce Consuma. It is not a pleasure for me; I need every year this return to my intimate *cittadella*. You are intelligent enough to understand what I mean when I say that Consuma is for me both a holiday and a spiritual retreat. And as I have taken the habit of it, every year I measure myself with it. Nothing as coming back to the same place after a long time may give you this feeling. I will come after the 18th, as Mary suggested.

No doubt I do not want to come with your other lady friends. I should be however enchanted to meet Desmond MacCarthy and your brother-in-law, though I am so shy that it takes me a long time to get used to new people speaking another language.

Forgive me if I don't send you my article. I will bring it myself and read it to you. In the meantime, I am sending you another one that I wrote on a French book, rather mediocre, which gave me the inspiration for an essay. I am in search of a subject, which means that I have to read a lot in order to find it. I have also read Italian books, for example *Barbara* by Marise Ferrero, but they didn't appeal to me. I am now reading Giraudoux. By the way, Gillet's son-in-law died after a long illness. Gillet himself wrote me a poignant letter about this loss.

Did I tell you that Malaparte wrote me from the island of Ischia where he is now confined? I heard he is the idol of the people taking their holiday there. He has a court of young ladies after him . . .

With love,
Clotilde

La Consuma
Florence
August 2, 1934

I am sorry your letter of yesterday oozes so much unhappiness and bitterness. I wish it were otherwise and that I could
do something effective to combat your despair. The worst is
that I seem to have lost what very little life-enhancement I
may have had for you. And I fear it is no use flattering myself that it will come back. Still I understand that you want
to come here (if only I were a bit more stupid I would be a
happier and more life-enhancing person!). And I trust that
the company of MacCarthy and Pearsall Smith will occasionally help you over bad places on your road. I shall rejoice
to see you and you must arrange to stay here ten days at
least, and twice that time if you can. I say "you must" because I am convinced you can always arrange to do what you
deeply want.

If I could flatter myself that you could be jealous over
me, I should reassure you about both ladies who may come
early in September. They are nearly contemporaries of mine.

Tell Pane that I greatly enjoyed his review in *Pan*. It is so
refreshingly free from humbug masking as ideas. I delight in
what he says about Picasso. Poor Gillet has an article in the
same *Pan* on French artists in Italy. How I wish you were
here in this heavenly breeze, temperature and light!

Yours,
B.B.

La Consuma
Florence
September 29, 1934

You are to send me at last a letter which from beginning
to end not only sounds real but vital, exciting, zestful. Why
have you never sent such letters before? One or two in the

last twelve months approached it but timidly. You appeared in colors that I liked, though I wondered whether you were showing your true colors. If only they did not fade, not too quickly.

You plead that you must be discreet where others are concerned. No doubt. But it leaves open a vent for every prevarication, forgive the word. Don't feel that I want any confidence about others. They interest me only to the extent that their relation to you helps me understand you. And that even, the understanding I mean, must be given freely and trustfully. I do not want to wheedle it out of you and still less force it. So . . .

Your picture of yourself with the children did my heart good. I am keen to see what you will do with the column of questions and answers to wake up children's curiosity. What if you turn out to be another Mme. de Ségour?!

What book of Mme. de Scudéry[38] are you reading?

Ojetti may now be capable of friendship even with a woman. The difficulty would be his wife. She would inevitably force it into being something clandestine, furtive. And inlovedness can put up with clandestine and furtive, and indeed most women never are really happily in love without an element of intrigue, but friendship cannot breathe except in the freedom of intercourse. Ojetti can be far too much the man of action to understand a friendship that is not a partnership. As long as one worked with him and helped him to get through with his own task and enjoy it, he would be what he would call a friend. I suspect he has no suspicion of what friendship means to me for instance. Hitherto at least

38. Madeleine de Scudéry (1607–1701), French historical novelist known for her accounts of life in classical Greece and Rome, and for her elaborations on the theme of seventeenth-century love and manners. Scudéry also hosted one of Paris's leading literary salons. Marghieri was reading Claude Aragonnès, *Madeleine de Scudéry* (1934).

he would have had no occasion to discover its existence. For him it is a partnership of reciprocal service. God knows that is good enough for all practical purposes. And I doubt whether he is given to cultivating others.

It is so enchanting here, and I have not in years enjoyed such uninterrupted weeks of normal life. Identifying myself with the landscape, living myself into my reading, cursing and rejoicing over my work, regretting every moment as it passes.

Morra has been here a few days and leaves tomorrow to go to the Braccis'. Mary returns today but to I Tatti, where I shall join her in a few days.

Beloved Clotilde, I have never been yours more than now, for all I am worth to you.

B.B.

La Quiete
Santa Maria La Bruna
November 20, 1934

Dearest, Darling Bibi,

My mother is better, and there is no immediate danger. I went yesterday to visit her and there is no reason for alarm.

The best about your letters is that I want to sip the juice of them until I have made them mine and can answer them. I carry them with me, both materially and mentally, and they are good company indeed. I say "carry them" because I haven't really done anything but displace myself between here, my mother's and Gino's. But then I got tired, not having the gift of ubiquity, and now I am here for my weekly article, and I feel lazy and unwilling.

My article this time is a *novella,* so I made a short description of a *ricevimento borghese* [bourgeois party]. I wonder if I shall have the courage to send it on to you. These things I write in an hour. Just the opposite happens with the articles, but wherever there is a little sketch, it comes out by itself. Knowing that I am writing for an *easy* public makes me free of a higher responsibility. I seem to obey to their taste and make things palatable for them. What do you think of this? Is it simply that I may be a good second- or third-rate writer? Answer, please. And as I know you will ask for it, well, this time I will send it, but you will read it by yourself and tear it up afterwards, won't you? It is just to show you what I am at my worst when the soft wind of Facility blows into my sails.

I am expecting Elena Croce, Pane and Ino Buonocore, a friend of Pane whom, miracle!, he wants to introduce. I haven't seen Pane for a long time, a month or more, but we often speak on the telephone. He is full of work and in good spirit. Elena Croce told me that this time you had taken a little interest in herself and she felt she owed that to me. I told her this shows how little she knows you, who do take interest in human beings by themselves.

But I rejoice seeing some bipeds with brains, as I really feel too much alone with nature. Days go by one after the other, splendid, and they are so beautiful that I tremble for fear they may stop. Love doesn't go either without fear. But if we did love for the it-ness, like a god, we should not have this fear. No, I can't realize that we may love "without asking too much whether we are loved in return." You say you do. I wonder, my dearest Bibi. See? Your letters fill me with the power of investigating, analyzing and introspection.

So much love from,
Clotilde

I Tatti
Settignano
December 1, 1934

No, my darling, not necessarily a third-rate writer but possibly a writer of stories or little plays or novels or romances. Let yourself, or rather let your pen go. Let it run and run until there is no more ink in your brain. Then examine and combine and still a little enlarge and enrich the pattern. One day you may discover that you are not a third-rate writer at all!

And if you were here! Is it not better to be happy if only a third-rate anything than a *rate* with vaguely lofty ambitions? One's ambitions should be to make the best possible instruments out of ourselves and to produce results and by-products. The rest is mere yielding to crowd-mindedness. Of course we could not live, we should have never been conceived and should be in another sense inconceivable if ninety percent of us were not subject to social factors. And yet we should fight tooth and nail for that one percent of liberty that is left to us, to some few of us who are not merely androplasm but *andros,* i.e., Freemen of the City of Art. And to be free means, as I said, to feel that you are perfecting and getting the utmost out of yourself—not striving to replace the favourite of the crowd. Don't say: "B.B. preaches but does not practice." I try constantly to practice what I preach. I refer to love as well as work. I try to love people as I love works of art and to love work for what it does to me, not for what return either may bring. I try to live for IT and if I succeed but moderately it is not for want of trying.

Write as often as the spirit moves you, if thrice a day.

Yours,

B.B.

La Quiete
Santa Maria La Bruna
December 7, 1934
Darling mine,

It seems so disappointing that I should want to talk with you endlessly and that you work on me in such a stimulating

Vittoria De' Pazzi,
ca. 1910

Clotilde Marghieri
with her son, Massimo,
Naples, 1923

Clotilde Marghieri
in a portrait
by Roberto Pane

Clotilde Marghieri,
Naples, 1930

left: Roberto Pane,
Naples, 1932

below: Villa La Quiete

opposite page

top: Bernard Berenson,
ca. 1935

bottom:
Bernard Berenson and
Clotilde Marghieri,
with Count Umberto
Morra di Lavriano (right)
and an unidentified
visitor, I Tatti, ca. 1935

Clotilde Marghieri
and Nicky Mariano,
Vallombrosa,
ca. 1950

opposite page

top: Bernard Berenson
and Clotilde Marghieri,
La Quiete, 1949

bottom: Benedetto Croce
and Bernard Berenson,
I Tatti, ca. 1947

Bernard Berenson,
La Quiete, 1949

way and that we have to live separated! Every letter from you gives me the *point de départ* of long travels in the world of thought and analysis. Only I suffer from aphasia, too, and I get tired before I can make an effort to express anything.

I agree with Vittoria. There is something demonic in you. She feels it in a literary way, influenced by a kind of D'Annunzian[39] interpretation of a personality complete and ready to live any sort of experience in the most intense way, in a refined frame, on a background of beauty and art. I feel differently now. You may have such an immense powerful richness of feeling, of heart, of brain, of sense; you are more than human because you have the power of living for a hundred men, and this power is what one feels near you as being *demonic*. Shall I tell you how I expressed myself about you with a friend of mine, more than one even, lately? I said: "He is not a man. He is a *semidio* [half-god]." I was astonished at my own words as if I had said a heresy, but I did say it. Vittoria may call it demonic. I think the two words are very near.

And now, tell me why you would like to love me differently. Do you feel passion as something heavy to support, something that takes away freedom from you?

I am so bored for having seen for two or three days people with no brain, women made of pettiness and snobism. This countess Picco who is nothing and nobody and has given me the spectacle of her vanity, is a contact that fills me with disgust. It isn't that I don't feel capable of understanding and indulgence, but I get so bored, such a violent

---

39. A reference to the flamboyant and charismatic poet and playwright Gabriele D'Annunzio (1863–1938). D'Annunzio is remembered as a type of modern Romantic hero fighting convention and alienation through his wild and highly visible political, literary, and romantic escapades. In 1919 he seized control of the city of Fiume for some sixteen months in the name of, and later in defiance of, the Italian government.

reaction. But to see the world with you, that makes it all different; so when I talk to you of people and situations they become the material for our studying, and then evil and saintly are indifferent as long as we look on them for our experience.

All my love,
Clotilde

PART THREE

1935–1939

Sainte-Claire Le Château
Hyères (Var)
January 14, 1935
Darling Clotilde,

I am so happy to hear from you and to have your news. I need not tell you how deeply, how tremulously I sympathize with you over your mother's condition. I must not speak about it for it tears off my skin.

On the other hand I am delighted that you enjoyed days in Rome of LIFE and that you felt as if you were cutting the finest flowers that the world has to offer. I can recall such moments out of my past and know how glowing and transporting they can be while they last and how much one can carry away from them.

And you have seen Gillet, and Gillet and Ojetti together? What language did they talk, I wonder, for in my hearing Ojetti is only half himself in French.

You ask me about Mauriac's *Désert de l'Amour.* Yes, I liked it very much. He plunges one like a thermometer into an atmosphere and you register its temperature until he sets you free. But what else he does I am not clear about. I like his *alto sdegno* [high disdain] with lukewarm Catholicism and I get absorbed in it. I am not sure, however, that his people are quite alive, even when most alive.

You ask another question at the end of your letter but you must have spilt ink over it for I cannot decipher it. You are wrong to think of my coming here as mere habit. Far from that. I come out of affection, loyalty, love of continuity, desire to see Norton and Lapsley and the Noailles, for the adorable landscape and walks and the talks, anything in short except habit.

Reading over your letter I see that Pizzetti invited you in Rome at his Fedra. That reminds me of a week in London. It must have been just before the war, perhaps earlier. One day I got an urgent message from Mme. Golubev to come and see her at once. I had not as much suspected she was in London, but I hastened to her and found her in a grand suite at the Savoy surrounded by musicians and dressed like a tragedy queen. She fell on my neck, in public, and told me at once that she had been entrusted by D'Annunzio with the honor of "creating" the part of Fedra in Ildebrando's (Pizzetti) opera, and that I must arrange to have her perform in at Covent Garden. I dare say I made a gesture of consternation and amazement but she paid no attention and began at once to sing the part accompanied by the musicians. I listened, getting more horrified at what was expected of me, for as I listened I realized that she was far, far, far away from being able to do it.

At the end she told me that performing the role was her only chance of keeping D'Annunzio and that if she could not she would kill herself. Well, I had enough influence at the time to get a serious hearing by Beauchamps, Lady Ripon, etc. Poor thing, she did not kill herself. On the contrary, she wanted me to make it worthwhile to live longer. And oddly enough she was not the only Arianna deserted by Theseus— D'Annunzio who wanted me to play the part of Bacchus!! Poor me . . .

> Lovingly,
> B.B.

I Tatti
Settignano
February 9, 1935

I can scarcely imagine what makes you fancy that I don't want you here. If you re-read my letters of the last six or more weeks you will see that I have been telling you how much I wanted to see you. If I was silent before (which I scarcely believe) it was only because I want to avoid seeming to put pressure on you.

Henceforth I want our relation to be more sincere. I want you to do nothing to please me, nothing except for love and hunger and thirst. If you do not feel a hanker for my society keep away. If you do come, the sooner the better; for I am truly hungry for you and should enjoy more perhaps while my appetite is so sharp.

Yes, if I had written down all that I have addressed to you in my mind, it would fill a library, perhaps one of the reasons why on meeting we are both rather numb and dumb, like a receptacle too huge for the neck through which alone it can pour out. At least that is so with me, except for the respect I have for the privacy of even the most intimate, and the fear of saying things about me of the least interest to you that I have not told you of, or am not ready to tell.

It has been snowing for 48 hours and the entire landscape is translated from the Italian to the Swedish or North-American. I love it for a change and have been stamping out in it at 70 almost as I used to at 7.

Maria Teresa and Vittoria have been here lately and look forward to seeing you. As for Sior Ugo [Ojetti] I have not as much smelled him since my return. I fear he is growing more and more into a public character with scarcely any avowable private life. Alas! How different from you, and how I love you for it!

B.B.

I Tatti
Settignano
March 12, 1935

I will in the first place tell you about Renée Vivien. Her real name was Pauline Tarn, she was an American and more than a friend of Nathalie Barney who has dedicated some pages to her in her *Aventures de l'Esprit*.[1] In *Ces Plaisirs,* Colette dedicated considerable space to her and I suspect the real Pauline is there.

She became the idol of my friend Salomon Reinach.[2] He thought her poems as good as Sappho's and argued that if only someone had done for Sappho immediately after her death what still could be done for Pauline, how grateful posterity would be. Wherefore he devoted himself to gathering material about her which is not to be published until the year 2000. I have heard a great deal about her from Reinach and of course from Nathalie. Nathalie is the lady who told me: "I was madly in love with you until I suddenly woke to the realization that you were a male." She long ago got over her feeling for me, and in the end she ceased being friendly.

As for Renée Vivien's verses, the best of them seems to me to be English poetry in French words. That perhaps accounts for her originality and charm.

Pane dined with us and was delightful, so gay and so good humored. Yes, I wish I could see him very often. Today Pancrazi lunched here. We discussed Moravia whom he is reviewing for *Pan,* and the ubiquitous *Sorelle Materassi*.[3] You must read the book for it is in parts very good. Only

1. *Aventures de l'esprit* (1929), by Natalie Clifford Barney, an American expatriate writer living in Paris and a close friend of Berenson's.
2. Salomon Reinach (1858–1932), French historian of art and religion.
3. *Sorelle Materassi* (1934), a novel by Aldo Palazzeschi (Aldo Giuliani), Florentine poet, author, and supporter of the Futurist movement. The book is about two unmarried sisters who pine for a male friend who has left for the United States, and their efforts to overcome the monotony of everyday life.

that Pancrazi thought much more highly than I did. To him, Remo, the hero, seems alive. To me he is only a function, a foil of the sisters. Finally he breaks them—as characters I mean—long before he destroys them through misconduct.

And thank you so much for the hymn to our friendship. Yes, it is so. I have above and beyond everything wanted to get under your skin so as to feel rather than to know what was going on inside of you. I was confident that not only would it interest me far more, but that I should love ever so much more truly and deeply. You seemed to put up all sorts of screens against this desire of mine, and that at times made me unhappy and at other times I was near disliking you. But I clung to my instinct and I now am getting my reward. We are over the threshold of a real heart-to-heart friendship where disguising and hiding and reticence and reserve have no place. Is not that so?

So, with more love than ever,
B.B.

Grand Hotel
Tripoli, Libya
April 3, 1935
Dearest of dears,

We have been here for more than 48 hours and feel already as if we had been here a long time. I rediscover the skies and air and temperature that we enjoyed so much four years ago when we journeyed in Tunisia. Only then we had Mary with us. She could not come and happily she seems to prefer staying at home worshipping her grandson.

The sea was boisterous and the night after I left you sleep was impossible. There was a such a clatter and racket. The following forenoon we spent at Palermo with my old friend Castel Maurizi and a dottoressa Accascina, an *ispettrice* who used to be attractive—I fear—but now looked like an over-fed pigeon. We looked at my favorite mosaics and at one we left again. Scarcely out of port the sea was in a rage.

Instead of being properly sick I walked the decks till dark admiring the headlands appear, approach and left behind. Walking was an acrobatic feat, and I enjoyed my skill. I had the decks to myself.

At 11.30 Monday we got into the harbor but did not land till 2.30 and they made us wait in the wind and dusk for the *Dogana* [customs] to be opened. Finally they did open and looked at nothing which put me in a horrid temper. We told the Governor[4] about it and he threatened to "cut off their heads."

When I unscruffled we went out for our first glimpse of the place. The "native" face is almost typically oriental, and the Arabs carry their togas with all the dignity of Roman senators and more grace. The young men look attractive and more than one made eyes at me. You know I have always been *l'homme fatal* for my own sex. We wandered through the souks, looked into mosques and finally sat down at a *café* and enjoyed the passersby. We then got into a cab and drove along the splendors of the sea-front, far more magnificent than anything in Europe.

The *Sovraintendente* called while we were dining and he adopted us there and then. He is the sweetest and dearest of the learned. He has taken us about in government cars to Tajur where there is an old mosque composed of nothing but antique columns, and all day today to Sabrata where he has constructed near the ruins the most enchanting museum in the world.

But the sight of sights was the Governor. "I care not what others may say . . ." but he is the most life-enhancing

---

4. Italo Balbo (1896–1940), the governor of Libya from 1934 to 1940. Balbo was one of four principal Fascist leaders who organized the 1922 march on Rome that brought the Fascists to power. From 1929 to 1933 Balbo served as the minister of the Air Force, but when Mussolini grew jealous of his fame and skill as a political leader, Balbo was reassigned to administer the colony of Libya.

creature that I have ever encountered. You observe I write in superlatives. The air has evidently gone to my head.

It was such a joy to see you in that freezing station. You were so sweet and perhaps I never before felt you so close and dear. But what a lark it was to hear you and Pane discussing like two lawyers! You Neapolitans are born disputatious.

With so much love
and as much again,
B.B.

Grande Albergo Municipale
Agli Scavi di Leptis Magna, Homs[5]
April 10, 1935
Dearest Clotilde,

We have had three days of the most satisfactory and enchanting days of a long life. One can enjoy sight-seeing here under ideal circumstances. This little inn is charmingly situated with perfect and decent food. You see almost no bipeds except in togas which they wear with the greatest dignity, and their occupations seem merely to attend to their sheep, goats and camels. Two kilometers away lie the ruins of Leptis.

They are among the most beautiful in existence, and although Balbeec and Karnac are more colossal and materially more impressive, these are situated between the bluest of seas and loveliest of palm groves. We have been enjoying them with the *Sovraintendente* Giacomo Guidi. He is the greatest treasure we have found here, and one of the most genuine, delicate, sensitive, and responsive people I have

---

5. Homs (or Khums) and Leptis Magna were among several Libyan sites where major archaeological excavations of ancient Roman ruins were underway. For the Fascist regime, these explorations revivified the symbols of Rome's imperial past and thereby justified an Italian presence in North Africa.

ever met. At Tripoli too we spent most of our time with him, seeing the sights in and out of town.

I will not attempt to describe or give impressions. You will find better than I can give in Bertrand's *Vers Cyrène, Terre d'Apollon,* just published. Read it and as it talks of the Italian colony, and in the most appreciative way, some papers may publish a review of it, if you cared to write one.

If you write within two days of receiving this, and put on an air stamp, address Grand Hotel Cirenia, Cirenaica. After that again to Grand Hotel, Tripoli.

I look forward already to seeing you at Siracusa, or Naples at latest. It will repay me for leaving all this splendor behind.

Love and love,

B.B.

La Consuma
Florence
July 15, 1935

How I wished you were here instead of Rome, Torre, Naples, or Lord knows where. No, families are not beds of roses. And you of all the women I know seems the last made for a family life. You belong to the variety of Aspasia, or Mme. de Espinase, or Mme. de Staël who although she had children seems to have had none. Children are only a *patior* [source of suffering] for you as they would have been for me. I thank whatever Gods there be, I thank them morning, noon and eve that I have no children.

Last Thursday we dashed up to Casenove[6] and spent some hours with Vittoria. I enjoyed seeing her in her retreat and I got a glimpse into her past that I had not suspected. No details whatever but a suspicion that she retired there at first because she was unhappy. After lunch her brother appeared with his wife. She seems a little birdlike creature, rather at-

6. In the countryside of Umbria, near the town of Spoleto.

tractive but one that might snap at your finger. He was pleasant in conversation. They discreetly led Vittoria and us to go off to Colfiorito. There we stretched out on a meadow under poplars and enjoyed an hour of Paradise. The following day we spent enjoying the frescoes of San Francesco in Assisi.

The verses about *Volupté* occur as an ode in La Fontaine's pastoral called *Cupidon and Psyche*. They are almost never printed separately along with La Fontaine's fables and tales. I repeat I wish you were here. It is so breezy, so still, so beautiful.

Your loving,

B.B.

La Quiete
Santa Maria La Bruna
July 24, 1935
Dear Bibi,

I was going to give you my address in Selva di Val Gardena, but Lucia is still ill and I shall have to delay. There is an epidemic of typhus in Naples and as soon as the doctor told me, my imagination lost all control.

You see, Bibi, I know that I am no different from the rest of humankind. I know that there are mothers so attached to their children as myself, if not more, in this only sense that they have no other world apart from that of their being mothers; whereas I know that I have the power of being strongly interested in the world for its own value, as something to be observed and never get tired of. Yet I have the immense dreadful certitude that I would lose all my zest, all my enchanting feeling of life if I should lose one of my children. It is something that I refuse to think as possible and yet, in a certain sense, my love and attachment to them is made of it. How much of physical mysterious, irrational there is in our love!

But why talk to you of the only one thing you cannot

realize, with all your power of understanding through mind and imagination? The fact is, as you say, that I was born to be an Aspasia, which I can admit, and that I have my children and they have entangled me in the most tyrannic way. Now that they grow, I see a new world of anxieties before me, and a new world of sensations. But I am not capable of having illusions about them—I mean I don't see them *in beau*—and this will be a great source of discontent for me. Then difference will be felt, difference between us, ambitions for them, vanity, and who knows what else.

And here I am writing to you, while Lucia is asleep so sweetly. She smells of nest, fever and bed, and I rejoice staying near her, feeling that she is alive. Yes, alive. Yet I know that there is a part of me which lives independently from my children, and I have had hours of perfect delight and absolute pain when they were absent. Complicated beings we are!

Thank you, Darling, for the little book you sent me. It reminds me of the poems I read at La Consuma, that beautiful *Ode à la Volupté*. And I miss the dialogues between you and the Countess Serristori: I was such a greedy listener!

Love and love,
Clotilde

La Consuma
Florence
July 28, 1935
Darling Clotilde,

The letter I received from you yesterday evening melted me into such a state of tenderness and love that I longed to be with you anywhere and at all costs.

And so I always feel now when you write from the heart, from the real depths, and give me a glimpse of a self which is surely not the whole, yet a genuine part of yourself.

Why have I this yearnful lust for contact with what you casually or even deliberately show? And perhaps nobody has inspired in me such a longing for spiritual nakedness as you, with such a hunger to know you as you are. Of course such a longing is based on the conviction that the better I know you the more I shall love you.

I am so sorry that your departure has been delayed by Lucia's illness. Intellectually I seem to fail to understand your feelings toward her and even to feel them with you. But the older I get, the better I understand such feelings. The difference is that I have never had the faintest line of fever over them, I have no craving for them, no anxiety over them. They remain, when well behaved, the most enchanting of toys.

But if you knew what I have gone through with Mary over children and grandchildren! And the end is not yet. Now it is the great grandchild. Mary should have given up her life to babies and children. She was made for that, while you would have been happier without them.

Nicky has left today for Sorrento. I am here alone with Morra. The countess Serristori and Sofia, her daughter, were here yesterday afternoon and regretted not to find you too. So do I. Tell Pane I hope he will come here for some days, when it suits him, and if I have room. Till *Ferragosto* [August 15] I expect nobody.

> So much and so much dear love,
> B.B.

La Consuma
Florence
August 15, 1935
Dear Clotilde,

The fact that the envelope was white and square, instead of blue and oblong, no doubt helped by the further fact that it was a long time since I had had a letter from you, made me fail to recognize your handwriting yesterday. My silence was neither vindictive nor punitive. I was alone, with Nicky, Mary and Alda away, and all the "institutional" correspondence to attend to (not a little) and the work which obsesses me more and more. It takes me the stimulus of a letter under these circumstances to induce me to sit down and write one. But Nicky has just returned and you may find more inclination to correspond with me, so that I may hope to avoid the danger of forgetting your handwriting.

Here it has been enchanting and after a break in the weather lasting a couple of days it is today more enchanting than ever but on a much lower temperature. How golden and ultramarine and silver is the world I look at!

This is to be our *grande semaine*. Not only is Nicky back but the Braccis have come for a few days. Johnnie arrives today, Trevy tomorrow, Barbara Parrott on Sunday, etc. etc. We shall have visitors until the end of our stay. But how restful it has been to be alone first with Nicky and then with Morra. He is a perfect companion. He read aloud to me first Moravia's *Ambizioni Sbagliate* and then Julien Green's *Le Visionnaire*. The first is well drawn, modeled in the round, clearly told, adequately written and altogether like the third-rate Elizabethan plays treating of Italian women. The second is boring and wistful, at times fascinating and charming.

By myself I have read the last two years of Croce's *Critica*. I am still puzzled by his theology and enchanted when he forgets his dogmas and writes appreciations of books and men and events like the rest of us. In a recent number of *Critica* there are estimates of Fogazzaro[7] and D'Annunzio that expressed exactly what I felt about them in better terms than I could have found. Croce doesn't quite say so, but implies that Fogazzaro is a Catholic and aristocratic D'Annunzio, and D'Annunzio a pagan and plebeian Fogazzaro. Nothing better to be said about either!

---

7. Antonio Fogazzaro (1842–1911), Italian novelist known for his Catholic-inspired, spiritual but melancholic treatment of inner conflicts over love and religious faith. His most famous novels include *Malombra* (1881) and *Piccolo mondo antico* (1895).

Pasquali[8] came to lunch, one day only *per curiosare,* like so many others, for he never came again. I found him worthwhile but in ordinary life he seems a bit of a clown. All tell me his wife is a beauty. Is she?

I am glad you are reading Eckermann[9] and the Goncourts. Of these last I read the *Journals*[10] as they appeared, excepting the very first, and I mean to read them all again when they are published without omissions. They have nothing like the observations of Ludovic Halévy,[11] who often treats the same people and events. What Gods were the Goncourts in my youth! With what pious feelings I used to read their novels, abandoning myself to a sanctifying *Ennui auguste!* I wonder what I would feel now. After my disastrous experience with *Madame Bovary,* I scarcely dare try. Perhaps *Manette Salomon.*

If only Mary was tolerably well instead of being so alarmingly ill, I could say to a morning like this: "Stay, you are so beautiful!"

Semper idem yours,

B.B.

8. Giorgio Pasquali (1855–1952), scholar of Latin poetry, philologist, and professor at the University of Rome.
9. Johan Peter von Eckermann (1792–1854), protegé of Goethe and editor of his works. His association with the poet is chronicled in *Gespräche mit Goethe* (1832–1848).
10. Brothers Edmond and Jules de Goncourt began writing their joint diary in 1851. Below, Berenson mentions one of their most famous novels, *Manette Salomon* (1867), about the conflicts between marriage and the pursuit of an artistic career.
11. Ludovic Halévy (1834–1908), French playwright and author of numerous operas and operettas. He also published an autobiographical work, *Notes and Souvenirs* (1871–1872).

Villa Plazzola
Selva di Val Gardena
August 24, 1935

Dearest Bibi,

The sun is shining again after more than a week of rain and mist. I also feel a little bit better, though I have come to the conclusion that 1600 meters is too high for me.

Yesterday I had the visit of the Fossis[12] and Pancrazi. The latter was here in Selva for a few hours only with professor Valmigli and Codignola on his way to a *refuge,* ready for mountaineering. He asked about you and then we spoke of the beauty of the Dolomites, and I was happy to hear that he, too, would give them up for a Tuscan hill. I hope to see him again tonight when he returns.

Afterwards we went to the Fossis'. The Maraini boy was there, Fosco,[13] and his fiancée, an Alliata girl, both very nice-looking, gay, and I enjoyed looking at them. So did Pasquali, who seemed in adoration of his young pupil, and although the *malelingue* [gossips] find much to say about his admiration for his disciples, I was quite touched.

Another young person was there, Paresce, coming from London. He told us how furious the English people are against us and how disagreeable it is—for an Italian—to be there now.[14] He even told me that friends of his had hardly greeted him on meeting him. He is something at our Embassy. Can English people be so fanatic? You know them, please answer to me. I was so astonished, although I think it comes from an imperialistic feeling which is genuine with them.

---

12. Florentine philosopher and writer Piero Fossi and his wife Nannina, née Rucellai.
13. Fosco Maraini (1912–   ) later became an important ethnologist, photographer, and documentary filmmaker specializing in the cultures of Tibet and Japan.
14. British hostility against Fascist Italy increased following Mussolini's declaration of war against Ethiopia in October 1935.

Yes, I finished the *Journal* of the de Goncourts and though I admire them I find they have a rather limited world, and they are too "nervous," too *excentrique*. Which is the book of Ludovic Halévy that you found so superior? Don't fail to tell me. How I wish you had told me more about your disastrous experience in re-reading Flaubert! How I enjoyed meeting him alive in the de Goncourts' pages . . . By the way, the *Journal* that I am reading has been recently re-published without omissions. I had it from Gillet.

I am reading another book, too: it is Gundolf's *Goethe*. I will tell you my impressions about it. I can't forgive myself for not knowing German.

Give my love to Johnnie, please. I don't think I know your other guests now that the Braccis have gone. Is Barbara Mary's grand-daughter?

Dearest Bibi, I am happy to feel that you are having a good time there and I wish you more of it. One of my brothers came back from Massaua [Ethiopia] for a while and is ill. Life seems totally absurd there.

Love and love,
Clotilde

La Quiete
Santa Maria La Bruna
January 10, 1936
Dearest Bibi,

I heard from Pane how he enjoyed your company and all of your Florentine acquaintances. I am glad and hope you enjoyed it too. I am only sorry I was not there too.

I went yesterday to Croce's to meet Pancrazi and there your name was mentioned several times. It wasn't a success as Croce was not talkative and Elena had two or three of her *mioches* of student friends, sort of giggling girls. So there was really no conversation. Pity . . . Croce has no taste and skill for it except if it is a monologue with an audience. Perhaps Pancrazi is coming here this evening with Elena but I don't believe he will, as he mentioned we will leave tomorrow. I hope to see Pane, however, so that I can know more about I Tatti. All my news have been second hand.

I also heard from Gillet that you are going to Paris, perhaps in February. Is that true? Listen to my great news!! I am going to Paris, if nothing God forbid prevents it, at the end of the month. I am simply crazy about it. I have just written to Gillet telling him the news and asking him to find a little hotel for my sister and me. Now, please tell me that it is true and that you are going to Paris in February. We want to stay there a fortnight if money lasts. We can't take more than 2,000 lire and 500 francs. This is the first time that I really go to Paris on my own, I mean to see and do what I want.

I wish you won't forget your promise if I went to Paris to give me a letter for your friend Claude Silve. I am reading her *Bénédiction*. You spoke to me about her in such a way that I should love to meet her. But of course, do as you like.

I am afraid it seems an awkward moment to go to Paris (so it seems to Vittoria at least), but my sister has a diplomatic passport and we should have no nuisances.

We are having wonderful weather. Settignano too was lovely, Pane said. I am having a delicious feeling of identifying myself with nature.

Write to me soon, dearest,

Clotilde

I Tatti
Settignano
January 11, 1936
Dearest,

No, I am not going to Paris but I am delighted to hear that you may. Be sure to let me know when it is decided so that I may send you word to Philomène and write to her at the same time. I should indeed enjoy being in Paris with you but I have got such an alarming series of internal chills that I simply must yield to facts and not venture North in mid-winter. If you return here no later than February 15 or so, you will find me here at I Tatti most happy to welcome you. Later I may go to Hyères.

Pane came up a number of times and was in splendid shape and we all enjoyed him. Twice at least he and I walked together. But much as he may have liked it here, I am sure he was happier at Alda's. Alda has now a great salon and gathers the most entertaining of the more intellectual younger males and suitable females around her. They have a grand time together and for several evenings together Pane was the favorite. I am delighted.

I do hope Pancrazi would come to Torre and see you alone. That is the way to get the best out of him, as it is of all people who are not orators, lecturers, teachers or—I have forgotten the fourth.

Our weather for months has been beautiful to the seeing eye but otherwise dreadful. It rains or is misty and damp. Luckily I can always take a walk because there is the high road going up which remains tolerable even after rain. The views are sublime.

So I count the rosary of the days with a faint but resigned regret as they pass. A septuagenarian must expect little if he is not too foolish.

With love,
B.B.

Paris
January 23, 1936
Dearest Bibi,

Thanks so much for your letter to Philomène. I am writing myself to her tomorrow to see if she can receive me. So many things rush out of my pen . . . impressions are so overwhelming that I hardly succeed in putting a little order in my mind. I am just coming home from the Musée Rodin and it is a lovely day that we just spent all along the Bois till sunset. I had never seen Paris in winter: how beautiful the trees! How lovely the *vitraux* of La Chapelle.

Gillet took us yesterday morning to the Louvre and first we went to see the painters of the nineteenth century, Manet, Cézanne, Renoir. My eyes are still filled with images, I can just close them and see all those wonders and try to understand what makes the difference in each work of art: why a *paysage de Corot* can be so beautiful and why a *paysage de Cézanne* can be so beautiful and yet so different.

Gillet is, I always thought and knew, like a prisoner. He gives us a few minutes, rarely an hour now and then, always worried with his work. I have the disagreeable feeling that he enjoys himself *sopra dolore*. Tomorrow I shall go to lunch there and I am anxious to meet his family. He is nice and devoted but we avoid talking politics, on which we easily become enemies.

I am writing to you again, dear Bibi, because I love to tell you my impressions and I wish you to understand them.

Lovingly yours,
Clotilde

La Quiete
Santa Maria La Bruna
February 16, 1936

So here I am, after all my wanderings, back to the starting point. Such a strange feeling, nothing has changed. This silence, calm, and the usual worries are the rule, and the impressions and beauties are the exception. I feel as if I had slipped into an old slipper, felt cosy and oldish, and . . . longing for a new escape.

On my way back I stopped in Rome but I did not see anybody. In Naples either I have seen no-one, but I felt in the family circle a silent disapproval for such a stupid thing as going to Paris: *id est* the city of *perdizione*, pleasure and *folies bergères.* But yesterday Pane came and we both enjoyed our talk. The only thing I did not like was his ferocity against Gillet; while I was talking about his tyrannic wife and his awful life of a slave, he kept saying: "Miserabile! Che Uomo . . ." [Miserable! What a man]. So I stopped him. But it was for him a chance to make a real *exploit* on the meanness of the bourgeoisie of every country, and the French in particular.

He laughed and he was happy as a schoolboy on holiday when I told him your words about the smile "of better knowing" of our Communist friend when he smiles instead of answering. He said you have freed him from him, that he used to get bored to death and his smiles got to his nerves. Now he will remember your words and whenever he'll see him smile he will be free of any resentment. We both started and went on and on with a hymn of praise for you and the opportunity you give to people to come out.

I have brought with me *I Vicerè,*[15] so this will be the first book that I am going to read. I feel rather out of my usual mood. This fresh wind of diversion has been like a new breeze in my quiet room.

Write soon, will you Bibi? I felt so happy in your home. It is really also my home.

Clotilde

I Tatti
Settignano
February 20, 1936

Thanks for your letter, my Darling Clotilde, and particularly for the enchanting last page. There you speak of the

15. *I vicerè* (1894), the major work of the southern Italian writer Federico de Roberto (1861–1927). Set in the period of Italian unification, the book chronicles the decline of a princely Spanish family in Sicily as it confronts the rise of parliamentary democracy and a unified state.

nostalgia for all you will not see again, for what you will never see, for all you never can see. "Infinite passion and the pain of finite hearts that yearn," that is the chord that most easily is set vibrating in me and to what ecstasy does it not carry one!

Yes, homecoming can be, and generally is a dreadful experience. How do I prolong an absence as to delay the return—like Dostoevsky's prisoners in the *House of the Dead* would put off, delay, delay and malinger so as to put off the lashing to which they were condemned. Particularly painful is to plunge back into an atmosphere where one breathes without the proper amount of oxygen.

You were simply enchanting while here and we all loved to have you and I more than I can tell. I could have kept you here for a long, long time. And in an hour I leave for Hyères. Do write me there to Sainte-Claire Le Château.

Here nothing unusual has happened since you left. The day before yesterday I had tea with Vittoria De Vecchi. She was simple, straightforward, aggressive and humorous that one could not keep highly approving of what she was doing, particularly as there is nothing in her activities that should not be done, and that is not done everywhere. I begrudge the myth, if that myth succeeds where otherwise there would be nothing.

Myths remain, however, what distinguishes our civilization and one individual from another. Scrape off or dispel the myth and what remains? Little but healthy or unhealthy animality having or not having free play and consequently good or bad, happy or unhappy.

We are reading aloud, Mary Walter Scott's *Guy Mannering,* and Nicky Fogazzaro's *Piccolo Mondo Antico.* The Scott's is a marvelous short story stuffed out with dull descriptions, Shakesperean glamour, and lots of North-British humour. I remembered it with rapture and read it now with a certain disappointment.

As for *Piccolo Mondo Antico,* it is a poor thing, meagre and edgy, although very well written. Not for a moment to be compared to *I Vicerè.*

Be dear and write to me at Hyères.

Love,

B.B.

Le Terminus Hotel
Nice
March 8, 1936

Dearest Clotilde,

I found Edith much weakened after her serious illness of last April but not aged. Our fellow guests were an English couple, the Robert Nicholsons, typical of a large British minority, cultivated, widely travelled, well read, experienced in politics, loyal and fair-minded. It is a tragedy that Continentals do not believe in the existence of this people and it is they, no mere tooth-and-claw imperialists, who now rule England and dictate her policy.

We are stopping overnight here and going on tomorrow to Florence. I shall post this in Italy so that this may reach you in less time than a week or more.

We had dreadful weather most of the time and whether it was that of old age creeping in me, I felt like a rag and did little but doze and read. I read Santayana's *Last Puritan,* a very long novel by the companion of my earliest years at school, college and afterwards in Berlin.[16] He has long ago become one of the most famous writers of the English tongue and the idol of the eye-brows. I hesitated to read his book,

16. George Santayana and Berenson were classmates and friends during their years at the Boston Latin School, Harvard University (where Santayana became a professor of philosophy), and at the University of Berlin.

chiefly because he is a professional philosopher and essayist and never has done any stories or novels. Once I began, I could not stop, for what he writes about is perhaps my world more than his. But I doubt whether the subject matter would interest you, and as art it is good, but not good enough.

You want to know about Gillet's visit. He was to come for about two or three days. Instead he appeared for luncheon and left at 5. And his wife was with him. She looked plump and rosy and was very much the wife of an academician. She sat next to me at luncheon but I did not exchange two words with her. She belongs to the world of the non-conductors between whom and me neither social nor any other intercourse is possible.

Talk had to be general and was rather insipid. After my nap, Mrs. Wharton packed Gillet and myself off for a private talk. So we hemmed and hemmed and talked politics and about his private affairs. These happily seem to have undergone a complete change. He told me he was wanted very much to go hither and thither to write up events, and that he could command almost any price he chose to ask. In fact his whole bodily attitude seems suddenly to be of a man fairly satisfied with his situations. I was greatly relieved, for I had for many years much concern over his situation. And at the same time I had the certain faint touch of regret to seem to perceive that he might become a bourgeois. I must add that he was dear and affectionate as ever.

Staying with Mrs. Wharton was an old acquaintance, the duchess of Manchester, whom I picked up again. A plump, pleasant little woman, as simple and direct as you make them.

At Mme. de Béhagues' was staying the duchess of La Rochefoucauld, a witty, quick, intelligent young woman whom I was glad to see again. Finally a new acquaintance, also a young and this time very attractive woman, the wife of an air commander. She had flown everywhere and had much to say of what she had seen and felt.

Mrs. Wharton read aloud her still unfinished novel. It is very good in her own formula and shows no diminution of power.

Let me have the letter you promised in your last note. You know how much I love to hear from you.

With so much love,

B.B.

La Quiete
Santa Maria La Bruna
March 30, 1936

Dearest Bibolinchen,

I was so desolate to hear about Bindo's death,[17] but I was surprised by the way you seem to face those events, feeling sorry for the survivor. Of course the survivor, but after all when we feel sorry it is also because someone has lost his life. For as full of pain and sorrow as life can be, it is better than "nothingness." I can't understand your feeling toward the dead as to say "He has stopped suffering." I remember the first time I lost someone I love, I could not stand to wake up in the morning and hear the birds sing. It seemed horrible, outrageous, that he could not hear and feel anymore. No, I am afraid I feel just the contrary: my dreadful dread of the death of a beloved human being is just in that feeling, more than how I shall miss him.

My mother has come back from Rome. I shall go there to see you after Easter, toward the end of your stay. Gastone and my sister rejoice at the idea of seeing you again. I shall give you their telephone number.

I am so happy I shall see you after such a long time.

With love and love,

Clotilde

---

17. Bindo De Vecchi, Vittoria's husband.

I Tatti
Settignano
April 6, 1936

Dearest Clotilde,

We are keeping our plan of going to Rome Wednesday at the Hotel de la Ville. We may stay till the 28th at most and may have to return earlier. Mary is so far from being well that I hate to leave her, although I shall scarcely find a better time for getting away now. Ray Strachey,[18] her elder daughter, arrived yesterday and Mary loves her beyond the rest of us put together. And this lady's daughter, Barbara, is here as well and this young woman's offspring, the little Roger,[19] whose acquaintance you already have made.

I dread Rome as I dread any place with many acquaintances. I like to see them but they tire me and fatigue is the plague of plagues. It leaves me helpless and depressed and ends in melancholy.

I am not surprised that you feel differently from what I do toward your friends who have died. My own attitude is puzzling to myself of heartlessness and insensibility. I excavate as deep as I can reach. My own sense of selfhood disappears, and it is difficult therefore to seize the noumenal selfhood of others. Individuality is such a faint line that it tends to vanish from my perception. And no doubt my feelings toward those who die result from inability to integrate selves. Of course there is also in my case a total contradiction between my own delight in life and the readiness to have done with it. I shall never get these matters straight for they are fundamental and beyond, or if you prefer this side of reason.

Your queer but loving,

B.B.

18. Rachel ("Ray") Strachey, née Costelloe, elder daughter of Mary Berenson's first marriage and wife of Oliver Strachey.
19. Roger, Mary Berenson's great-grandson, was born of Barbara Strachey's first marriage. At the time of this visit she was di-

La Quiete
Santa Maria La Bruna
April 26, 1936

I am sure you haven't missed my letters in the actual life you are leading right now. All the same I am sorry I did not write at once as you affectionately asked me to do. I have been overwhelmed by various things, one of which was Mme. Hombert's visit to Zanotti at Foce del Sele—where once again we arrived too late to see anything but the diggers!! This time it was Mme. Hombert's fault . . .

Mme. Hombert found Zanotti an incarnation of a Greek hero; she said he looked like a statue she had seen at the museum in the morning. Zanotti, knowing how Fascist she is, kept a different attitude but showed her almost a hundred photos. And then she was in a great hurry to go away, though she said all the time: "C'est la perfection même." It was killing . . .

Paola Montuoro was charming and simple and slightly skeptical and amused at the whole thing. Mme. Hombert told me that a cousin of hers had insisted on her meeting Zanotti as "tout ce qu'il y a de mieux en Italie." So much for Mme. Hombert.

A few nights ago I went to a concert and met Elena. She whispered in my ear that she had got a telegram from you for congratulations for her engagement. "Oh," I said, "one of the many gossips. I wonder who did it this time!" And she said: "You know it is true: I *am* engaged." I could answer nothing because the music was loud, so I just looked at her in amazement. "Yes," she continued, "but you know, I am just the same . . ." She told me he is twenty-four and that the story was going on for years. "I should have guessed it," I told her, "You look *innamorata!*" And in the end, enig-

---

vorced. Later she took the name of her second husband, Roger Halpern.

---

matically, she told me: "We could never decide. Shall we do it or not?"

What a strange human being. She puzzles me and interests me. I told her I could not congratulate her as every engagement is for me a step into the dark, something so serious for which I always find more reasons to worry rather than rejoice. She looked at me quite puzzled, and that was all we said. Do you know him? He is a nephew of the Albertinis, she told me.

I hear you have seen Pane. I am glad. Write to me, dearest, as soon as you come back to your quiet home. And have all my love. I enjoyed these three social days very much, as only half-hermits *malgré soi* can.

Clotilde

Hotel de La Ville
Rome
April 28, 1936
Dearest Clotilde,

I must snatch a minute to thank you for your delightful letter and the account of Mme. Hombert's visit to the Foce del Sele. Here she has had an interview with the Duce who promises the realization of her heart's desire.

We are leaving for Florence Saturday, May 2, and I almost wish we were going at once. For I have used my spare energy and without exuberance there is no zest and without zest spinning about like a top on its last rounds is no fun. But I have enjoyed it more than I could have imagined. Yet when I look back, what I have most enjoyed, besides the impersonal glimpses of you, has been the Serristori. She has come with us this morning and a more stimulating companion would be hard to find.

I have managed to find the time to read Colette's *Mes Apprentissages*. It calls up so many personages and events I was all but in touch with in my youth, and it is as usual most exquisitely done, given her subject matter. She is as Greek as if she wrote in Greek and in Athens of the 4th Century.

Now I must rush if you please to Mrs. Strong's to meet the Sarfatti!![20] Be dear and let me find a letter to welcome at I Tatti.

Ever so much yours,

B.B.

I Tatti
Settignano
June 3, 1936
Darling,

I am glad to receive such a cheerful letter and to feel a vibration of animal happiness between the words. And I am so happy that you mean to come. Do translate your intention into execution. There is no time to lose for July 2 at latest I shall be taking flight.

There is no mystery although there is no little uncertainty. Mary leaves at the end of this month for London. Nicky and I are going first to Dalmatia then as much into Yugoslavia as wind, weather and old age will permit. I

---

20. Archaeologist and historian Eugenie Strong (1860–1943), wife of American philosopher Charles August Strong. Berenson frequently visited them at their house in Fiesole, near Florence, and she often accompanied Berenson in his travels.

Margherita Sarfatti (1883–1961), Italian writer and journalist and important figure in high pro-Fascist literary and cultural circles. Sarfatti left the Socialist party for Fascism and became literary editor of the daily *Il Popolo d'Italia*. With Mussolini—reputedly they were lovers—she cofounded and directed the regime's authoritative cultural and political magazine, *Gerarchia*. In 1926 she published *Dux,* a biography of Mussolini. Critical of the newest trends in modern art, Sarfatti was a vocal proponent of the conservative literary and artistic movement known as *Novecentismo*. A Jew, she was forced to flee Italy for the United States after the declaration of Italy's racial laws in 1938.

should like to push way into the Balkans and explore monasteries with Byzantine frescoes. It may prove far too fatiguing, in which case we shall drift northward and pay visits in
Austria and land up in London about September 1. That
month I should like to spend in England. After that, utter
uncertainty for the present.

As for here, I am seeing almost nobody. I cannot bear
communal emotions of any kind and most of our common
friends are now immersed into them.

If you come I'll let you have a look at Sylvia Thompson's
Third Act in Venice and it will give you a notion of how
smart and flashily and yet at moments so delicately the fashionable society novel is now written in that sink for all the
vials and waters of wrath, England.

Morra is leaving us Sunday. He is expecting Moravia
who has brought from America two entire books and I don't
dare say how many articles.

Come then, complete incompletation.

B.B.

I Tatti
Settignano
June 25, 1936
Dearest Clotilde,

Thanks for your dear kind words and the expression of
your wishes to come here before we leave. You would be
ever so welcome.

Here we are rather under the weather and I am already
in the nervous, *désouvré* state of mind preceding a journey.
And if we carry out our program, this will be an adventurous
one, more perhaps than any yet undertaken by me. For even
Konia [Turkey] was on the railway and we knew there was a
possible inn, whereas in the heart of Serbia there are apparently no roads leading to the places we want to see, nor inns.
And we cannot find out because there are no guide books

that speak of them. And I long to reach them because I have a hanker for Byzantine architecture and frescoes, just as others might have for strawberries or mangoes or Château-Lafitte or . . . we shall stop before comparisons get too hot.

And I have begun writing. It is a sort of prolegomenon to the big book I have in mind to do. I am rather pleased to get back to writing, but *facciamo per noi* [we do it for ourselves], because nobody is likely to read me.

Shall I say *à bientôt?*

Lovingly,

B.B.

Hotel Excelsior
Dubrovnik, Yugoslavia
July 31, 1936
Darling Clotilde,

Thanks for the beautiful letter which you can always write when scalp-hunting is entirely our of your mind. How dearly you write of the De Vecchis, angelically!

We got back last night from 13 days spent in the Turco-Slav Orient still all but unspoiled. The scenery was marvellous and of every possible kind. We saw almost all I came to see, slept in monasteries *chez l'habitant* and in *gendarmeries,* but we fared not badly and I am, I trust, no worse for it although it was by far the roughest and most daring journey I ever undertook.

Here the heat is tropical and one sweats like a pig. Most people, including elderly and fattish damas, go about semi-nude. Nicky and I keep up appearances. She reads to me in the hours it is too fiercely hot to be out. We are re-reading *Genji* from beginning to end. His was one of the lives I should and perhaps really have lived. So far above the clouds, so voluptuous, so spiritual in his sensuality, such a lover of beauty that he reduces all life to a ritual, and such a lover of life that he does not outlive being alive. By myself, I read very counter-irritating stuff: Hans Delbrück's *Geschichte der Kriegskunst*.[21]

So much love and appreciation from the B.B. who adores what is real in you.

Always and always yours,

B.B.

Cava dei Tirreni
Salerno
October 5, 1936

Darling Bibi,

Massimo is going back to college the 18th. I am really distressed at his departure, and not only for myself. Not only because I will not see him or follow him and so on, as this pleasure is also mixed with criticism (and the criticisms at one's own children can be cruel and sharp). But I will be sorry for him, too. I physically suffer to think he shall have to be there, shut up in four walls, among stupid priests and certainly not refined comrades. When we speak of it, he just pulls his face to keep away the thought of something intolerable.

I shall resent the fresh air breathing freely on my face and a nice bed where I shall delay in the morning and enjoy a good breakfast, while he will be there in his ugly clothes. I shall think of him kneeling in a cold church at 6.30 in the morning, a church where all his fun will be that of imitating the Father *Rettore*. So, physically, I shall really feel his departure, because for the rest I know that it is not good under certain conditions for him to stay at home.

I should like to tell you more about him, but if only you knew him a little bit, it would be easier.

Darling Bibi, I do, do hope he can come to you and that

---

21. Hans Delbrück, *Geschichte der Kriegeskunst in Rahmen der Politischen Geschichte* (1911–1921), a four-volume history of warfare from antiquity to modern times.

you can talk with him. We shall then speak between us and as freely as you can imagine. I don't think I have a mother's complex, so to speak. I can be free as an observer from the outside. At least I think!

Write soon, give me some news about English books, and don't forget me in your success!

Clotilde

16, Fitzhardinge Street
W.1. London
October 8, 1936

Darling Clotilde,

I write to warn you that we leave Monday the 12th for Paris and that our address there will be Hotel Plaza-Athénée, Avenue Montaigne.

I am very tired and discouraged. I see that I can no longer attempt to put in four years of London shopping, sight-seeing and society in four weeks. I have seen many people but, as I wrote already, in the unsatisfactory way of meeting and parting. I hope it will be better in Paris, although there too, except that I do no shopping, I try to put four years into four weeks.

I am truly glad that Massimo has been so enchanting, promises to be satisfactory to you and happy in himself. Of course I shall be delighted to see him and offer him every chance.

You must never mention the word "success" in my hearing. I don't know what it is. Since boyhood I never desired it, and since manhood I should never recognize it if I saw it, and now if I could encounter it, it would be utterly out of place. But I have enjoyed and continue to enjoy life and even hope to enjoy the last experience of all—dying.

Meanwhile, long life to you.

So much love,
B.B.

Hotel Plaza-Athénée
Paris
October 24, 1936
Darling Clotilde,

I envy you the paradise you are having at Torre. It is wicked to be away from Italy in October. Here, as in London, it is already autumnal enough for the sun seldom to shine unveiled and bright, although for the season the weather is almost exemplary.

Gillet and his wife lunched with us two days ago along with Mrs. Wharton and Frau Sarra. The last is the wife of a famous Berlin oriental connoisseur and is herself very much of a society lady with fine manner and, in German, most pleasant speech. She happened to be there when we arrived and have been going out together to museums and dealers. Gillet was in excellent form, but visibly older and I must add so much more distinguished-looking than when I saw him last February. His wife looked more bedraggled and tired more than ever, and I fear I neglected her. I can't help turning to the most interesting person near me anymore than a sunflower can help turning to the sun.

On my rare but repeated visits to Paris the person who pleases me more and more among women is our beloved Philomène, and among men Georges Salles.[22] He is your contemporary, perhaps a little older, and he is like Maclagan in London, a full Citizen of the City of Art. He commands all its wards and, so to speak, knows every house and every inmate. And he is besides very good looking, very much a man of the world and very much in everything that goes on here in every field of activity. We had a wonderful dinner

22. Georges Salles, French archaeologist and curator at the Louvre. In 1945 he was named director of the Musées de France. Salles also edited the *Revue des Arts Asiatiques* and wrote *L'histoire des arts de l'Orient*.

there a couple of days ago with people very much in the know of the present cabinet.

Paul Valéry dined with us yesterday and was too enchanting with his verbal wizardry in recounting and his apt quotations. My dear *Abbé*[23] will be back in a day or two. Abel Bonnard and the Noailles are here too. And how I wish you were here too! I think I could help you have a good time, but it will be joyful to see you in Florence. I can't tell you how I look forward to seeing your dear face again. Write and write immediately. Thanks for the photos.

Love
B.B.

La Quiete
Santa Maria La Bruna
November 5, 1936

Dearest Bibi,

This is my last letter to Paris. When you are back in Florence I shall feel you more for me, though I know by experience that the more we are stimulated the more we love, despite of distance.

Something similar, but in the opposite way, happens just now with me and Pane. He is unhappy as things are not going well with his girl, and he is less and less friendly with me in particular. I understand it, and try to be friendly and detached and indulgent. Love and friendship really are great teachers of the art of living, but I shall tell you more when I see you.

Darling Bibi, you must have lots of things to tell me when you come back. I won't be able to stay long, but in a

---

23. Arthur Mugniér (1853–1944), French priest known for his work among the poor. He also frequented Parisian intellectual and literary circles and was a friend of Marcel Proust's and Joris-Karl Huysmans'.

week there will be time enough, I hope. It will be lovely to see I Tatti again. I shall be there the 18th.

Your always loving,
Clotilde

La Quiete
Santa Maria La Bruna
December 20, 1936

Darling Bibi,

I have been reading *The Way of All Flesh* and found it very interesting. A little slow, meticulous, but full of sharp *tratti* and a humorous vein underground. I don't catch it all yet, but I will when I read it to the end, and *Erewhon,* which I have in English.

I have read another book, but don't be shocked: the letters from prison of Rosa Luxemburg. You can't imagine how poetic, beautiful, human and pathetic they are. No rhetoric of any kind and a gift for writing, too. Something of the best Katherine Mansfield and, as far as letters go, no trace of fanaticism. You should read them, and I can send them to you.

I am planning to come after the so-called *feste.* I hope you will have room for me, but I will always announce my-self a few days before. My love to everyone at I Tatti and greetings for Xmas.

What weather Bibi! What sunsets!

All my love,
Clotilde

Sainte-Claire Le Château
Hyères (Var)
January 1, 1937

Dearest,

It has just struck twelve and I did as you bade me and I hope it reached you full on the mouth. If only we were to-gether you beloved of my soul and my heart, you my sole sovereign of that Region of Beauty and wonder and longing and hope that lies between the actualities of life and those dreams that lure us on to live.

Do you realize what a realm it is you rule over? You rule over that spirit which in each of us, through countless ages, has changed man from the biped he was to that to which some of us are beginning to be already, to that which some day may humanize us so completely that we shall be like gods.

Yes dear, you are my soul, too precious to be kept in my body and entrusted into yours. You are you as well, and because for me you are at once you and me, I love you so at once passionately and soberly, selfishly and disinterestedly.

This that I have been saying is not rhetoric, to which no doubt you have been treated ad nauseam. It is a worst aphasia for, at least, I have so little gift for communicating my exact meaning that I have to make dashes at it. And no matter how I may sound, although to your ears I hope it will sound right, there is genuine meaning behind every phrase, every word.

I had a letter yesterday from Gino, did he show it to you? He talks of his difficulties, his preoccupations, and what an oasis we are for you, how refreshed you come when you come back from us. It is a bitter but not a mean letter and it ends like that:

> Se le dico che invidio Lei, Berenson, che riesce a costituire per Clotilde come un'oasi di serenità e di benessere alla quale lei guarda con malinconia e nostalgia, certo comprenderà quanta gratitudine e quanta amicizia io abbia per lei.
>
> Suo, Gino Marghieri [24]

---

24. If I told you that I envy you, Berenson, you who manage to constitute something like an oasis of serenity and well-being for Clotilde, to which she looks with melancholy and nostalgia, certainly you would understand how much gratitude I feel for you. Yours, Gino Marghieri.

I answered at once and hope my answer was not too inadequate. Tell me if you know.

January the First is as enchanting as ever this forenoon but I don't enjoy it. I have a headache, I feel grumpy, I am frightened. Of what? Why frightened more than usual? I walked too long and enjoyed it too much yesterday: the radiant beauty of the scrub under our feet, of the Titianesque horizons, of the crystal sky and the pleasure of the walk with Norton. *Tout se paye.*

Half my holiday is over: I should regret it but for the thought that the day that passes brings me nearer again to you.

Have I sent you *Main Street* by Sinclair Lewis? His ex-wife has just published, thinly disguised as a novel, the story of their marriage life. Like all American novels, it is still an epic phase of literature but it has an extraordinary crispness and freshness and modernity not so much in method as in the selection of topics. And of course it gives a striking picture of life among writers and has one or two passages pointing to a more advanced, lyrical stage of literature. I can acquire a copy and will send it to you. Yours for keeps

B.B.

I Tatti
Settignano
February 22, 1937
Dearest Clotilde,

I have just received yours posted the 19th and hasten to thank you for it and the photos you took of me that Ralph Perry brought. Everybody likes them and I do too, but I find Nicky's a masterpiece, a Vermeer of a snapshot. You Siren, you of course captivated Ralph and he looks forward rapturously to see you again here, as I hope, or when he sails from Naples.

I am so glad you are rediscovering Mérimée. He has

been my favorite since boyhood. I love his rapier-like elegance and his steely dryness, his soft-hearted cynicism and his fundamental romanticism.

We have had so many non-Italian guests that we have had to neglect my Florentine friends so that I haven't seen Vittoria since you left.

I seem to be reading nothing. Oh yes, I have re-read Jules Laforgue's *Moralités Legendaires* and Bacchelli's *Amleto*,[25] and I am perusing Marie-Laure's first book which reached me yesterday. Laforgue enchanted and fascinated me, and I find in him all that Cocteau and T. S. Eliot and Sitwell try to give, but in a way that delights instead of repelling me.

I hope you have received the copy of Rosa Luxemburg's letters that I forwarded from here.

Write again and write very often, if you wish for worthwhile answers.

Love

B.B.

I Tatti
Settignano
March 11, 1937
Dear Clotilde,

I was so glad to hear from you. It seemed a long time since your last note and I am beginning to believe that our friendship is reaching the stage where there is little to be said by letter. Is that so? It would seem so seeing how seldom you write and how little you have to tell.

I read in this morning's *Nazione* or *Corriere della Sera*

25. Laforgue's *Moralités légendaires* (1887), a collection of literary-historical stories, and Riccardo Bacchelli's novel *Amleto*. Bacchelli was also a poet, journalist, literary critic, and a translator of Voltaire and Baudelaire. He is best known for his historical trilogy *Il mulino del Po* (1938–1940), about three generations of millers, from the Napoleonic era through 1918.

that Manacorda[26] has been received by Hitler. "Birds of feather flock together." But I see him, Manacorda I mean, as a possible Goebbels. Nowadays all is possible. Apparently Goebbels in his earlier years seemed quite as silly as Manacorda seems now.

I envy you being able to swallow book after book. I fear I am losing the habit of continuous reading owing to the perusal of so many reviews and so many papers.

Marie-Laure de Noailles has sent her first book *Six Ans sur la Terre*. It is fantastic and very uncertain but done by a person born to write. She will have to find something definite to write.

Ralph Perry reads out his *Life of W. James* and it interests me and absorbs me. In a sense it is my own history, for the milieu described therein was my own *bouillon de culture,* as it were.

Mary's brother sent us the first five chapters of his own autobiography. It is really about Mary more than himself and very entertaining, although I am not so sure that strangers would enjoy the fun as I did.

Mary's granddaughter Judith Stephen is staying, a strapping girl of 18 looking like a periwinkle and with a beautiful lucid mind free from misinformation and prejudice.

With love, even though
thou failest me,

B.B.

La Quiete
Santa Maria La Bruna
March 17, 1937

Dearest Bibolinchen,

No, don't say I failed you. It hurts me to hear you say so. To write is more difficult than to talk, and I am so rarely

---

26. Guido Manacorda, scholar of German literature and professor at the Universities of Naples and Florence. He founded the journal

in that sort of inspired concentration that when I try to put down written words, all seems monotonous and unsatisfactory.

I have a new German (female) guest: a girl I met four years ago and who stayed with me for some months.[27] She is so sweet and pleasant and a joy to look at, she moves like a sylphid and her body would make Venus jealous. She is very intelligent, too, and has a lot to say about life in Germany today. I feel like I want young people around me again; does it mean that I am getting old, as if I wanted to retain near me what I am myself losing?

I have seen Pane very often these past few days. It is not to be said, but his affair with the young lady was broken off. She did not feel to adventure in a difficult life with no money on either side. Pane was very upset, but not desperate. He feels a sort of anger, and he pours out with me all his indignation with the bourgeois education which allows a young girl without anything of her own to claim for a rich husband . . .

This girl was not very vital, anyhow, but she has much suggestive charm in her face. She is very young, a child in fact, and a spoiled one. I dare say that Pane would have after a while thrown her mother out of the window . . . And I wonder what would have happened to the daughter who hangs on to the mother like an oyster. At bottom, I really believe that it is much better for him, though her sweet face made him dream . . .

If you want to know how I feel about all this, I should tell you that I was pleased for a sort of wicked pleasure, and for him. Things are now the way they were before, only I know that in a short time he will crystallize himself in an-

Giovine Italia (1917) and published a novel, _La selva e il tempio_ (1933).

27. Lieselotte Wiedebach-Woidjusky, a German friend of Marghieri's. She later emigrated to the United States.

other marriage affair, because he has decided that *that* is what he needs.

I just finished Watteville's book. I shall send them all together back. It raptured me and kept me for several days in a mystical atmosphere, and increased if possible my love for nature. It made me look even at my dog with more comprehensive eyes.

Good-bye dearest. I shall never fail you. I get too much joy out of you.

Love and love,

Clotilde

La Quiete
Santa Maria La Bruna
April 15, 1937
Dearest Bibi,

As I promised, I write to tell you all about Ralph. I went to the station to meet him and he arrived late for dinner here. We talked of you and I Tatti. My young German friend, Lilò, was there and she made at once a very pleasant impression on Ralph. We went early to bed as we all were very tired.

The next morning Ralph and I went to visit Leopardi's house[28] and walked through the vineyards and the pinewoods talking about nature, of my feeling of harmony in it, and my contemplative mood. He understood everything I meant to say, and said on his part how much he loves to live through sensations and feelings, proving to himself that he is

---

28. Giacomo Leopardi (1798–1837), major Italian Romantic poet, philologist, and classicist, known for his philosophical writings about the inability of man to overcome the pain and illusions of everyday life. His most famous works include *Le operette morali* (begun in 1827) and *Canti* (1835). He lived for some years in Villa La Ginestra, close to Villa La Quiete.

not only a thinking machine. I felt the whole time as if I had known him for many years.

After lunch we went to Ercolano with Pane and one of my *cavalier serventi,* who took us all in his motor-car. Ercolano was splendid and with such a dramatic light that gave to each mosaic and each piece of marble and stone a wonderful aspect. Then we went up and down the motorway as the sunset was too lovely and we couldn't decide to come home. At last we did.

In the evening we talked all gaily. A young nephew of mine came to dinner and he was very shy but wanted to talk with Ralph about politics. He helped him enormously, showing us his good-hearted nature. After dinner . . . we danced!! Can you believe it? Pane was dancing like a *bersagliere*[29] and we laughed at him, but he did not take it badly.

This morning the three of us, I, Lilò and Lucy's Fraülein, accompanied Ralph to the boat. *Les adieux furent déchirants.* Ralph promised to stop here in June of 1938, and as we wanted to give him a souvenir, he asked for cigarettes called *Tre Stelle.* We filled his pockets with cigarettes and saw him become a small silhouette whilst we waved our hands and handkerchiefs. Quite pathetic . . . but he is really a dear and he has such a soothing simple nature.

I don't think he really came in contact with Pane, though Pane talked a great deal. I dare say Ralph was more turned to the feminine side, and he took a great fancy for Lilò. He said he would have liked her as his sister-in-law. And I felt that he liked me just as I liked him, and that therefore we could become good friends.

I heard from Ralph that you have been seeing a lot of people and are now ready to leave. Do let me know where I

29. A member of the special Italian military corps whose energetic, feather-capped soldiers run instead of march, usually to the sound of trumpets played on the run.

must write. Is there any hope that you might stop in Naples?

Gillet writes, every now and then.

Do enjoy every moment of your journey, but think of us longing for your return. I am eager to see you again.

Lovingly,
Clotilde

Nicosia
Cyprus
May 5, 1937
Darling Siren,

For what is it that you are piping to enhance us; and now you have enthralled another victim. Oh such a happy one! I thank you for the delightful letter and the snapshot. Ralph will send you his book, and I shall put you through an exam on it some day.

Here we are in Arcadia, an island of the Phoenicians, an earthly Paradise, the most unspoiled of the Mediterranean lands. The landscape is of the most appealing loveliness on both coasts, and the romance of it is real. Real Gothic castles crowning almost inaccessible crags whose magic casements look across to Asia, Gothic cathedrals and deserted Venetian fortresses and castles by the sea.

I love your letters, so write as often as the spirit moves you.

Ever so much love,
B.B.

La Quiete
Santa Maria La Bruna
May 11, 1937
Darling Bibi,

You unsatisfiable! If I hide you my good fortunes (I speak like a man . . .) you say that I am secretive and mysterious. If I tell them to you openly and candidly, you say I am piping to enhance you. Man, man: how shall thou be handled?

I just addressed a letter to Nicky to Cipro-Famagosta, a long letter with the description of our lives and adventures. I addressed the letter to both of you and wrote it in Italian, as I feel more free to express myself.

I don't know how to answer to your letter, if "such a man" is to be called happy who is enthralled by me. I am afraid I can only give fleeting, rapid joy. Unless he consents to become a friend, if there is a chance. I am afraid I must be quite a disappointing siren, first of all because I am the first to be disappointed. My amorous cycle is very much like that of some insects and, on the whole, very true to nature. Much desire, lots of imagination, a life-enhancing state of expectation, and then nature, having accomplished its duty, produces fatigue and delusion. Love is for me a *passerella* [footbridge] to friendship. If there is nothing on which to build a human relation, it is better to throw the slave from the tower, as in that Oriental story you once told me. There is no use being scrupulous about men; they all do just the same thing. And if this is obscure to you, I shall try to explain it to you when we meet.

I see quite a lot of Pane who has taken a great fancy for Lieselotte, my young German friend. She is awfully sweet and quite a human being, but I am afraid Pane prepares himself for another disappointment. You can't imagine what an amiable, comprehensive and indulgent and always more intelligent friend Pane has become since our relationship has reached its supreme freedom and liberality.

Dearest of dears, I long to see you again. Come back soon, and give me the opportunity of meeting you in Rome or in Naples.

Love and love,
Clotilde

British School of Athens
Villa Ariadne, Konos (Crete)
June 3, 1937
Darling,

I was so happy to receive a letter from you here and such a subtle and yet such a sincere one as even you have seldom written, to me at least. And the same post brought the letter you addressed to Nicky at Cyprus.

Yes, creatures so sensitive to nature and so in harmony with it, who understand its moods as well as a lover does the mistress in his arms, such creatures are a wonder and joy BUT not companions. We can admire them and love them as we love nature, art or children, but not as friends, not as companions.

A friend and companion I could make of a Neapolitan whom I met here yesterday evening named Pugliese, a pupil of your friend Pane, to whom by the way my affectionate regards and thanks for a letter. This Pugliese is an intellectual as cultivated and at the same time as delicate and subtle a young man as I have ever met. He will be returning to Naples soon; do try to meet him.

Also I have met a Signorina Banti, neither young nor good-looking, nor possessed by any S.A., but so able, so gifted, so candid, so straight and with such a passionate love of nature that out of sheer joy in discovering such a person I could take her in my bosom.

But it is symptomatic that she has scarcely heard of D'Annunzio and that neither she nor Pennisi, the head of the Italian mission here, had read *La Città Morta*.[30] And yet Knossos and more still Paesthus breathe the atmosphere Gabriele meant to convey. He, D'Annunzio, is all but forgotten, has become a mere name in his own life-time.

---

30. *La città morta* (1898), one of Gabriele D'Annunzio's earliest works, is a drama set in the Greek city of Mycenae.

Don't let anything interfere with your coming for a long stay at Consuma. I believe that at bottom we agree on our case. Only naturally you see it from within and as unique, whereas I study it from without and therefore am subject to the law of averages. To get the two views to coalesce is impossible for many reasons, among others that there remains a vibrating dolorous nerve that must not be touched, which is yet the key to the situation.

I wish as were promised we could go straight from here to Venice instead of having to return as we shall tonight to Athens and spend a day there and embark in the evening. Athens is no place now for a day. It has become too huge, overgrown and a bustling town, and my old Athens is almost lost in it and would take time to uncover.

My address in Venice will be Albergo Monaco. I shall be there till the 12th, on which day I hope to reach I Tatti. This I shall post in Brindisi.

Despite all that intervenes, I press you to my heart with real love,

B.B.

La Consuma
Florence
September 17, 1937
Sweet darling,

I was very happy to get your letter. It was fascinating. Gino must have a great deal of S.A. for I understand that your lovely friend has not been able to resist him, and now this equally lovely and far more interesting and gifted *Autrichienne*! The one, is it not, that turned down Pane?

I remember coming into a drawing room in Paris with my heart beating excitement and my arms prepared to embrace a woman who was there. She is perhaps the most beautiful I have ever loved, the most *femme du monde* in the grandest and most refined and most fashionable order. She was also one of the most cultivated and "brainly." Well, when I entered I saw that she was flushed and beside her stood a beast of a man whom we all knew to be a vulgarian and a crook. They obviously had been kissing. Since then, the man by the way was a few days later expelled from France, I have remained friends with the woman but the ecstasy and the passion left me instantly, realizing as I did that though she was expecting my visit, she could not resist the advances of another male. And what a male! Yes, but from my point of view, not hers. Or is it so difficult for females to resist, and must one be so indulgent as one is to other physical weaknesses of our loves and friends? Perhaps.

On the other hand, in this particular case what offends you? Is it your dignity as *épouse,* or jealousy as *donna?* There is an absurdity so well characterized by Oscar Wilde when he said: "How many things we would drop if we were not afraid somebody else would pick them up." Or, what I have often speculated over!, does Gino still have more sex power over you than you admit to yourself?

How are plans shaping? When do you expect to go to Paris and shall you stay with Marthe?[31] And have you squeezed out of her information on a trifling but essential matter we touch upon here?

I must stop or you will get tired or perhaps bored. My heart is so full of love for you that my body aches with it and I go sleep with it and wake with it, and wake in a state not to be described in words. How is it, sweetest of sweeties, that you have completely bewitched me and that I am so happy to be your victim?

B.B.

31. Marthe Ruspoli, friend of Jacques Truelle's, a French diplomat who was a close friend of Berenson's.

La Quiete
Santa Maria La Bruna
September 20, 1937

Darling Bibi,

Your letters are such a joy, and a nourishing joy. I feel as if I ate and drank them. Does it sound brutal?

Angel, I am going tomorrow to Rome with my husband to settle this affair of Lucy's college. I have had with him a long, calm talk about our settling. We agreed that we better go on like this, that is not living together, as he said our modes of life are too different, which I could not deny. And in order to preserve and save the sincere affection that we have for each other, it is better to go on considering ourselves friends to whom we can go with pleasure and for help.

This is what I think is the best, a supercivilized, or perhaps not so "super," way of conduct. If only he means it, or conforms his actions to it! I have not omitted one occasion to show him my affection and kindness; and should he be with me as I can be with him, I could even live with him, but so much the better like this.

He seems worried about my solitude here after Lucy will be in Rome, and is also perhaps afraid of what I might be tempted to, pushed by solitude and loneliness. But I dare say I shall not lose my head, shall I?

Lucy is happy thinking she is going to an Eden. She does not know that she will long for her family. My various *Proci*,[32] as my brother calls them, are probably waiting for my entire freedom to see if they can get something out of it . . .

As far as the S.A. of my husband is concerned, I do not think I am under his sex power. I really do not think so. I can even be in the next room knowing that etc., etc. and sleep quietly. But I hate it when he denies things and invents stories and lies. As for this case, I happen to know that she

32. Penelope's suitors in Homer's *Odyssey*.

kissed him—the lovely *Autrichienne*—and the feeling I have is a sort of curiosity toward her, my husband's siren, astonishment and a sort of jealousy. I wanted her to myself and this puts a barrier of silence and secrecy between us. Pity! Sometimes I feel like telling her: "Darling, I know you are lovely, away from friends, playing the role of a governess; you who are such an exquisite woman who could be and are a lady, why not kiss a man whom you think loves you? But I know *you* don't."

All my love for ever,
Clotilde

La Consuma
Florence
September 23, 1937
Dear Sweetie,

Your fascinating letter of the 20th reached me, but you don't say where I am to address you, whether Cava or Torre. Wherefore I shall address this c/o Raffaella in Rome, hoping to reach you sooner that way.

I have given up Venice. I was going there for two or three days, but have discovered it will be full of cosmosnob acquaintances whom I could not take.

Now for the substance of your letter. You have all my sympathy for the loss of the constant presence of Lucy, the sense of intimacy with her, and the joy of seeing her blossom. It is often the most attractive children who are madrifrugal. One must submit, as one does to the loathsome behavior of one's intestine.

You make me eager to meet Hilde, your fascinating Austrian friend. You should not be hard on her. Some sort of sex-relief is at her age like a *besoin physique* and utterly impersonal. Any male not too disgusting will satisfy it. It is a matter of propinquity and nothing else. Wherefore it should be thought of as on the excretatory and not the amorous plane, and psychology should not enter in it. You understand, I am sure, and I understand that given the way we are made, a certain awkwardness comes despite reason.

Here since the departure of Walter Lippmann, whom I am very anxious to have you know, I have had Placci only among the people you know of. We expect Albertini and Morra for lunch today and Pellegrina with her *caro ben* for dinner.

It is already too cold and stormy here and yet I hate to leave. I shall carry away pleasant memories of the summer, the pleasantest of all being your visit.

If this reaches you in Rome, remember me to the Guidottis. Let me have a letter at Gazzada.

Love and no end,

B.B.

Hotel Bristol
Vienna
October 7, 1937
Darling of Darlings,

Yes, you can say everything to me that you say or that you don't quite say to yourself. *B.B. sum. Nihil Clotildae alienum puto.* There is nothing that can shock me, nothing sexual, nothing erotic, and what is so often at the bottom thereof. Nothing that you will tell me will shock me. Remember the bitterness I felt because of furtiveness, secretiveness, an invincible sense that you were pretending frankness and yet not really frank. I say this not resentfully but historically. So please henceforth be opener with me. It can be done.

I understand your being between, *vorrei e non vorrei,* about Paris. It is awful to leave Paradise at Torre for the unknown and doubtful joys of Paris. Yet I fervently hope you will go. Poor Gillet would be so grieved if you did not. You after all are not obliged to stay with Marthe. You could go to a modest hotel and keep free. I repeat my offer of two or three thousand francs if you need the sum. You would of course accept it, for it is your own. You could explain to

Marthe and promise to be with her when you were free. Of course socially there would be real advantages in staying with her. You certainly would see more people and more variation.

By the way, would you like me to write to Marie-Laure de Noailles about you? She might be "gracious" *per sbaglio* and show you some of her friends.

The famous Dr. Neumann is a great dear, and I fear as expensive, and is treating me an hour each day sticking all sorts of things in my Tartar nose and equally complicated things onto my throat, and injecting things into my arms, and exposing me to all sorts of rays. As yet I feel no different and smell has not come back. I fear I shall have to stay here for the rest of the month, particularly as at the same time I am having my teeth seen to by a real dentist and not by the horse dentist that we have at home.

Lots of fair women, some of whom I like and enjoy, and such music including Toscanini. And the shops . . . I could buy them all up, such cravats and sweaters and socks and such leather. And books, books, books! How we should enjoy each other here, you beloved.

B.B.

Hotel Bristol
Wien
October 17, 1937
Belovedest,

Your letter from Torre is most fascinating and this account you give of Siegfrid makes him so attractive that I want to know him at once and add him to my menagerie of pets. As for the one who sings *Ich heisse Mahmud. Ich komm aus Yemen und mein Stamm sind jene welche sterben wenn sie lieben,*[33] this one I have no use for and when you have taken

33. Paraphrasing Heine: My name is Muhammad, I come from Yemen, And I belong to the Asra, those who die when they love.

his scalp I advise you to let him go to a hair specialist *a rifarsi i riccioli* [to redo his curls]. No, I can smell the perfume he misuses, I can see his eyes as brilliant as Smyrna plums, his whole attire so exquisitely and subtly ill-matched and overdone.

Perhaps in earlier incarnations you were a cat, but Venus happened to like you and had you born a woman. Once so often the cat in you wakes up and you have to chase and capture and devour a mouse? Not quite! But long, long ago in our acquaintance I recognized in you Diana the Huntress. It is the chase that you are after and not the game. Surely that explains so much of your impulse and urge and eventual conduct. Not all your conduct by any means, but the feverish, flustered, restless state described in your last, so characteristic of conflict between ideal and impulse, and two dreads of inhibition and the anticipated weariness, disappointment and even disgust following on letting oneself go.

Darling mine, I have indicated the theme and I could embroider it for many pages, but you can do so for yourself and we can do so together in tranquility when we next meet. Today there is no time, for I don't like to put off writing for fear of missing you in Rome. Write from there if possible and when in Paris as often as possible. I shall be so eager to hear and know what you are up to from day to day.

Love to Guidottis. To you every *tendresse* and devotion.

B.B.

Hotel Bristol
Wien
October 18, 1937

I hasten to assure you that you can express yourself in fullest freedom to me. You will not only find no censor in me, and no *jaloux*. I shall rejoice in your satisfactions and sympathize with your deceptions, and try to amuse you when you are tired, bored and weary with the chase and want to find comfort in the bosom of somebody who loves you and desires and enjoys your sex and mind together.

If you were born for Cytherea, no use your trying to live up to the standards of Thebaide. I believe in an Absolute and always have, and have never lost sight of it as my lodestar. But there are all sorts of ways of revolving around it. Yours may be one, and thus far it has perhaps seemed to move away into the void. Let it. I am confident that one day you will have enough of the chase, either through fatigue or through arresting satisfaction. I shall always be at your side, ready with tender sympathy.

Only you must never, never, never hide anything from me, nothing of any sort or from any plane. Let me see the drags of the depths and let me help you touch the bottom in yourself. When you do touch it, we shall have a wonderful time together.

So I send you to fresh fields and new pastures, and tell me every detail of your commerce with Cherubino [Louis Gillet] in Paris and all the sundry other adventures encountered.

Your true,

B.B.

55, Rue de Turenne
Paris
October 30, 1937
Dearest Bibi,

At last a letter from you! I was getting quite anxious and felt horribly neglected. So my Angel, my first days in Paris . . . I have seen this morning for lunch Marie-Laure de Noailles. She at first did not make a good impression on me. It was only toward the end that something in her struck me as not *antipatico*. The people she had there were uninteresting; a young girl, a musician; a compatriot, also a musician, and a man whose name I did not catch. On the whole, I did not get a good impression. She did not seem to be very real.

As for Gillet, I have seen him alone only yesterday. We went to see L'Art Française together and that I enjoyed immensely. Then we had tea together and he was happy and I was, in his words, *déglée*. You may easily imagine how icy cold I was at his home with his wife, daughter, son-in-law and various boys and grandchildren!!! He was talkative, first on art, showing me the best to see, and then complained about himself, his life. He is a dear, so candid, so exquisitely sensitive but one must go through his *corazza* [armor] which habit and necessary hypocrisy have set on him. When I see within his family, I have a feeling of repulsion. How can such a man let himself be suffocated and altered like that?

Marthe has gone for dinner to the Pertinax's tonight. That's why I am here alone and can devote myself to you. I shall enjoy my own self and a little *détente*. I need it, indeed I do. So now I shall read and write.

Mme. Salandra has asked me to Bruxelles but I don't know whether I should go. I am reading Halévy's delightful book on Paris, but have not seen him yet.

Love and love,
Clotilde

Hotel Bristol
Wien
November 2, 1937
Dearest Clotilde,

Marie-Laure is very *journalière* both in looks and response. Certainly, when she telephoned to you and wrote to me about it, she seemed eager and happy to see you. You must see her again, leaving your card or something. By the way, don't fail to ask Gillet to take you to see the exhibition of French manuscripts at the Bib. Nationale.

Why don't you go to Brussels? If you do and want to see wonderful things, ring up the Stoclets[34] and tell them I sent you. And don't run away from Paris now that you are there. If Marthe can't keep you go to a hotel.

---

34. The family of Belgian banker and art collector Adolphe Stoclet.

If the Focillons[35] are still in Paris, ask Gillet to introduce you. He is the best professor of the history of art now writing in any language and they are a delightful couple.

Here I continue submitting to real torments at the dentist's and so listening to a great deal of music and seeing people, Biba whenever I am free, and the glorious beautiful Dorothy and some very interesting men, none comparable to my doctor, H. Neumann. Tell Gillet that if he comes to Vienna he must not fail to meet this man. He is marvelously well-informed, as no other in fact, for he knows everything from every part of the earth.

I am here till the 15th at least. Write as often as you can, for I love to read you even when you have nothing in particular to say, and tell me what you have done with the lovers you left behind you.

So many kisses,
B.B.

55, Rue de Turenne
Paris
November 4, 1937
Darling Bibi,

You must have found my letters unsatisfactory. Perhaps I am living a double life, one in Paris, eager to see and contemplate, and another—to use your words—with those I left behind. We shall speak in freedom and leisure, for it is too complicated to explain it in a letter, and I shall put my heart on an anatomic table, where we can look at it with subtle eyes.

I am disgusted with this strong mechanism of the heart, I mean that "don't-know-what" which gives me so much trouble. I feel I am at an age when I should look around and ask myself what I have been experiencing, where I am going,

35. Henri Focillon (1888–1946), French historian of Roman and oriental art and member of the French Academy.

what I am capable of doing. Perhaps it all began when Lucy left and I realized that, despite of all my friends, I missed a real home.

I went the other day with the *ménage* Gillet to Chaalis, going first to Chantilly and Senlis. I was really in rapture with this quite different and for me new beauty of the world. It was a wonderful autumnal day, and you can easily guess what glory was in the woods, noble, enormous trees. Chantilly had the color of pearls and Senlis struck me as a perfect sanctuary of peace and meditation. On everything was the magic of a light so exquisite, caressing, like a *pudique* [chaste] smile from within.

Sometimes I see Gillet *en cachette*. We go seeing Paris, looking at old hotels, walking in narrow streets, and he tells me how unhappy he is and how sweetly fond he is of me with whom, he says, he feels so free. A unique experience in his life . . . What a prisoner he is. I really feel sorry for him.

Last night we had here for dinner Pertinax and Julien Cain with their wives and a certain professor Dubré. Pertinax left at once after dinner because he had to work, so I did not have a chance to talk to him, and I wanted it so much. But he did say he liked Gillet's book on Germany. By the way, Ojetti wrote me furious against poor Gillet, whom he attacked in the *Corriere della Sera*—did you know?—because "si è permesso di scrivere contro l'Italia, facendo dei chiari accenni nel suo libro sulla Germania" [he took the liberty of writing against Italy, making clear references in his book on Germany]. But then he ends by saying that he never wrote the article on *Cose Viste* as he had promised. *O vanità umana!* Gillet simply ignored the article; he seems to ignore all kinds of hatred against him. He is truly *très élevé,* though often so childish.

All my love, my beloved,
Clotilde

P.S. I wish I could meet your friend *Abbé.*

Hotel Bristol
Wien
November 6, 1937
Beloved Darling,

You are really trying to *mettre votre coeur à nu,* and I shall treat it with the tenderness due to any new-born thing. I shall help you in every way to let it wax healthy and strong. Only you must never be furtive or surreptitious again.

Yes, Gillet is all that you say. None of my friends has a finer nature and none of them has continued improving as he has, getting more and more free in his mind and more capable of describing what he encountered and expressing what he felt. I am sure that among his feelings none are sweeter to himself and more delightful to me than what in his heart he has for you.

I am so glad he guides you to the beauties of old Paris. How I envy you in Chantilly! The Wiener Wald may be as lovely with the amber translucencies of the northern autumn, but I have never had the leisure to go up and see them. Practically all my day-lit hours are taken up with doctors.

I am afraid I have no means of getting you to know Mugniér, excepting by being in Paris myself, in which case it would be the easiest thing in the world. I dare say—no, I am sure—Jacques [Truelle] could do it. He is on the best terms with the *Abbé.* I am sure he would be delighted.

I shall be here another ten days, but I hope no longer. I can't tell you the torture I go through at the dentist's, hours everyday . . . *forse è già l'inferno* [maybe this is already hell]. Many caresses to you and for you, my dear, dear Clotilde.

Lovingly,
B.B.

I Tatti
Settignano
December 4, 1937

Darlingest,

Of course you must come, unsatisfactory for head and nerves though it may be to see you for 24 hours only. But come, come, come and perhaps you can, once here, stay longer.

Let us know by what train to meet you.

Lovingly,

B.B.

Via Virginio Orsini, 18
Rome
December 9, 1937

Darling Bibi,

I can't tell you in what state of nervous breakdown I am.[36] I measure it through the agony of my indecision: should I or should I not come to Florence? I already have the ticket.

I have never felt like this before. It has become a nervous illness, I know it, I can see it, and I can't do anything even with all my will power. I hesitate to come because I am afraid of making things even worse within me by speaking about them. And if I am alone unhappy, sympathy makes me weaker and in a way takes away my last resources of forbearance.

And yet I know that I love you, and I know that you love me and mean so much to me. My dear and beloved Bibi. Isn't it absurd to think that I have the treasure of your affection, that you are there, and only to imagine what would happen if you were *not* there . . . What misery and disaster it would be. Yet I know that you could not help me. Do try to understand, I know you can.

---

36. Her depression was provoked by the sudden departure for Africa of a man with whom she had been conducting a stormy relationship.

The fact is, in its simplest terms, that I feel desperately lonely, and with no center, lacking an axis around which may turn the wheel of my life and all my energies. All my vital powers lack an aim.

I should work, but I have never felt so disgusted with myself and with so little faith as a writer. The worst is that I have a dreadful, cruel clearness in my mind! It seems *aiguisée* [sharpened] by my morbid physical condition and I spend hours condemning myself. To realize that I am not coming to you, that I do this with my own hands makes me feel even more miserable.

I have come here to see Lucy, but I feel like a robot. Everything else, including my departure for Florence, pushes me in a *mare magnum* of pro and contra. I can see myself sitting on your bed telling you everything. I know what you would say because you are so much identified with my *inneres Ich,* so much so my dearest, that I know it would not help me!

I must get out of all this. I know what is the only remedy, if I can't manage to overcome it with my own powers and strength. Pane, whom I have seen lately, is too strong a medicine for my illness. He lacks mercy, and as far as condemning me . . . I have enough for myself. He is, that is true, a wonderful friend to me, but has little indulgence for my womanly weaknesses and this can make me miserable. *Au fond,* I avoid him. Torre is also too lonely for me, and I hate to stay in Naples even if with my mother. She is always dear and present except in the moments of real need and difficulties. The others don't exist. They are there to hurt.

My dear, do tell me if in your life you have gone through such a misery and what helped you. Was it the extreme strength of pain or sorrow that helped you? Perhaps I must go to the bottom to be saved. But what I hate is that I can't even have the pride of this flight with the devils of weariness and feebleness, because I do see that all degenerates into morbid neurasthenia and crises of tears.

Bibi darling, my only real human comprehensive friend, I feel a little bit comforted for having told you all about my misery. With you I don't feel ashamed. Please write at once to Torre. I shall remain in Naples a day or two only. I need your words more than anything.

Clotilde

I Tatti
Settignano
December 10, 1937

You suffering Darling,

I am glad to receive your letter and need not tell you how disappointed we all were not to see you here yesterday as expected. And even now I am distressed beyond words that you have not come. I can assure you of my complete, undiminished, untarnished sympathy in everything. But sympathy is cold comfort when unaccompanied by the warm presence of the sympathizer.

And sympathy is no help. It is manifest that you have got yourself tied up in some sort of Gordian knot and that by yourself you may find it difficult to extricate yourself. If you came, I could perhaps help you untie it. It looks to me as if because of pressure from without or timidity from within, you were shy or even afraid of seeing me. If the latter is the case, you are making a great mistake. If you came and told me all, positively all, I might be able to help you out in many ways. I can do nothing of use unless I know what has caused your present state.

It cannot be that you lack the deepest and tenderest affection. I give it to you and you should have heard Cherubino talk about you and know how in the few hours I spent with him it came back talking about you. Not enough, he was so full of you that he who so seldom writes, wrote me when I had scarcely left him behind at Vienna. By the way, I am forwarding two letters of his for you, addressed here.

So it must be something definite that has upset you and I

fervently hope is nothing savage, although whatever is the case you should come and tell me all, all, all.

I myself find it hard to settle down to work. The days drift by so swiftly and nothing gets done. I won't worry too much.

So lovingly,
B.B.

I Tatti
Settignano
January 9, 1938
Darling Clotilde,

You have been dangerously near to committing the sin against the Holy Ghost by sinning against Love. You have said it yourself, otherwise I should have not the heart to tell you so in your face. At first, it nearly broke my heart, then I got rather indifferent, but since our new understanding I acquired the conviction that you would come to see for yourself where you were going, and that then and then only would you hold back, perhaps turn back. I hope you will take the turn, I hope it with all my heart, yet I shall not despair if you fail to do so this time. I am sure you will end well, provided some unfortunate disaster does not overwhelm you.

Did I ever tell you the story of the man who saw a black man struggling with an enormous fish that he had hooked and was trying to land and how this man asked: "Is the nigger fishing or the fish niggering?" I am sorry the *Waldvogel* [forest bird] has fled from your woods. He sounded so genuine and I should have liked sampling him and getting his flavor. Perhaps he will return undamaged.

I am ready to believe anything about Gillet's sensitiveness, sympathy and delicacy. I am glad his defunct father-in-law did him the turn of preventing his becoming editor of the review. It is a place for mummies and Gillet is still what in America we call a "live-wire." Life is still capable of holding out for him adventures of the mind and of the heart, utterly incompatible with such a charge as editorship of the *Revue*.

And you beloved, what are you going to do? Why return to Torre just now instead of coming here at once? You would be so welcome and left so free, hours and hours to introspect, to investigate, to meditate and if the spirit moved you, to write. I do not urge you but assure you of a welcome.

All good wishes, my Darling Clotilde,

B.B.

I Tatti
Settignano
February 4, 1938

Darling Clotilde,

I have not changed in any way from what I was toward you when you left me last summer, but I confess I am in a mist about you. From Paris I began to feel out of touch and sure that I have no idea where you are mentally and spiritually and not only spatially. You have become an enigma, and I confess that enigmas soon exhaust me. I have not got the brain to cope with them.

I am glad to hear that you are consigning your inner life to a diary, if you feel you cannot consign it to me. But perhaps you will let me read the diary in a state of nature, unpurged and unarranged.

I have not seen Ojetti since our return. Indeed he is seldom here now. He is so much on the wing.

You will always pick me up where you dropped me, dear Clotilde. I understand you and I understand me as well—*quand même!*

Ever yours,

B.B.

I Tatti
Settignano
February 17, 1938

Darling Clotilde,

Ever since you first took me to Torre and talked of Capri
I have been longing to go there with you. We must realize it
someday. You have no idea how eager I am for it.

Alberto Albertini I really have seen but once. That was
at Vienna. He was alone and came to tea. His *Creso* I like for
its talk which is very good for its kind. But Pancrazi and
Morra are of your opinion about it.

There was an entertaining article by Praz[37] on contemporary Italian culture in the last *Criterion*. Presumably he expected no Italian to read it. You may remember Morra wrote
a rather harsh review of Praz's manual of English literature.
It led to very unamiable letters from the former. How touchy
and provincially oversensitive men of letters remain here! We
never turn a hair.

Moravia was here the other day, looking more like a
rajah than ever with his demonic look. He is writing a novel.
You know of course that his *Indifferenti* is having a great success in Paris as a play.

My love to Werfel, and for you that much besides.

Devotedly,
B.B.

La Quiete
Santa Maria La Bruna
March 22, 1938

Darling Bibi,

I am anxious to have from you some news of Werfel. I
am dreadfully sorry about him. I saw him a few days before

---

37. Mario Praz, Italian scholar of letters and languages at the University of Liverpool and Manchester, and of English literature at the

the horrible thing happened in Austria[38] and he was worried. What a tragedy for so many! And how bitterly you must have felt it.

I must talk of plans, as I have after your last letter the clear feeling that you don't care to write as before, that you have lost contact with me.

Is there any hope of having you my guest here? I am having the bathroom remodeled which makes this offer a bit easier. Is there any hope to take you to Capri? It would be heaven. I am having just now as a guest Edwin Cerio, the "king of Capri." So *lieb,* genuine, such a marvellous *causeur* in many languages, you would love him. He is in love with Lieselotte and I can't tell you how pathetic the whole thing is, for the moment at least . . .

He is 70 years old but clearly belongs to those men who go through a renewed adolescential stage. In his own way, he is also full of humor.

Could I come to you before Easter?

> Your always loving,
> Clotilde

I Tatti
Settignano
March 24, 1938
Darling Clotilde,

Come just as soon as you can and you must stay as long as you possibly can, but before rather than after Easter. The more so as in every probability we shall be leaving toward April 25 for Asia Minor and be away till June.

University of Rome. A specialist on British literature, he also translated works by T. S. Eliot, Paul Valéry, Arthur Rimbaud, and Berenson's *Aesthetics and History in the Visual Arts.*
38. Marghieri is referring to the German annexation of Austria in March 1938.

I can't tell you how much I should love to come and stay with you at Torre. Perhaps in October. And I long to be in Capri with you.

If you will open yourself up, I am sure I shall understand you. If you do not, I shall have to guess. The worst of guessing is that as I don't have much confidence in it, I soon abandon it, and with this my interest tends to sink. My feeling for you is not likely to change in kind but in intensity. It must necessarily cool and dim, if not fade.

So come, come. Let us know the day and the hour. You shall see how welcome you'll be.

Yours,

B.B.

La Quiete
Santa Maria La Bruna
March 28, 1938

My dearest Bibi,

Your letter has strongly disappointed me, just in the moment I was anticipating the joy of my visit. Is it necessarily fatal that your love for me must "cool and dim if not fade"? You seem to have professed your life to the contrary. There is no use writing when we are going to talk very soon.

But if you really felt that your affection has to go through this diminishing cycle, why should I come? to become aware of it? If it isn't so, why say it? You shall have to explain all this, please, beloved Bibi.

Yours lovingly,

Clotilde

I Tatti
Settignano
March 30, 1938

I don't know what in the world you are talking about. I urged you most lyrically to come and you try to pick a quarrel about a matter of which I have told you and written a hundred times. Namely that even the dearest loves tend to fade and fail if I don't come in physical touch with them and so often. As Antaeus needed to touch earth to go on living, I need to touch the object of affection if I am to go on loving it intensely, convincingly, in short: physically. And you know as well as I do that such is the kind of love you want from me besides friendship, and that friendship alone would not satisfy you.

If it would, say so and risk it. The risk is there. If you provoke or stimulate me, when we meet, to discuss this and kindred subjects with you, we shall be entertained.

Still as ever,

B.B.

I Tatti
Settignano
April 23, 1938
Darling Clotilde,

I have never had you out of my thoughts since you left me. So much did the little I saw of you impress, distress and interest me. I think I understand to a degree what you are going through and you have my sympathy to the depths, and every desire to give you a helping hand. How? I could only do it by your being with me a great deal. By letter it is not easy, at least not for me. I have no *jolie plume,* nor a particularly comforting one either.

We leave Tuesday and stop over to dine with Mrs. Aldrich in Rome. If the Guidottis still are there they might come to see us off at the station. We embark in Bari Saturday morning and are due in Smyrna May 4.

If you write there, address c/o British Consulate General, Izmir, Turkey.

With true love,

B.B.

In camp near Strabonicca
Turkey
May 13, 1938
Darling Clotilde,

I think of you continually as we drive along through this enchanting land macerated with every kind of poetical and historical association. I wonder whether you are getting over the blow to your self-confidence that you still were aching from when I last saw you. It was a nasty blow, but you can turn into a caress if you take it the right way.

You may be in Rome today seeing the Guidottis off. They came to the station when we passed through and Gastone was interesting. I hope they will be happy at Belgrade.

Did I tell you that only two or three days before we left we discovered that Poggio allo Spino was sold? I felt lost. We have taken the Corsini's Casa al Dono and I hope you will join us there. You must.

Of this voyage that we are making I can scarcely begin to tell you. It would make a book to describe each day's subjective reactions to the things that pass. We are four: Nicky and I, Sir Robert Greg, an English diplomat, and a Smyrniote Englishman who leads us. We sleep under tents and travel in a car with a German chauffeur. Nicky works about four hours a day like the spouse of a very poor man and makes me perfectly comfy. Tent life is sheer slum life, and like a Gipsy you carry the slum with you. It is not only materially so, but this wandering life far from cities, far from the towns, with nobody but shepherds and peasants to encounter, cattle and sheep and goats to hear, and birds and piping, such a return to a pastoral existence affects the mind. It ruminates, it muses, it dreams, but it does not think, does not want to read, scarcely wants to know where one is or what happened there, gets indifferent to everything, and not only careless but oblivious of the world's doings. Thus, all this business of Hitler's coming to Rome to inaugurate his Reich, the third Reich, none of us gave a thought.[39]

Do write me, beloved Clotilde. It takes five or six days at utmost. Address c/o British Consulate.

Je t'embrasse tendrement,

B.B.

La Quiete
Santa Maria La Bruna
May 23, 1938

My darling Bibi,

No, your letter took seven days to reach me, and when you sent yours you had not yet received mine sent on the 8th. It seems we are distant and by now lost!

I have just come back from Rome where I saw the Albertinis. We went to Torre in Pietra, the lovely place you know, so captivating and such a lovely house. There I saw the *ménage* Gillet after his lecture on D'Annunzio. We dined together at Villa Medici with his cousin Gilbert, a musician who did not impress me too much. He had not shaved, and he spoke of Signora Ojetti as a genius. As always, Mme. Gillet was unbearable and he, under the spell of his wife, was insignificant. He told me he had been in Naples for a few days, had dinner with Croce, and had asked Pane to dine with him. I found it very generous and very "cherubin-like" and I thought, once more, how much more worth is his indifference to enemies compared to the obstinate hostility of self-asserting people such as my good friend Pane.

My beloved, I don't know if I am getting over the blow. Certainly it has not transformed into a caress. I feel lacking

39. Hitler's visit to Rome and Florence, May 3–9, 1938, was intended to consolidate the Rome-Berlin Axis created in October 1936.

enthusiasm, as if my *joie de vivre* was fading. I am not indulging in this agony, but inside I feel rotten. What shall help me?

Always to you with love,
my Darling Bibi,
Clotilde

Cava dei Tirreni
Salerno
September 5, 1938
Darling Bibi,

I am so upset by what is happening around us. I can't hide that I am nourishing an awful fear: the fear that you, disgusted, might want to get away. This idea puts me in a state of desolation. I never realized before how this worry can take a hold of me, what you being here, where six or seven hours of train can carry me, means to my life. I wanted to write you about it, yet now I fear your answer.

I am reading Julien Green's book and find it intelligent but obvious. I want to read the last of Alvaro's books; some people said it is very good. Have you read it?

The weather is rainy here, and I am afraid is damp over there in Florence too.

Full of love for you, my Precious One,
Clotilde

Casa al Dono
Vallombrosa
September 8, 1938

Not yet, my sweet Darling, but who knows what may happen the next hour.

I am better but not yet my normal self, little though that is. The worst is that the least effort tires me, so that little by little I am drifting into the disinclination to make any.

Do you refer to Julien Green's *Journal*? I too found it rather presumptuous to publish such stuff—most of it. Who

214

cares to read that this work came hard or easy on a certain day? His notes in America interested me more. Oddly enough relations of his from over there were here the other day.

Marthe Ruspoli had been quite ill. She is with her parents in the Lozère. I am expecting Alda today and the Doro Levis. I rather dread seeing and hearing them. There is nothing to say that has not been said a hundred times.

I love you very much,

B.B.

I Tatti
Settignano
October 28, 1938

Dearest Clotilde,

I have read your play[40] and liked it very much indeed as literature. I say "literature" because I can have no opinion on its adaptability to the stage. As you know, I almost never go to the theatre and know nothing of its technique.

As "literature" then, the progress you have made since the little sketch about the house in Capri, the last I recall reading, is enormous. The first act is perfectly charming as genre, exquisitely delicate and atmospheric. When the masculine element appears the play loses, for me, much of its initial fragility and refinement. The third act, perhaps the stagiest, I liked least. That does not mean I did not like it. I liked it a good deal, but nothing like so much as the first act.

You have made such immense progress that you seem capable of a great deal, a very great deal more. Come soon, bring the play and we'll discuss it further.

With admiration and love,

B.B.

40. The play, *Caccia piccola,* was never published.

La Quiete
Santa Maria La Bruna
November 30, 1938

Darling Bibi,

I was most delighted to hear your favorable judgement
of my play. Gillet had read it and said exactly the same thing.
Only he added that I should have written a central dialogue
if I wanted the whole to make unity. And so that is what I
will do. I had to laugh whilst writing: there slipped from my
pen the word *lotta* [struggle]. I smiled amused at your likely
comments . . . but I must be myself. Although *the word* can
be changed, it reflects all of my youth's *Sturm und Drang*.

Darling, I shall go to Rome to accompany Lucy towards
the 6th or the 7th, and then remain there a few days. Then, if
there is place for me in the room (I know there is in your
heart) I shall fly to you.

Your loving,
Clotilde

Hotel de La Ville
Rome
March 30, 1939

Dear Clotilde,

I cannot wait till tomorrow to tell you that I have read
your article on Katherine Mansfield's letters and liked it. I
am almost startled by the facility with which you can write.
It amounts almost to virtuosity. Beyond question you could
be a writer. Your difficulties would not be mine, but the
contrary. You would have to restrain your eloquence and
your rhythms.

The contents of the article were as delightful as the style,
and no small revelation. I confess that I should not have expected you to be deeply moved by these letters. I should
have supposed the genre to which they belonged was too

well known in perhaps better examples. For you they of course have the attraction of contemporaneity.

Enchanting letter that I enclose from your friend.

Till tomorrow evening and always,

B.B.

Cava dei Tirreni
Salerno
September 5, 1939
Darling Bibi,

Your letter was such a consolation to all my worries, as I had feared you were gone. At least I know that you are here and who knows, perhaps you will stay. I know nothing more exasperating than this state of uncertainty and reclusion. As for what has already happened and all the evil that it brings along, no words are necessary between us.

We have decided to stay here as the place that Gino considers our real home. Anyhow, it is a larger and safer house than Torre. My sister has come back from Belgrade with her English nurse who did not want to leave them. My other sister, Rosanna, will settle in my house in Torre and I will envy her. Lucia will stay with us. *Hélas,* she is very sorry and Massimo after his exam will probably be drafted as *avanguardista*[41] for local services here or in Naples. Gino thinks that he will be mobilized too, and this is not a gay perspective.

My friend Lilò left Capri where she had been staying the whole summer and is now here waiting for the events to develop. Her brother, who was in Capri, was also called in by the army and she thinks she may be forced to return as well. All houses and villas in Cava are requested by Neapolitans who had to leave the city and we shall give up our *dépendance.* Unhappily, no nice people have come in the neighbor-

---

41. Member of a militarized Fascist youth organization.

hood. It seems difficult to work or even to read. One gets only eager for news.

I had a sort of farewell letter from dearest Gillet, and who knows when I shall hear from him next. He said he hoped you might be our *boîte aux lettres* [mailbox]. His four sons were all called in the army.

Pane is getting married the 11th, only a civil marriage. I haven't seen him yet. He seems ferociously happy, not for his marriage but for the atmosphere in general.

These are my news. I am longing to hear yours, and to follow your decisions, so important to me.

More than ever attached to you,

Clotilde

I Tatti
Settignano
September 15, 1939

Darling Clotilde,

I do hope you will come here soon. It would make me so happy!

From England I have received no written words since September 1st. *The Times* struggles in irregularly. From France it is the same. The only sign of life from there was from Marie-Louise, a devoted and loving friend despite appearances to the contrary.

Marthe I know nothing about. It must be nearly a year since I have heard from her. Vague rumours reach me again and again that she is off with Jacques. They must be in Washington.

I feel deeply touched and much cheered by your affection, my Beloved Clotilde. Do come as soon as you can.

B.B.

I Tatti
Settignano
October 24, 1939
Darling Clotilde,

I enclose a note just received from Cherubino, first in two months. Please return it.

I am so sorry you have had further annoyances, troubles and perplexities. Surely "life is one damn thing after another." Perhaps I can harden my heart and go to Rome fairly early in November. I say harden because Mary has just come back. I wonder though how much *cash* pleasure my company gives her and whether she cares more than the comforts I Tatti offers her.

The Croces have been here, he unusually affable. Others came through. Number of Germans all telling tales of the same privations and drear misery under the Nazis. Let us hope we shall keep them and their ways very, very far from us.

Much love and devotion,
B.B.

PART FOUR
1940–1955

I Tatti
Settignano
May 4, 1940
Darling Clotilde,

We have been so alarmed that our thoughts in so far as one could think at all were all concentrated on plans of getting away. This is why I did not write sooner to thank you for the letters of a week ago.

Your sister did come and we were so happy to see her, but she too was frightened and depressed. Think of it, I was planning to go to Yugoslavia! However, there is *compensation à tout,* and Nicky and I are planning to go to Rome in a fortnight or so. And you know what you mean to me there. I look forward to seeing you and learning how at least you are fulfilling yourself. I am sure it is true, but I want to know just how.

I had a call this morning from our (USA) Ambassador,[1] who comforted us greatly.

Ever lovingly,

B.B.

1. William Philips, United States ambassador to Italy from 1936 to 1941.

Casa al Dono
Vallombrosa
August 12, 1940

Dearest, Darling Clotilde,

So near and yet so far, you should be called Daniela, for you are thriving in a lion's den! How different from us here in the heart of the forest where we hear only the wind in the trees, the birds singing and brooks babbling. We have no visitors and very few callers. Among these is the Empress of Lesbos, *la civile* Nathalie Barney, so enchanting that I forgive myself for having been so much in love with her more than 26 years ago. And she would have returned my flame had I not been—as she discovered to her horror—a male. She comes up with Romaine Brooks, one of the *maîtresses authentiques* of D'Annunzio's.

I read a great deal, do some writing and much loafing. If the queer little bipeds crawling over the Eur-Afric-Asiatic land mass were not misbehaving so naughtily, I could enjoy the blessing wherewith the gods are cramming my old age.

Darling Clotilde, you know how I should love to see you here and keep you. So I say no more.

No word from the country that once was France.

With love,
B.B.

La Quiete
Santa Maria La Bruna
October 9, 1940

My darling Bibi,

I woke up during the night in tears. I dreamt you telephoned me to say farewell, and then you said other things at a very low voice and I couldn't hear you, and so I asked you to repeat, but you replied that it was late, that you had to go . . .

I wish there was no truth in it, but perhaps there is. Please let me know when you go to Rome because I would certainly come. In fact, I am going there the 14th, perhaps only a few days, but if you came I would stay longer. I must, if only for a few days, come to see you and feel comforted by your love and affection.

It is only too beautiful here, we never had such an Autumn. But my mother's cries [at the death of her first son] make me go mad, I can hardly physically stand it. And no news from Cherubino, another thorn in my heart.

All my love and affection,
Clotilde

I Tatti
Settignano
October 15, 1940
Darling Clotilde,

Your dear letter posted at Santa Maria La Bruna has just reached me, Tuesday October 15, at 11.30 a.m. I hasten to tell you how I hope that you will prolong your Roman stay so that we can find you there when we get there in eight or ten days. Needless to say how much we want to see you.

Your dream may come true. If it were not for Mary I should risk sticking here whatever happened, but she is getting afraid and I can feel her alarm increasing. Friends from America implore us to leave and friends from here likewise. But I perhaps foolishly keep cherishing my hope that there will be no declared war between my two countries.

We have seen no common acquaintance since we came down ten days ago. Few are back, or I am sure they would have come. Mary is better and madder. Nicky tries to look calm and unconcerned but feels worried and there is reason to be.

Dear, dear friend, do try to stay in Rome till we come, or to return.

Most lovingly
B.B.

I Tatti
Settignano
December 16, 1940

Darling Clotilde,

My last news of Cherubino are not very good. In June he had an attack of lung trouble and moved South with his wife. He is better now and living with his daughter Demanguel, Rue Baroussuat, Montpellier. I wrote him a long letter yesterday giving him your news and your present address.

We are having divine although very frosty weather and I wish you were here with us. We see very few people but those very companionable. We talk and read a great deal. Have you seen Moravia's volume of short stories,[2] just out? It has one, "La verità nel caso di Ulisse," which takes rank with the best he has ever written.

I have you constantly in my thoughts and carry on a long dialogue with you. How pleasant it is despite, despite all around us.

Ever so much love
and every good wish
B.B.

La Quiete
Santa Maria La Bruna
September 14, 1944

My beloved, Darling Bibi,

It seems a dream that I may be able to write to you again! God bless you, dearest of dears. I heard at once from Captain Stone, who was in our villa at Cava dei Tirreni and with whom I am in frequent and pleasant contact, that you were "alive and well." But after this message I heard no more. Nothing about Nicky and Mary (although I presume that Nicky is with you), and nothing about my beloved I Tatti. I am sending this letter . . . but shall you receive it?

---

2. Moravia's *I sogni del pigro. Racconti, miti, allegorie* (1940).

Do please address a word to here and to Rome, Via della Consulta, 50.[3]

It has been an agony to think of Florence these last two months, and Florence means you and Nicky first of all, and what I cherish most in the world of beauty and friendship. I won't talk with you about Florence and its destructions, for we would bleed together in the same intensity, but I must know about I Tatti, about Alda, herself and her family, and if you are back at I Tatti.

From Commander Lowler I heard that Johnnie Walker was coming to Italy. Perhaps he is already here. I would be so glad to know that he is with you.

I found everything at Torre still *in piedi* [standing]. La Cava is injured but habitable, so much so that Captain Stone and other English officers are there. My darling, there is so much to say that one does not know where to begin from. I should love to fly to you but it is not easy! You know that one of Gillet's sons came to Naples to meet Pane?

So Bibi, you are still of this world, so this world is still full of meaning and delight for your friends. And first of all for your faithful,

Clotilde

I Tatti
Settignano
October 4, 1944[4]
Darling Clotilde,

Malavasi[5] came to lunch and brought us your letter. It quieted and comforted us for we were perplexed and anx-

---

3. Marghieri's new residence, on the Quirinale hill of Rome.
4. This letter was not delivered until November 1944.
5. Achille Malavasi, Italian journalist and writer in charge of press relations for the prefecture of Florence during World War II. He later translated into Italian Berenson's *A Sienese Painter of the Franciscan Legend* (1909), about Renaissance painter Stefano di Giovanni Sassetta.

ious to have had no word from you since our liberation.[6] I had a very bad upset after it and could not write, but Nicky wrote at length. It is clear that you never received the letter. At the same time she wrote to Croce and to Titina, and tried to send it in the same way. Perhaps you could find a way of letting them know that we wrote to them almost as soon as we could.

Yes, beloved dear, we are back at I Tatti, having returned ten days ago. I got a fresh glimpse of it September 2, and it looked so squalid, so uninhabitable that I dreaded to return and remained in our retreat for another nine weeks. Since then, miraculously, the house is almost itself again. The greater part of the works of art occupy their old places and yesterday books and photos returned from their hiding places and are being put back on their shelves. The more important works of art were with us at Careggi where we spent an entire year in perfect comfort. The books and photos were at the villa of Quarto on the slopes of Monte Morello.

Unfortunately, thirty pictures and some sculptures were stored in what seemed to be the safest of all places, namely Alda's flat. These were buried under the ruins of that part of the town. Happily 26 pictures have been recovered in fair condition and the other four may be restored. On the whole we have come out of this most devastating of man-quakes with little loss, just to sign us as having been there.

But Alda has lost everything: furniture, crockery, silver perished or stolen. The Anreps spent the year we were away here to see to the place and to mollify the Germans who occupied it a hundred at a time. No doubt that it is their tact with the Germans, and knowing how to deal with them in their own language that saved this place from sacking and pillaging to the full extent, as occurred elsewhere. The Anreps are still here but mean to migrate to our villa by the church as soon as it is clean enough to receive them. Mary

6. Florence was liberated in August 1944.

never moved. She is a bed-ridden invalid now. I can only see her in the rare moments when she is not suffering acute pains.

Nicky and I spent the whole year with the Serlupis,[7] cousins of Pietro Pancrazi, and as I said in perfect comfort, almost luxury. We enjoyed a Riviera climate, had hot baths every day, central heating and abundant and excellent food. The grounds were extensive enough to afford pleasant walks and the Serlupis themselves and her mother, a baroness Ritter, a French woman, were good company. He loves to read aloud, does it beautifully and made me acquainted with a number of recent Italian playwrights, poets and story-tellers who were scarcely names before. So there was no lack of company. There was a good library of French besides Italian authors and I had several hundreds of my own with us. I read a great deal by myself. Nicky read aloud in English and German, and the baroness in French. Nicky read the whole of Shakespeare and Milton and a good deal of later English verse and much Schiller and Goethe. I wrote a little every day, a kind of journal which I may publish under the title *Rumours and Reflections*.

Now I have a lusty appetite for work. I want to re-write two or three books I have composed during the last forty years and go on with *Decline and Recovery*.

We had a cable from Johnnie three weeks ago but he did not mention coming over here. Thus far I have not seen one English or American old acquaintance except a cousin, Robert Berenson, in our army here.

I cannot tell you how much I want to see you, and more than see you, to talk, to think, to be silent together in the dear familiar way of our past. May it be soon—the sooner

7. Marquis Filippo Serlupi Crescenzi, lawyer, art collector, and ambassador of the Republic of San Marino to the Vatican. Protected by diplomatic immunity, Serlupi turned his villa over to Berenson, providing him, his artwork, and papers with a safe haven from the Nazis.

the better! And how I long for Pompei and Paestum and Naples! But that for the moment is out of the question.

So much love to you,
my Darling Clotilde,
B.B.

Via della Consulta, 50
Rome
November 25, 1944
My darling, beloved Bibi,

I am just arrived in Rome and had the joy and surprise of seeing Pietro Fossi, finally someone has *seen* I have been waiting and waiting and waiting every day, for months, to hear from you directly or from Nicky, but nothing came. I wrote several letters, two of them sent by hand, and I was sure those would reach you. Did you ever get them? Do please write, if only a word.

From tomorrow I will look at any opportunity that will lead me to Florence, although I have heard that it is very difficult to reach Tuscany. Nonetheless, I will try all that I can. I long to come and see you.

My darling, what bad news. I can hardly believe it is true about Pellegrina.[8] I had the news from Vittoria two weeks ago. I can't think of anything else, but I won't believe it unless I know for sure what happened. What do you know, and what do you believe? What can be done?

I had news of Massimo. He is in a prison camp[9] and he wrote to say he was in touch with Ralph Perry. He also

---

8. According to Nicky Mariano, Pellegrina Paulucci de Calboli was shot by the Germans for having sheltered a messenger sent from behind the Allied lines to Resistance forces in northern Italy (see Mariano, *Forty Years with Berenson,* p. 266). Pellegrina had earlier been taken prisoner and held in jail at Forlì. Her husband, Raniero, was also shot by the Fascist forces.
9. Massimo Marghieri's regiment was defeated in Libya. He spent fifteen months in prison camps in Amarillo, Texas, and Boston.

228

wrote that he [Perry] is in a hospital, very ill. Bibi, this is not a letter; Piero is here and I am writing a few words for him to bring to you. I write in a hurry as Piero has to go, but I want to be sure that this time you get this letter. Dear darling, life is still good if you are still under the same sky. Then . . . little by little, letters will follow. And then I will come to you, I must come.

Clotilde

I Tatti
Settignano
December 5, 1944
Darling Clotilde,

It was good to receive your letter of November 25. I cannot understand what happened to the letters we addressed you. I wrote three times at least and at great length and detail, and Nicky likewise. Let me hope at least this will reach you and bring you the assurance, if indeed your heart needs it, that I love you not less but more than ever. I cling to real friends and you surely are second to none. Come as soon as you can, and your presence will do a good way to making up for many wants we suffer from here, as no doubt you do in Rome.

I am glad that you have satisfactory news of Massimo and I hope that they will continue to be so. As for Ralph Perry, the latest rumours to reach me were very grave. He may no longer be alive. Yet I go on hoping, as indeed I do about Pellegrina. In spite of the accounts to the contrary, I cannot help hoping that she has not been killed and that we shall see her again. [. . .]

I hear that Vittoria is flourishing and that her daughters are always with Allied officers. Vittoria wants to come up here but there are no buses or other public conveyances, and I can't afford to send for friends unless it be you. If you come, you no doubt will stay with her and I shall see her then.

Piero I have not seen since you have. With no telephone

and no transport it is far from easy to meet. In fact we see scarcely any of our Florentine circles. But we are social enough; Allied officers come a great deal, all are agreeable and some interesting. Only they take up time, with the result that I neglect my work, for I am too tired to write. I read a great deal but only in connection with events. It is interesting, but after all not my job.

Darling Clotilde, come very soon. I long for your company. What talks when you come!

Ever and ever yours,

B.B.

I Tatti
Settignano
January 9, 1945
Dearest Clotilde,

I share your distress over Pellegrina and like you I cherish a hope that it is not true and that we shall see her again alive. A British officer who was going to Forlì promised to make full enquiry.

Why do you avoid seeing Allied people? You surely cannot be obeying some surly grudge propagandized against them by incurable political idiots. I would urge you to frequent Anglo-Saxon and French. You would find a surprising number of *Unsereiner* among them.

I am truly disappointed to learn that you think there is no prospect of your coming here very soon. I so long to see you, to feel your dear presence, to prattle and chat together.

We are much taken up with callers. They begin to come as early as 10.30 and the latest may be here at 7.00 p.m. It leaves little time for my work or reading except of periodicals. We have found the Roman weeklies worthwhile, as well as *Mercurio*, *Aretusa* and *Il Mese*. I have enjoyed the French reviews that have reached me, *Fontaine*, and *La Re-*

vue. The books in English to reach me are nearly all political and topical, to me excitingly interesting but I doubt whether you would care for them. There is an English monthly that would amuse you, if you could get a hold of it. It is called *Horizons;* it is clever, witty, subtle, rather leftish not only in politics but in every respect, and on the whole well written.

Plenty of books appear in England and America but it is next to impossible to get them. Communications are still so uncertain and so slow for us civilians. The reading matter I procure I beg from military acquaintances and I receive odd copies of *The London Times* and *The Spectator, New States-man,* and *Time and Tide* as well as the *New York Nation, New Republic,* besides books on current problems. They keep me busy. For three quarters of an hour, every morning, Nicky reads aloud something literary, just now is Matthew Arnold.

Do your utmost to come here, my beloved Clotilde, and write very often.

Lovingly,
B.B.

I Tatti
Settignano
February 27, 1945
Darling Clotilde,

Cecil Anrep returns to Rome tomorrow or the day after and I seize the fresh and safe occasion to write. Yours from Torre reached me and Nicky safely. Trevelyan brought me your note written in Rome. Much as I love to think of you in the Virgilian world of Naples and as much as I long to stay with you, unless I am there with you, I prefer to know you are in Rome: Rome the so much more accessible, now particularly when posts take more to Naples than they used to . . . Australia.

I am delighted that the rumours heard months ago about

Gastone going to London is verified. If you are going to be in touch with him soon, give him my greetings and tell him I should be very happy to send him my introductions. Sibyl Colefax,[10] Kenneth Clark[11] and Henry Harris[12] could open all doors to him. By the way, we have met Gastone's sister and I found her profile fascinating. I had little speech with her because her boss, the commissary for the town, Col. Mitchie, absorbed my attention.

Darling, how well I understand all you feel about Pellegrinchen. You will be glad to hear that there is again a ray of hope that she is not dead. It seems her wedding ring has not been found on any of the bodies dug up. But being the only valuable one, being the other female victims of humbler station, it is likely to have been snatched off her finger by a German trooper or the grave diggers.

Ben Nicolson was seen the other day. He had a severe contusion on the spine and is now in plaster at Barletta. His far more brilliant, dashing, extravagantly handsome brother Nigel, who brought this sad news, is here for a day or two. You know of course that they are the sons of Harold Nicolson and Vita Sackville-West, both distinguished writers.

Of course, dearest, I never thought for a moment you could avoid Anglo-Saxons for nationalistic reasons. I feared the nagging pressure of Gino. If that danger is over, or has never been, I shall be happy to send people to you. Here we are overwhelmed by them. They leave me almost no leisure.

The young Trevelyan, for instance, like many others, came the forenoon and yesterday evening. There were new-

---

10. Lady Sibyl Colefax, née Halsey, wife of Sir Arthur Colefax and prominent hostess in London circles.
11. Sir Kenneth Clark had once been a former student of Berenson's. He later became the director of the National Gallery in London (1934–1945) and the Surveyor of the King's Pictures. On his friendship with Berenson, see his *The Other Half* (1967).
12. Henry Harris Wilson, scholar of history and politics and author of several articles on the media and public opinion.

comers at late 7.30. Not all are worth my while but they seem to enjoy the monument from a distant past that I have become, and I have not the heart to refuse them.

Yes, Mme. Gillet wrote several months ago and it was I who assured her that her husband must have been the greatest letter writer of his time. I shall let her have all addressed to me but I cannot flatter myself they can even remotely have the interest of those written to you. Keep them for the day they can be printed without disturbing survivors.

I am in bed with one of my Gargantuan colds. If I am well enough in these days to lunch with the Uzellis, I shall probably find there Vittoria De Vecchi. She too seems at last to have seen the light.[13]

How I hope that you can come. I yearn for your dear presence and our talks. There will be so much to remember and discuss the moment conversation begins to flow. I am so tired of the obvious chatters suggested by events and I long for words that touch bottom or rise.

So lovingly,
B.B.

La Quiete
Santa Maria La Bruna
April 1, 1945
My beloved Bibi,

I just heard from Col. Mitchie about Mary's death.[14] I do not tell you anything. We know what words are in these circumstances. I have gone through it myself; for her it must have been the end of so much horrid, useless, cruel suffering. But how much of oneself goes away with those who shared our life, were part of it and ourselves. I wish I could be near you, my dearest of dears.

---

13. A reference to Vittoria De Vecchi's political views and earlier support of Fascism.
14. Mary Berenson died in late March 1945 and was buried in the private chapel at I Tatti.

You know my affection, my love and my devotion to you. Although I am here, my thoughts are with you and I share your feelings, I guess them. Did she suffer a great deal at the end? Or was it peaceful? I do hope it was so. Dear Mary, what part of the house she was. My memories of her are so various, so different according to the different periods. Yes, we do live on memories and it is really like another life that goes on along with the actual one. And sometimes memories seem even more real than reality.

I am staying here for two or three weeks and if there is a chance to come to Florence I certainly will. As for Rome, my Darling, my house is so small but if you still are in a war-time attitude towards practical life, you can have a bed for you and one for Nicky, a bathroom near your room, simple food and a car at your disposal as we have the permit and Gino is getting new tires. As soon as he actually gets them, I will let you know.

You know I should be so happy to have you here. Nicky would sleep in Lucy's room and you in Massimo's, and Lucia would happily stay with Gino, who lives in the opposite street and is very near. Nicky knows my apartment and so does Cecil, so they can help you visualize the place and then you can decide. You know I would be so happy to have you here.

The weather is divine and this place supreme after so many days in the town.

Lovingly,
Clotilde

I Tatti
Settignano
April 20, 1945
Darling,
Your wonderful letter remained unanswered till now because I did not know how to convey it. This will be brought

by Morra who has been here a fortnight and returns to
Rome tomorrow.

You understand without me telling what the loss of
Mary means to me. On the lowest level it means breaking of
threads that have tied me to her for over fifty years. On a
higher plane it is the loss of the lodestar toward which my
activities pointed, which indeed guided them.

The end was peaceful and I was there to take her last
breath as she had asked me months before. She looked heroically beautiful in death.

It all happened just four weeks ago.

Do your best to come here and bring Lucia with you. If
we alarm or bore her she can take refuge with Vittoria's
daughters. I am eager to sample her for myself. I hear so
much about her from others, all very favorable.

Let me thank you for the offer to lodge us if we came to
Rome. It would be a delightful solution of the problem and
would make me happy to see so much of you. But, dearest, I
feel too broken up to face people and all the hurly-burly
capital. I must put it off for the present. By the autumn
Rome will be emptier and I stronger. Then I should like to
make a longish stay.

I must not forget to tell you that Ackroyd[15] appeared
yesterday and that we had a good talk which I enjoyed very
much. He is a free and intelligent spirit.

Have you heard from Mme. Gillet? She wrote she would
keep in touch with all Louis' friends.

Dearest and dearest love,

B.B.

15. James Ackroyd, British art historian. He and Marghieri met during the war, whereupon she introduced him to Berenson. Ackroyd became a frequent visitor at I Tatti before departing for India, where he lived for many years. He continued to correspond
with Marghieri and Berenson.

La Quiete
Santa Maria La Bruna
April 29, 1945

This letter is to tell you that unless something unexpected and unpleasant happens, I am going to visit you in the near future. In some ten days or a fortnight Benedetto Croce is coming to Florence and I asked to go in the car with him. This is the only way for me to come without a permit. I am looking forward to coming and I am astonished to realize that I am looking forward to it with the same thrill and expectation of nearly twenty years ago.

Unhappily, Lucia won't be able to come, but we must arrange it for some other time. You may be sure she won't be bored. She is dreaming eagerly to come in touch with I Tatti. And I am happy with her today. I know she will appreciate I Tatti and enjoy every bit of it. She has been quite a revelation to me these past few years and a real company.

Now Bibi, may I ask what have you done to enchant and bewitch my friend Jimmy Ackroyd, who came to me last night quite under the spell of I Tatti? We spoke till late about you and Florence and the first thing he said was: "I must go back to I Tatti as soon as possible. I must speak with B.B. again." And it is likely that he will come while I shall be there. I should like it immensely if he does. I should love to tell you more about him. He is more complicated than what appears, and often indeed he is a puzzling being, queer and disappointing, but sometimes wonderfully responsive. His love for Italy is touching, yet till now he knew too little about Italians, at least of the good sort. I felt on myself the burden of being the only representative of my country!

Nowadays politics prevents me from reading other stuff. By the way, I should, when I will come to you, let you know a very young friend of mine, a pure Florentine youth, extremely intelligent and intellectual, like I have seldom or ever encountered.[16] More in the political and in the philosophical sphere than in any other, and with a rigorous historical culture, a precise language, a sharp judgement—perhaps too much of it, at the age of 21!

Will you excuse me with Nicky and Alda if I did not write? I shall be there soon enough to have with them all the talking we wish.

> My very best and deep wishes
> and love to you, Bibi mine,
> Clotilde

I Tatti
Settignano
May 4, 1945
Darling Clotilde,

Your beautiful and fascinating letter of April 29 has just reached me and I hasten to assure you that you will be no end welcome for as long as you can stay. The longer the better. You will find nearly every comfort and convenience minus two, namely telephone and transport. At last we have fixed a wreck of a *balilla* [an inexpensive model of car] but as it is of extremely delicate health, we use it only for indispensable trips. So once here, you will [be] something of a dearly beloved prisoner.

I hope the weather will have returned to decency. At present it is so windy that we have had to restart heating again. I am looking forward to it for I am *der Leuten müde* [tired of people] and eager to get back to work and intimacy, and to the very few friends who really count and you foremost. If you knew, but you do know, how eagerly, how impatiently we look forward to seeing you.

> Love and no end,
> B.B.

16. Marghieri refers to Giovanni Sartori (1924–), Italian political scientist and author of numerous works on party systems and

I Tatti
Settignano
June 30, 1945
My Darling Clotilde,

How could you fall ill so soon after leaving me and so far away! I fervently hope you are enjoying full convalescence in your divine landscape, a landscape which perhaps more than any other haunts my memory and imagination. How do I long to return to you within it. I could wish to breathe my last breath there and to lie buried in your ground. I wonder sometimes whether mankind did not reach its highest happiness on your slopes and whether it does not still retain possibilities of it that the industrial age has driven from the rest of our world. Here too is beautiful, but with a beauty that I have to help on, while yours lifts me on its wings and carries so far without leaving its horizons.

We have had more visitors than ever because of my 80th birthday and still they come. We mean to go to Casa al Dono before July 20th and look forward to your coming for a long stay. There we shall converse with and without words. We shall read together and breathe together. Much as I love this place, its comforts and luxuries, I shall be glad to get fresh new air and farther away from the miscellaneous crowd.

Ever so much love,
B.B.

Casa al Dono
Vallombrosa
August 6, 1945
Darling Clotilde,

Yours of the 16th brings me the very disappointing news that you are not coming. I cannot blame you, for un-

democratic theory. Formerly a professor at the University of Florence and at Stanford University, Sartori is now at Columbia University.

less you have a car to bring you here, the journey would be beastly. But Nicky and I shall miss your visit.

One says little by letter, at least I do. Therein I am not a bit of our beloved Gillet, *le meilleur épistolier de notre temps,* as Jerome Tharand characterized him recently. In the same article there was described the touching funereal ceremony over the fall in Alsace of François Gillet. No, I am not a writer, not even of letters. To come to full expression, I require somebody like you to draw me out but from different angles, for I am polygonal perhaps to a degree unusual. But you, Darling, draw me out as few do and I love your stimulations and your subtle solicitations.

It is so quiet, so silent, so unpeopled here! No neighbors nearer to the Orlandos. In fact, no other at all. And to come up from Florence means car-potency given to few.

We read a great deal, politics chiefly, including novels and poetry. It is impossible to send books, so there is no use telling you about them till you come here and I can put them into your hand.

Much heart-felt love,

B.B.

I Tatti
Settignano
December 16, 1945
Darling Clotilde,

I hope that Torre will restore your normal condition, after which you will find an occasion to come to us. I long to see you and want you alone to ourselves.

Now I want to tell you that your Lucia is the most promising young girl I have ever come across. She is only too cerebral if anything, and I have urged her (but I fear in vain) to turn from too much abstraction to things concrete and empirical. She has read prodigiously and digested what she has read and can talk it all intelligently. She can hold her own in any argument.

If you see Pane, tell him how much I enjoyed his too short article about the Americans of Naples.

Best wishes for a happy new year. May we meet often in 1946!

Love,

B.B.

I Tatti
Settignano
January 2, 1948

If Lucia turns up I shall do my best, but winds of doctrine are hard to cope with.[17] They seem to work like the *Spagnuola* [influenza epidemic] in 1918 which affected the strongest men under thirty. Ideas are as contagious as other and manifestly more physiological infections. It is hard to deal with them for it is not their minds that are affected but their will. The will to believe. And an old English proverb says: "A man convinced against his will is of the same opinion still."

The abler the patient, the better the dialectician, the harder to evince from him a false position which engages his will to believe. And of course sex subtly and treacherously has hidden cards that it supplies to the argument. Ever since my 12th year I have suffered from the experience that any amounts of evidence will not affect convictions. And recent years have confirmed it. Most of my acquaintances were unpenetrable to any argument that touched their beliefs, no matter how flimsy, how absurd they may be.

I envy you the slopes of the Vesuvius and the quiet life there. *Ich bin des Treibens müde* [I am tired of the bustle]. Hinks[18] stayed here for a couple of days: he would be horrified if he knew that I believe him full of complexes and

---

17. In 1947 Lucia Marghieri joined the Italian Socialist party.
18. Art historian Roger Hinks, director of the British Museum and coauthor with Naomi Royde Smith of *Pictures and People* (1930).

futile ambitions. It is a pity because he is so gifted in all sorts of ways.

Morra is leaving today, Carocci[19] lunched here yesterday and today we expect Bianchi Bandinelli[20] back from Mexico and the U.S.A. And he, as you know, is a declared member of the Communist Party. So is Luporini.[21] How to account for it? Come soon and we will talk to no end.

Much and dearest love,

B.B.

La Quiete
Santa Maria La Bruna
February 23, 1949

My Darling Bibi,

I went to the Pasquiers'[22] to hear Pane's lecture on his Parisian impressions as a painter, and it was quite a success. All intellectual Naples was there. We stayed for dinner and the conversation fell on Stendhal, Gide, etc. We sharply disagreed about the ending of *Rouge et Noir,* which some considered missed; others, like Morisani[23] whom you know, thought it perfect.

One of the women whom I have most admired in my life as a work of art in her beauty, for her humanized, lovely face and figure, the princess of Fondi,[24] was there. She must

19. Alberto Carocci, literary critic and playwright.
20. Ranuccio Bianchi Bandinelli, historian of ancient art and classical archaeology. In addition to directing the journal *Antichità e Belle Arti,* he was cofounder of the journal *Critica d'Arte* (1935) and of the political-literary *Società* (1945).
21. Cesare Luporini, philosopher, literary critic, and scholar of German and French philosophy and nineteenth-century Italian literature.
22. Jean Pasquier, French consul in Naples, and his wife Ninette Pasquier.
23. Ottavio Morisani, art historian at the University of Catania and the University of Naples.
24. Princess Giuseppina di Fondi, née Viti.

be 62 but near her, every youth, even sparkling of beauty, seems insignificant. It is a human face rich with age, fascinating with the remembrance of a noble past. I can't tell you how she fascinates me, and now perhaps more than when she was young. We talked of you, for she knows a lot about you but has never met you, and she asked me for a book of yours.

So I have lent her my copy of your last accompanied by a letter which flew from my pen with easiness after years of inhibitions and difficulties in writing. I had to think over this episode.

I am reading Graham Greene. Do you like him? Nicky the angel sends me the reviews; when I find your "To Clotilde" written on it I feel like I was in the next room waiting to see you at 11.30, and it gives me a thrill of nearness.

All my love, Darling, and thank you for existing, again and again,

Clotilde

I Tatti
Settignano
February 26, 1949
My beloved Clotilde,

How happy it makes me to receive word that you have come to life again so fully, so vitally, so joyfully. It makes me long to be with you in your ambiance, Naples and the Vesuvian slopes.

I should love to meet the princess of Fondi. Every day I grow more aware of how much people mean to me as works of art—mere works of art as passive, as intransitive as pictures on a wall. Thus, a few hours ago, I received a youngish German Jew whom I helped getting started in America. Fresh from Germany, he appeared to me by a certain ascetic distinction on top of personal beauty within his type. I saw him now flabby, common-looking, vulgar almost. No doubt he is more than ever a fine scholar, but what do I care!

No, I do not know Graham Greene. I do not like his work. It is based on a notion of Catholicism which is not genuine, besides being repugnant to me. Pseudo-Mauriac, pseudo-Bernanos, etc.

Roger Hinks is going to learn to hate another country and people while with them, and to regret the one he left. He plans to pay us a visit before he shakes the dust off his feet. *Wo ich nicht bin da ist mein Glück* [Where I am not, all joy is there.]

I kiss you feelingly,

B.B.

La Quiete
Santa Maria La Bruna
April 2, 1949
My dearest,

Your most delightful letter compels me to further discourse. How right you are as for most of the talking being mere vanities! I see very little of people, so it is a bit different in my case. I come out of my monologues anxious for otherness, and each one person represents, even at the lowest level, the opportunity to get a plastic feeling of myself, realizing my contours. When I am too much alone, I seem to become "fluid." It is often a temporary feeling, but this is what generally pushes me toward others. As for real talk: how rare! It is all that I dream of now, all passions spent, at my very ripe age. But for you, Nicky and me, the dream has been realized; don't let us deprive each other of it.

Do you really see a possibility to spend some time at Torre? I shall have to talk to Nicky about that, for fear of nourishing a tender pigeon in my bosom and wake one day to the bite of a naughty bird taking his flight. I should be too happy and from the 15th of May on, it would suit me very well. It is only in June that my mother comes here, and besides I would not advise it for my place can be very hot already in June. It can also be too dusty for your eyes, used to the sweeter atmosphere of the Tuscan hills. But how should I love it! There is space for Emma[25] next to your room and you wouldn't need Parry for I can offer you the motorcar.

I met Sylvia Sprigge[26] last night at Raffaella's. I liked her and I felt stimulated by her. So do you, and I fully understand.

Always yours,
Clotilde

I Tatti
Settignano
April 8, 1949
Darling Clotilde,

It would make me happy to spend with you the second half of May. I doubt whether it will be feasible. I am in the midst of a stream of work that is carrying me provided I do not abandon it. And ever so many other reasons. But why don't you come here instead? You would not interrupt my work and we could spend hours together that would be delightful in act and nostalgic to recall.

I expect Hinks next week. He is to stay five or six days before he shakes African dust from his feet and runs to paddle and quack like *canards* [ducks] in the *canaux* [canals] of the *canailles* [scoundrels], as Voltaire epithetized Holland and the Dutch. Roger was the victim of a shock when he was deprived of his post of antique Greco-Roman sculpture in the British Museum, having failed to see that reliefs were being chiselled by unauthorized restorers. He has physically loathed all Mediterranean art ever since and logically transferred that distaste for everything Mediterranean. An ex-

---

25. Berenson's personal maid.
26. Sylvia Sprigge, journalist and frequent visitor at I Tatti, author of *Berenson: A Biography* (1960).

traordinary gifted, learned, thoughtful, ultra-British individual, but not satisfactory because no reliable friend. Which does not prevent my making the best of him and enjoying his society. I confess I find more to my taste in vanishing obsolescent British cultivated aristocracy than in British intellectuals, perhaps in all so-called intellectuals.

But why all this to you, darling Clotilde! Incline your heart to my solicitation and join us here *im wunderschönen Monat Mai.*[27]

So lovingly,

B.B.

I Tatti
Settignano
April 19, 1949
Darling Clotilde,

I should love to hallow your abode with my presence and ever since you showed it to me I have been longing to stay there with you. Some day I shall, but I doubt it will be next month. So you had better plan to come here anytime.

Sibyl Colefax will be here till May 15, after which we may be alone or have day guests only. Sybil will enjoy you and you her, once you have got accustomed to her voice and pronunciation.

Roger has left us and Italy. Pretty gloomy and taciturn on arrival, he cheered up toward the end and has been genially human during the last talk just now. But it was sad to hear no word of appreciation of anything in Rome, blind to all its splendors, ignoring its marvellous associations and utterly negative. And although over fifty he has not understood that his attitude is adolescent and if not cured is punished by privation of enjoyments and happiness. He remains

27. A phrase borrowed from Goethe: In the beautiful month of May.

dandiacal and proud of what he does not like or does not understand.

We are busy correcting proofs of Italian versions of my diary.

Tenderest love,

B.B.

La Quiete
Santa Maria La Bruna
April 26, 1949

Darling Bibi,

Roger's letter from I Tatti ended like this: "We English don't understand you. You don't understand us. We understand each other better when we understand you. This is just a fact of nature and I see no point in trying to glaze it over even if to you it seems like *une comédie de la sincerité Stendhalienne.*"

One sentence was for me incomprehensible. I am sure that while writing to me he was addressing many more persons, and perhaps posterity. But I don't think it was either good manners, nor kind.

My dearest, from your lips I have heard that this month you shall not come, and I do not dare to ask you in June for fear it might be too hot. Would it perhaps be possible in October? As for me, I should love to come in May. If you have people coming unexpectedly, you should not hesitate telling me. You know that I have friends in Florence and you should feel quite at ease.

I saw Maria Teresa yesterday in Naples where she has come with her husband and Angelica to spend ten days. We talked over memories of thirty years ago, when she was a young girl and gave a concert and all Neapolitans were at her feet. In the light of our remote memories I saw her at her best; in Florence she seems almost too heavy a weight to lift, all the various layers of fat that cover her hidden light.

246

People here, including myself, are anxiously waiting for some rain. As always in these cases, pilgrimages are made daily to Pompei. But I hope to find Taormina in the sun. I have never been there.

All my love, dearest,
Clotilde

I Tatti
Settignano
May 2, 1949

Darling Clotilde,

Why should not understanding one another be a cause for repulsion rather than attraction? Take the case of Roger. I don't understand him at all and it is perhaps what most draws me toward him: curiosity, a desire to solve the enigma of such a tormented and problematical personality. With people, in multiplural as well as singular, the desire to understand them draws us far more than when we think we do understand them. For me, every individual personality is infinite, and as for a people—say the Italian—*c'est la mer à boire* [there's a sea to imbibe]. *Aber doch, lass den Roger* [But still, let Roger be].

Rain at last for you I hope, as I hope for us, and being summer rain it has great beauty as well as refreshment. I look forward almost as a bridegroom to your coming. We expect no other guest after the 15th except our architect and beloved friend Cecil Pinsent, who however is the least interfering of mortals. There doubtless will be visitors for lunch and tea but except for house guests we try always to keep evenings free. My friend of fifty years, Sibyl Colefax, is with us till the 15th. Have you seen her?

Loving expectation,
B.B.

Casa al Dono
Vallombrosa
September 26, 1949
My beloved Clotilde,

It looks as if at last my dream of a visit to you at Torre will be realized. Nicky will write dates. This is simply to jubilate at the prospect of seeing you again so soon and in your own paradise where there will be none of the snakes that each has in his own paradise.

And yet it will be heart-breaking to go away from here. The moment is from every point of view so exquisite. But nostalgia for what one leaves enhances the eagerness for what one moves to.

Yours ever and ever,

B.B.

Cava dei Tirreni
Salerno
October 23, 1949
My Darling Bibi,

Dearest, it is almost impossible to convey the feeling of happy radiance which is connected with this bundle of days spent together. They are and will remain the happiest of my life. Perhaps they are the only through and through serene moments of my life.

It struck me as incredible that it would be so. So much that I dread to go back there, for I shall taste the bitter feeling of acute nostalgia. But rich memories are a nourishing dish for a solitary nymph, and now I want everything in the house to remind me of you and Nicky. From your and my room, to the dreadful *scalino* [step] and the records at night, and every other detail.

I am looking forward to coming to Florence about the 3rd of November. Meanwhile, I shall certainly write again for at Torre, where I shall be on Wednesday, the road is going to be paved and that means even more possibility for you and others to come as guests.

All my love to you and Nicky, always dearer and dearer to me, closer and precious,

Clotilde

I Tatti
Settignano
October 26, 1949
Darling friend of my soul,

Your dear letter was wonderful and leads me to tell you that whenever I am not busy with doing things, my mind scarcely harbors a thought, or my heart a feeling that is not for you. I long for you as much as when I first was in love. Only now while it remains a desire it is sweet and not at all tormenting. It is quite a new experience to be in love again with the same person, to have her come back from the middle distance, as it were, to the very fine edges of my undaunted meditation and dream.

So I look forward with longing to seeing you oftener and oftener here or at Torre.

Dear, I love you,

B.B.

La Quiete
Santa Maria La Bruna
December 10, 1949
Darling Bibi,

It isn't that you are asked to partake of a dish you do not like. It is that when I happen to admire a book I wish you would join in my admiration, and if you don't I get uneasy.[28]

I went last night to the Roberts'. We were sixteen people of whom the Schwarzenbergs, the Robertis, the Bonners, the Boncompagnis, the Guidottis, Flavia Gherardesca, Igor

28. Marghieri refers to Graham Greene's *The Heart of the Matter* (1948).

249

and John Mallet. Some were curious to meet me, as they heard about me through you, and as John Mallet called me "the lady who sits on the lava," I composed a limerick which follows:

> The lady who sits on the lava
> Was asked to dine with the grandees.
> They wanted to see what it's like
> A lady who sits on the lava.
>
> A velvet dress, too tight and stiff,
> A jocund smile pinned on her lips.
> That was all the grandees could see
> Of the lady who sits in the lava.

Being in a way introduced by you, and you and the lava being my claims to distinction, I was much asked to comment on the *Sketch for an Autobiography*. And Bonner, for instance, very abrupt and straightforward, harassed me with all sorts of questions. À vis à vis I had Flavia Gherardesca who, it seemed to me, had been at I Tatti enough to gather false impressions, which proves you received too many people. The result was that I became silent, which provoked after dinner a very flattering approach from the Schwarzenberg, who came to me and said (she was at the table somehow far from us): "Permettez moi de vous dire mon admiration pour la façon avec laquelle vous avez répondu et pas répondu à propos de B.B., vous qui étiez la seule à vraiment le connaître."[29]

Mallet was so inquisitive to ask me abruptly if you had provided for Nicky in a convenient way. For they all (?) hope you have, for if you haven't that wouldn't be approved, etc. I hope you don't mind me telling you this. You imagine, I did not tell them anything, I just answered I did not know

29. "Allow me to express my admiration for the way in which you answered, and did not answer, questions concerning B.B., you who are the only one to really know him."

in detail. Do tell me if this is the American way to put questions, so direct. My impression of Bonner is of a man *sans finesse* in our sense . . . Am I wrong?

All my love, darling,
Clotilde

I Tatti
Settignano
December 18, 1949

You need never fear to be indiscreet. Our new dispensation, "all passions spent," in favor of true love, must be based on the confidence that nothing we communicate to each other will be misunderstood.

Too much to say about Nicky for a letter. So we shall keep it for our next meeting (may it be very, very soon). Perhaps the bottom reason why I did not propose marrying her is that it never occurred to me. Marriage, except for young people, and for social reasons, seems to me a repulsively insincere affair.

Morra was here with Silone[30] and they came up together. I gathered from the talk that at last Morra has ceased to be a Sovietist. Yesterday I got a letter from him. It was the first on politics he has written since the war. But it is so confused that I cannot make it out. I fear he is eager to get somewhere but keeps stumbling over piles of rubbish, and falling into pits. His psychology is beyond me, unless it be like that of the usual fellow-traveler who cannot understand what it means to understand.

---

30. Ignazio Silone (1900–1981), novelist, journalist, and politician. Author of the modern classics *Fontamara* (1933) and *Pane e vino* (1936), Silone is famous for his compassionate descriptions of peasant life in his native region of Abruzzi and its fate under Fascism. A founding member of the Italian Communist party, with which he broke in 1930, Silone was active in the labor movement and in the anti-Fascist resistance.

John Mallet? Attractive, well-groomed sartorially and mentally, but I fear very much taken with women of "clank and fashion," snobbish that is. Be with me as sincere as possible, and fear not that I resent or betray you. I love you and trust you mean well by me.

All good wishes. By the way, my *Sketch* is out in Italian. Where shall I send it to Gino?

Lovingly,
B.B.

I Tatti
Settignano
New Year's Day, 1950

Best Beloved,

Thanks for the good wishes sent from Cava and to Gino for his kind words about my *Sketch*. We, I in particular, look forward to your visit and to resuming our cosy, pointless, unaggressive, inconclusive talks. They are the only kind I ever enjoyed and now more than ever.

Harold Acton, Loria and Trevor Roper[31] are staying here. The last is a wonder of historical and political culture and insight, and a great gossip.

Je vous embrasse tendrement,
B.B.

I Tatti
Settignano
February 27, 1950

My Darling Clotilde,

Derek [Hill] came back drunk with the delight of his visit. The time, the place and Clotilde all together. He will never get over it. Thank Heaven.

31. British historian Sir Harold Acton, Italian historian and philosopher Arturo Loria, and British historian Hugh Trevor Roper.

Yesterday we all went to see Katherine Dunham[32] and I was completely hypnotized by the tam-tam effect of it all, its appeal to what in one is almost pre-human. There lurks in me a stern Puritan whom all this alarms; yet I could not help enjoying it, like Saint Augustine's penitents who confessed they could not help enjoying it when raped by the Vandals.

As for Katherine herself, she is a fascinating creature, gifted in many ways and highly civilized, even intellectual and not more negroid than many an Egyptian. And what a body! As beautiful as any bronze.

I long to see you again, my Darling, and talk as we can with such hearts' care when you come to my bedside in the morning!

B.B.

La Quiete
Santa Maria La Bruna
March 28, 1950

My Beloved Bibi,

I heard from Derek that Katherine Dunham is coming back from Paris to say farewell before she leaves. Instead of feeling jealous I felt admiration for her . . . and envy. Yes, a sort of envy not of her affection for you, not of yours for her. But of her youth, beauty, energy, health and spirit of enterprise, *vitality* in a word, which in her must be developed to the fullest, and in me is declining. And now I understand your admiration for her, and her nostalgia for the world you represent. How I should have liked to meet her and see the two of you together!

---

32. Katherine Dunham (1910–   ), black American dancer and choreographer and a leading proponent of Afro-American dance and other dance traditions of African origin. Dunham toured widely outside the United States as a dancer, lecturer, and artist-in-residence. Her influence on modern American dance now extends through the works of her former students, including Alvin Ailey.

It is a pity that she does not sail from Naples, for I would have given her my homage, too. If she is still there, give it to her from an unknown admirer . . . And tell me about her, please, tell me more. Let me share your life, I seem to be in a desert, or so my universe appears to be at present!

All my love,
Clotilde

I Tatti
Settignano
March 31, 1950
My Darling,

I fear I must disenchant you about Katherine Dunham. She has not come back from Paris but only from Milan and not for ME but to see a film which her impresario insisted on showing her. I doubt whether she has any feeling for me of a "sentimental" nature. She may feel a bit better for being treated as an equal by a countryman of a country where blacks are not received in private. It may be a feather in her cap to be known as frequenting I Tatti.

On my part, I admire her as an artist just as you would, and with a little sex feeling. She has, as you say, great vitality and elegance and creative taste. I was entranced by her performance and it still haunts me. Last time I saw her, two days ago, her husband, a white Canadian who does the costumes and scenery of her performances, was talking to Salvemini[33] and Raymond Mortimer. She sat apart with me and began to tell me how she feels with her personality absorbed completely by the institution she has herself created. And the tears flowed as we talked.

---

33. Gaetano Salvemini (1873–1957), historian of Italy, politician, and a major figure in the history of Italian Socialism. An ardent anti-Fascist, Salvemini was stripped of his citizenship by Mussolini's government and spent several years in exile in the United States, at Harvard University.

soon as I succeed in having the necessary leisure to enjoy a
work of art. Thanks, my Angel.

My dear, I am absorbed in an overwhelming book. I
wonder what you think of it. It fascinates me while reading
it. When all finished and re-thought at a distance I shall
know better. It is called *Attente de Dieu* by Simone Weil.[41] If
you read it we must speak about it at length.

I am planning to come in February. I want it very much.
And may I tell you in confidence that there is one person
who would love to be asked to stay a few days at I Tatti, and
it would do her a lot of good for she needs it, and that is
Ninette Pasquier? Perhaps we might come together? Answer
very frankly. I wanted to mention it to Nicky in my letter
and I have forgotten.

All my love, dearest, and please write.

Clotilde

I Tatti
Settignano
January 18, 1951

A few days ago I wrote to Mme. Pasquier suggesting
that she comes here for a few days. So you see that I anticipated your suggestion. If she comes with you, all the better.

Yes, I have read Simone Weil's *L'Attente de Dieu* and was
impressed, fascinated. But time has given me time to reflect
and praise *Dieu* that there are not many Simone Weils. One,
dann und wann [now and then], is enough.

You know there are two books of hers. One is a treasure, a real work of art. I wish I could have it on hand for

41. *Attente de Dieu* (1950) by French writer and philosopher Simone
Weil (1909–1943). Weil was a labor activist, a member of the
International Brigades fighting for Republican Spain, and supporter of the French resistance while in exile in England, where
she died of tuberculosis.

years and years. We have few like her in our journalistic world.

There is a chance that when you come here you will find me toothless and mumbling, as I have to go a major operation on my teeth. Pray for me.

Give my best to Raffaella and the Guidottis and all my good wishes for their adventure.

Love,

B.B.

La Quiete
Santa Maria La Bruna
March 16, 1951

My Darling,

It was absurd and yet how like us! We talked of everything and all, but never of your tooth operation. Somehow I must have thought it was postponed, and now I hear from Ninette how horrid it was. Oh my Darling, I wish I had known, just to be able to be with you in my thoughts and share your sufferings. How I hate physical suffering; so useless, so hostile, so meaningless! I know what it is and how I loathe it! Do give me news, Angel, and tell me how soon I can come.

The Guidottis arrive tonight but it appears they will not be leaving until the 22nd, for the *Vulcania*[42] has to be repaired and they are postponing the departure. I dare say they will stay here for they have no longer a home, or will they come to Florence? I shall know it tonight. But this is the reason why my home shall be full during the Easter week.

Pane was enchanted with Papi.[43] Pity I was not there. Ninette was in good spirits, happy over her Florentine visit, full of affection for you and Nicky.

42. A transatlantic liner.
43. The writer Roberto Papi or his wife, Vittorina.

I read and sent back the first volume of Turnell which I enjoyed immensely. And now the second one, and the Nightingale biography:[44] fascinating, what a vivid world even if, as long as it regards my writing, a mediocre realization of an urgent need. It is always on the bounds of my real home, after such a dissipating *scorribanda* [incursion] in the realm of *le coeur* . . .

Darling, write a word. I need you more than ever, for you are my real world, the only one without the danger of shipwrecking.

All my love,
Clotilde

I Tatti
Settignano
March 19, 1951
My Beloved,

I know you would suffer too much if I told you what awaited me about my teeth. I feel I shall have to undergo no little pain and annoyance before they are in relative order again.

Here visiting is a curious young female who began a "fan correspondence" with me when my *Sketch* appeared. Most unexpectedly she has come on from New York to see me in the flesh. She has a beautiful body but an indifferent face and does not know whether to paint, to write or to act. Has left her husband and a lover and now does not want to go back to New York. Is daughter of a famous actress and psychoanalyzed and fearfully up-to-date, puzzling, charming, tenderly but not amorously affectionate.

Today arrives a couple of Boston fine *fleurs,* and how I wish you met them. She is the daughter of my dear friend,

---

44. Cecil Blanche Woodham Smith, *Florence Nightingale, 1820–1910* (1950).

older than I am, Mrs. Chanler,[45] and he, Pickman, a sort of historian of intellectual movements. I can't tell you how conversational one feels with them, spiritually how at home.

The *Florence Nightingale* is a dream of human experience and contains even literary matters of interest, as for instance about Clough and Fitzgerald. Do by all means write about it and let me know what you write.

Dear, I love you
with all that is in me,
B.B.

Hotel Manin
Milan
June 24, 1951
Beloved, Darling Clotilde,

I have no news, nor any sage comments to make. I write with the sole purpose of assuring you of my love, deep, deep love and yearning for your intimacy. You must try to join us at Casa al Dono. We leave in an hour for Venice, Hotel Europa. Do write me there.

I have had an interesting time here. We met your young friends at the Bompianis[46] and liked them very much. I was taken up by others and had little talk with them, but Nicky found them sensitive and responsive.

The most interesting ever since you left has been rereading Stendhal's *Lucien Leuwen*. The first part is a beautiful lyric against a background of stupidity, malice and meanness. The second a painfully cynical exposure of parliamen-

---

45. Daisy Chanler, friend of Edith Wharton's. An American, Chanler was raised in Rome.
46. The friends were Italian journalist and novelist Ottiero Ottieri and his wife Silvana. Ottieri's novels focus on the pathologies of modern society, including unemployment, class snobbery, and technology. Valentino Bompiani was a playwright, founder of the Bompiani publishing house (1929), and the editor of the theater journal *Sipario*.

tary government as produced in France in his days. Do re-read the first part.

Love and choicest vintage,

B.B.

La Quiete
Santa Maria La Bruna
July 21, 1951
Darling Bibi mine,

How my heart flew to you seeing your handwriting after a long absence and privation of it! Like hearing one's own language in a foreign country. I was waiting for this moment to come. Knowing you at Casa al Dono, where I can *see* you, I can follow your hourly occupations almost as if I was there with you.

Here I enclose Silvana's letter which I pray you to send back. Angel, you must be open to her. You know you can for I deserve it. I can understand everything and have no silly complex about anything. If you did not like her, and you justify her feeling of being "dropped" by you, she does seem to have resented it. But it is you that I am interested in, and I ask you. Sometimes I may conclude from experience that you are not interested or perhaps have a prevention against my young friends. I have quite a few and find them stimulating, pleasant, sometimes cruel, hard, sometimes fatiguing, and I feel impatient. But I get over it for they always stimulate me, even if in a clearly irritating way. Let us go deeper and find out what is our real attitude toward them.

Write, Angel dear! Before the summer is ended I shall come and share a week with you. September, the beginning.

All my love, as always,

Clotilde

Casa al Dono
Vallombrosa
July 25, 1951
My Beloved Clotilde,

Thank you for letting me read Silvana's letter, beautiful and so well expressed. The facts are as follows. She did sit next to me at the table when I was very tired and neither stimulated nor stimulating. Besides I had my hostess to think of when we got up. I was kept busy talking to Bompiani and his guests wanted "to meet me." I had no chance to approach Silvana again.

If interlocutors stimulate me and I feel I am stimulating, they have no age for me, nor station, nor much sex. Indeed I have lost numerous occasions of love-making because I got too interested in talking to caress. I have no prejudice for nor against the young as such. But I love them when they are responsive and promising. I enjoy seeing the young as a rule, more than conversing with them. They so seldom let me forget that they regard me as what I am! a great grandfather. So all in all I feel more at home with people of your age and up to 70. Older than that?!?

So far I now can foresee that there will be room for you the first week of September. I mean room in the material sense. In my heart there is always room for you, and so much.

B.B.

La Quiete
Santa Maria La Bruna
October 21, 1951
My Darling, Darling Bibi,

This time your departure has been a real ache to me. And be sure, please BE sure, that this is no exaggeration. It is the simplest truth. And so much must you have felt it that you urged me and advised me not to go to Paris. For it is true: more than ever I now need affection, tender love and a shelter. Yes, I need a nest and there is no place that I dream of as much as I Tatti.

Near you and Nicky I feel at home. All others have become strangers and strange casements from which the soul has departed, and for soul I mean my own in its creative, joyous mood, or if you prefer *dreaming* mood. When my son and daughter were children everything was different, for they did make the house a home, but now? Each goes his way and in Rome especially I have the feeling of a house where *il focolare è spento e la cenere muta* [the flame is spent and the ashes are pale]. It makes me shiver . . .

My angel, how I treasure every word you said to me! Write soon. Tell me how you feel coming home again. But I expect for you it is home wherever you are with Nicky near and, dare I say?, with me.

> All my tenderest love,
> Clotilde

I Tatti
Settignano
October 24, 1951

Thank you for your *Herzensausguss* [outpouring of your heart], so deep, so complete, and how I sympathize! The truth, my Darling, is that you must start *Neues Leben* [a new life] without *Neue Liebe* [a new love]. Not *Liebe* in the way young and youngish people understand it. If you can weather a crisis and settle down to a life of work and the affection of friends, to enjoy the exercise of freedom and *l'amitié amoreuse,* you still may have wonderful years before you. And *l'amicitié amoreuse* I can offer you and everything to help you through the present slough of despond. Even if we cannot always lodge you here, we can always see you daily whenever you can be in Florence. The oftener, the happier I shall be.

Home-comings are always confusing but we have a houseful of guests, fascinating and fatiguing . . .

With dearest love,

B.B.

I Tatti
Settignano
January 1, 1952

A happy new year, my Beloved Clotilde, and may every wish of yours be realized.

Gastone lunched here yesterday and we had a delightful talk. We were quite alone; he, Nicky and I could *cracher nos coeurs* freely. Only it was about politics, although of course I got satisfactory accounts of Raffaella and the girls.

I am so glad that you feel you have turned the corner and can face life again with joyous expectations. That is as it ought to be. I could be there at 86 and a half and over! Life is a gift that most of us throw away, unconscious of its value. I cannot understand howling against it; what you have done is to be in the swim or to see only its inevitable, seamy, lower animal side.

Last night there was a great jamboree at Alda's while I with Nicky, Ritter and Yashin[47] spent the hours looking at my Chinese paintings. Yashin was my pupil thirty and more years ago and is now at the head of everything to do with art in Japan. I compare him with Chen who was here just a year ago and so different, although brought up to Chinese classics. But the Japs even of Yashin's class have something exotic about them that the same quality of Chinaman has no more than any other European.

I heard from Ninette and from Jean separately, both delighted to be with you at Cava.

Love,

B.B.

47. Japanese art historian Yukio Yashin.

Via della Consulta, 50
Rome
February 23, 1952
Darling Bibi,

I have been so near to coming to you, had it not been for
Gino's illness. I have been very worried and now I know that
he shall have to fight with this constant enemy. I have been
staying by him all the time for this is my wife's role and
it felt so strange to be useful and necessary. But at night I
have been going out and did not lose my contacts with the
outer life.

Last night I finally met the Guttusos.[48] With them was
my latest English acquaintance, Lewis Way, whom you
would like had he not a hearing difficulty. I know you don't
give much credit to my judgement, but he is *Unsereiner*. He
only lacks outer *brio,* unless in certain moments. But intense
and spiritual life he certainly has and one feels it near him.
And when he talks, he always has something to say. Ask
Guttuso.

As for Guttuso himself, I find him adorable. Somehow
he did not catch how near and close you and I are, and with
I Tatti, as I heard him say that "I knew you"!! I found him so
fascinating, open, human, enthusiastic. How I hate not to be
there when they come. I should give anything to see you together. I dare say one can even talk with him about politics;
he seems to be a gentleman with nothing of the *énragé.* Am I
wrong? About her, I am more reticent. Do please urge them
not to drop me, for I like this sort of stimulating people even
when . . . well, I wish I could talk to you at length of the
adventure of coming in touch with people and so on.

48. Mimise Guttuso, née Dotti, and Renato Guttuso (1912–1986),
modern Italian painter known for his depictions of contemporary
social problems and the ordinary aspects of everyday life. A member of the Central Committee of the Communist party, Guttuso
was critical of Soviet-style social-realism, believing that the committed artist should work outside the realm of political ideology.

After Torre and the Colacicchi's [49] visit I shall be flying to you. I need it.

All my love as ever and ever,

Clotilde

I Tatti
Settignano
March 2, 1952
Darling Clotilde,

> *Home sweet home,*
> *thro' pleasures and palaces*
> *though we roam,*
> *be it ever so humble,*
> *there is no place like home.*

"Home" is not a place but a person and for married couples after children have left the nest, the gallant pursuits have passed, it is the husband and wife one returns to as to a HOME. So I am glad to hear in your letter that Gino is absorbing your affection. Given the human lot and our human condition, Gino is worth your return.

I wish you were here with the Guttusos. He is a truly captivating person despite his *foi de bûcheron* [woodcutter's faith] in *Unum Deum Stalinum sedentem in Kremlino.* I know her less well and no wonder she is possessive having fought so hard, sacrificed so much for him and being older. I get the impression of a very good sort.

Gabriel Marcel comes here to stay for a few days. You no doubt will hear him at the Pasquiers where he is due the 13th. I will expect to go to Ischia about May 12th.

Ever and always your loving,

B.B.

49. Italian painter Francesco Colacicchi.

Via della Consulta, 50
Rome
March 13, 1952

My Beloved Bibi,

   Your letter left me *pensierosa*. Your words "your return to Gino" etc. I kept them in my mind as a great question for which I could not find a real answer, an honest one, true to my own self. What I am trying to reach, innerly speaking, is to stand on my feet, if I can say so, and mostly try to accept the ultimate solitude which is at the roots of everything, which is the last word of many lives, perhaps of all lives. Certainly I feel it myself, although I have wonderful moments of nearness and even complete harmony with other human beings, as I have with you—complete and serene. But I do not have, I cannot have a real Home-Sweet-Home any more. And it was absurd and foolish to have hoped to build another one on the ruins of the previous one, ruins in which I can still find shelter.

   So shelter is the word that I would give to my home. I am willing to have Gino share it with me for as much as he may wish it and perhaps need it. For he is getting old, too, and I am grateful to him for having accepted me and allowed me to make my experiences. The same I did to him, as you know.

   I am glad to hear that you will meet Pompeo Biondi.[50] He is life-enhancing and vital as few. I hope he will not be shy—it may happen!! Nicky told me you are full of guests, but as I want very badly to spend a few hours with you, to come in nearer touch, I will go to one of my Florentine friends and then come and visit you. I miss you in my intimate core, I need to be in touch with not too long silences.

50. Pompeo Biondi, professor of political science at the University of Florence.

All my deepest love, and perhaps you might destroy this letter.

Clotilde

Cava dei Tirreni
Salerno
July 28, 1952
My Beloved Bibi,

Seems absurd that I could leave you so long without a direct word from me. Through Nicky, however, we are always in touch. I have been ruminating about all that was between us: phrases, sentences, encounters with other people. I had quite a lot to brood about. Somehow I have a slow digestion but more and more I realize that our lives, though not always shared, still have a common roof, and the more I advance in age, the more I feel it. Our love, affection and friendship shall remain the one thing in my life, together and alongside with married life and motherhood, to carry with me if and when we die. All other things are like Schubert's *Incompiuta,* more dramatic and passionate, but between us I feel the marriage of minds, and certainly to nobody in life do I owe so much as I owe to you. You have been the salt of my heart.

Dearest, I do hope that you will feel what I am telling you in such a way as perhaps never before, for it is a truth that has become ripe in me, almost as if I were dying. It has been filling me with a peaceful sense of thoroughness since you left Naples.

I am now in the midst of family life. Lucia, her husband, her sister-in-law, and a charming little boy were here and have now left, only Lucia remaining. It was an awkward reunion of which I can only give you a caricature by saying that Gino got furious with the cook because he bought *L'Unità*[51] for Lucia's family, and Gino said: "I will not pay

51. *L'Unità,* daily newspaper of the Italian Communist party.

for it!!" *Zum Lachen!* He likes these self-assertions. The others laugh at them.

I am wondering how it will turn out with the Guttusos. I have offered them the house at Torre for a while. He would love to paint there and I shall be staying with them now and then, as Cava and Torre are so near. I did not want to impose myself on them all the time, because I do not know how it would turn out with Mimise's *présence,* very present at all times and even menacing. I understand her only too well, but all the same . . . So I put it this way: we shall see.

I shall tell you about it. Meanwhile, this will be my headquarters and from here I shall be going there on a visit and sample the possibility of a longer stay. I want to talk ideas and politics with him and see by myself what their world is. I cannot do it with Paolo because of Lucia's reactions. So, *au fond,* this is a *détour* to reach the same end.

I have written to Rosamund[52] about plans for September and October. Darling, be well! I know you have written a charming letter to Father who enjoyed it like a refreshing spring, a touch of a richer life. Thank you, my Darling.

Clotilde

La Quiete
Santa Maria La Bruna
August 4, 1952
Dearest,

I love to discover in myself that when I plan to come to I Tatti and stay with you my heart beats quicker and I still feel a thrill, isn't it wonderful? To come then, to be welcomed by all of you (including the maids), to feel at home in

---

52. English writer Rosamund Lehmann (1903–), whose novels include *Dusty Answer* (1927) and *The Weather in the Street* (1936). Influenced by Henry James, her writing focuses on the world as seen during childhood and adolescence.

another home. In fact I have two, Torre and I Tatti. It thrills me with an everlasting feeling of part and continuity.

I shall have so much to tell you about my impressions, experiences and reactions to this strange month which I shared with opponents of various faiths and pseudo-religions. Tonight we expect Pane and I already smell black powder!

I shall talk to you when I come with Rosamund. I had a wonderful letter from her. This present, too, I owe to you.

Yours ever,
Clotilde

Casa al Dono
Vallombrosa
August 20, 1952

Beloved Darling,

Thanks for the wonderful letter with such a penetrating appreciation of both the Guttusos, and so just. I envy you having seen so much of him. I loved him instinctively.

And your plans? After September we shall be quite free and ready to devote all our leisure to you. Walker has just come and leaves soon. He will be followed by the Hamiltons but they stay two nights only. After that, as yet, nobody to stay, although a day seldom passes without visitors.

I work as hard as I can on re-editing my *Lorenzo Lotto,* first published nearly sixty years ago. It is humiliating to be doing nothing better. In fact I find I have little to change, although a great deal to add.

What of Rosamund? It is a long time since I had news from her or even of her.

I wish I were with you,
B.B.

La Quiete
Santa Maria La Bruna
December 8, 1952

My Darling Bibi,

I wish I could tell you my real feelings about all these old friends and figures leaving us: Croce, Orlando, Borgese.[53] Words are poor and inadequate. I had received a letter from Borgese four days before his death in which he told me that Croce's death struck him deeply, and I know what love-hate-hate-love had always been in his heart. He must have felt it dreadfully, I am sure. His last article on Siena I thought very beautiful, except the end that was too mystical. I think that death came in time.

It is strange how death puts a conclusive seal to a man's whole pattern and that we discover what was always there. Why didn't we see it before? Why are we not more attentive to the secrets and mysteries that each of our friends conceals? I was put off these last days by the *côté spectaculaire* of Borgese, for instance. And when he told me the whole story about his son and his relationship with Croce, I did not, *au fond,* listen to him, really share his tale. I was distracted by the exterior side of his confidence, if I may say so. The ges-

---

53. Benedetto Croce died in 1952. Marghieri also mourns the loss of Vittorio Emanuele Orlando (1860–1952), conservative jurist, politician, and pioneer in the field of constitutional law. Orlando served in the Liberal governments of Giolitti, Salandra, and Boselli. Following a brief attachment to Fascism, he moved to the opposition, and later negotiated the postwar accords between Italy's King and the Committee of National Liberation. Also dead is Giuseppe Antonio Borgese (1882–1952), journalist, novelist, and literary scholar. In addition to writing literary criticism on nineteenth-century Italian and European works, Borgese wrote historical novels and was editor of the newspapers *La Stampa* and *Il Mattino.* An opponent of Fascism, he left Italy for a long self-imposed exile in the United States, where he was a professor of literary theory and comparative literature.

tures, the screaming, the rolling of the eyes. I was amused and at times revolted, and did not pay him any deeper attention. I do not even remember all that he confided me. I resent it about myself.

And somehow this is now my real feeling toward the dead: that we neglect to take from the living all that they can give to us or are willing to give, and we miss our chances, forgetting how mortal we all are.

I spent the day yesterday with Katherine. We went to Paolo Gaetani's.[54] He was alone there with a friend of no importance. He was charming and caressed his dog all the time. Katherine was rather disappointed and did not like him. And as for the lovely house she said she liked mine better because it was lived in. I dare say Paolo was shy and *gehemmt* [inhibited]. I am afraid he is like this when he "smells" people of another kind and quality, yet he loves to smell them.

The Albertinis bought a house in Naples, a lovely house. But he looks so . . . dead already! Whereas Borgese was still in the prime of his energy and vitality . . .

All my love, Bibolinchen,

Clotilde

I Tatti
Settignano
March 16, 1953
Beloved Clotilde,

In the sea of life enisled
We mortal millions live alone

All of us, Darling. Not only you. The only way to conquer some of this stellar solitude is to try to escape from this Robinson Crusoe Island where we are all monarchs of all we survey but without equals. Relative happiness—it can never

---

54. Neapolitan count Paolo Gaetani, host of an intellectual salon in Naples.

be complete—comes with work of no importance, so long as it is hypnotizingly regular and better still in identifying one's interest with the interest of others. In short, to get away from one's Me First. I have succeeded but partially. When I do, reading, writing, talking, loving beauty in people and nature and things, then and only then do I feel at peace with myself.

Of course you always will be welcome. Only if the crowd is too much and I can't dedicate myself to you alone, that is what I dread.

Ever lovingly,
B.B.

I Tatti
Settignano
November 14, 1954

If only we could live the life of lookers-on, it would be ideal even now. And in fact I still live such a life. I have always taken everything—except my work—as a spectacle, my work and the very few human beings necessary to my existence.

What has saved me, relatively, is that I have put work first, before all love, even those necessary to my comforts, my functioning and my happiness. I should approve and worship you if even now you can live the life of a looker-on, nothing but a looker-on, without getting mixed up, committed, tangled-footed like a fly-paper with the life of others. All this sounds very solemn. Far beyond my intention. At bottom I am a frivolous old man, yet very serious in my love for you, darling Clotilde.

Yours,
B.B.

Via della Consulta, 50
Rome
February 3, 1955

It was delightful again and every time more to be at I Tatti and feel that our 25 years and more of conversation goes on, increasing in easiness, freedom and understanding.

Sometimes I want to console myself for not having produced nor created anything in my life, but I have universes of friendship which count for me as *temples vivants*. And of these temples you know you are the Parthenon. I may have in my landscapes some romantic ruins, yes of a more pathetic kind, but . . .

Darling, since more than twenty years I come to I Tatti to gather energy or to focus on my own self, and I have never came back disappointed. Now I go back to my mother, whose end of life I must sweeten as much as I can. And then I rush to my grandchildren, who move my soul and make me feel like a young mother again. Time goes on and we still try to extract all its juice. I have not given up the terrible "why" and try to explain everything, but I try not to be enslaved by this search. It is perhaps my turn of mind, the one you don't like in me and which I should not encourage.

Darling, be well and keep well. It will not be long before I come again to you.

Endless love and affection,
Clotilde

I Tatti
Settignano
March 19, 1955

Dear Clotilde,

This is what Alex writes about you: "First of all your friend Clotilde, in whom I have discovered *une nouvelle amie d'enfance*. Sometimes one meets people and it is as if one had always known them. She is one of them."

I hope to be strong enough to go to Tripoli. The plan is to return by way of Sicily and Calabria, with a good stay with YOU, first and last. But I have not recovered my strength, perhaps I never shall again. The least effort tires me. I can't sit at my table because my ribs and back begin to ache. On the other hand, if I lie down, I am bedsore!!

Friendship, affection, stimulus of heart even more than of mind, but both together are what remain at my age, and the Gods have given me this and much else in loving friends like you.

What a beautiful world today. I wish I was with you in your Realm of Gold.

B.B.

✤ I N D E X ✤

Designer: Wolfgang Lederer
Compositor: G & S Typesetters, Inc.
Text: 10/12½ Bembo
Display: Bembo
Printer: Maple-Vail Book Mfg. Group
Binder: Maple-Vail Book Mfg. Group

I look forward
already with real
Sehnsucht to seeing
You again. We must
meet oftener,
dearest, darling
Clotilda.

? Back to Paris

Ever lovingly

B. B.